THE PERMANENT HOLDOUT

THE PERMANENT HOLDOUT

JACKSON BROWNE, HIS MUSIC, HIS AMERICA

CORNEL BONCA

ROWMAN & LITTLEFIELD
New York • London • Oxford • New Delhi • Sydney

ROWMAN & LITTLEFIELD
Bloomsbury Publishing Inc, 1359 Broadway, New York, NY 10018, USA
Bloomsbury Publishing Plc, 50 Bedford Square, London, WC1B 3DP, UK
Bloomsbury Publishing Ireland, 29 Earlsfort Terrace, Dublin 2, D02 AY28, Ireland

First published in the United States of America 2025
Paperback edition published 2027

Cover design: Sally Rinehart
Cover image © MediaPunch Inc / Alamy Stock Photo

Library of Congress Cataloging-in-Publication Data
Names: Bonca, Cornel, 1958- author.
Title: The permanent holdout : Jackson Browne, his music, his America / Cornel Bonca.
Description: Lanham : Rowman & Littlefield, 2025. | Includes bibliographical references and index.
Summary: "Known for albums like Late for the Sky, The Pretender, and Running on Empty, Jackson Browne was a master of capturing the counterculture ethos of the late 1960s and 70s. This book dives deeply into his music, long career, and activism within the context of American life, revealing a remarkable musician still fueled by ideals of love and peace"—Provided by publisher.
Identifiers: LCCN 2024040359 (print) | LCCN 2024040360 (ebook) |
ISBN 9781538172872 (cloth) | ISBN 9781538172889 (epub)
Subjects: LCSH: Browne, Jackson. | Rock musicians— United States—Biography.
Classification: LCC ML410.B866 B66 2025 (print) | LCC ML410.B866 (ebook) |
DDC 782.42166092 [B]—dc23/eng/20240828
LC record available at https://lccn.loc.gov/2024040359
LC ebook record available at https://lccn.loc.gov/2024040360

ISBN: HB: 978-1-5381-7287-2
PB: 979-8-216-46510-2
ePDF: 979-8-8818-6461-3
ePub: 978-1-5381-7288-9

Printed and bound in the United States of America

To A, A, A, and N,
Again.

CONTENTS

ACKNOWLEDGMENTS

Many thanks to my editor, Michael Tan, ever supportive, who gave me all the freedom I wanted to write the book I wanted to write.

I want to thank Dicky Barrett, a friend who lit a fire under me at a time when I was ready to give up. Also, great thanks to Louis Maeux, whose uncanny understanding and steadying advice sustained me through two years of going up and going down.

I wrote this book alone in a room surrounded by other people's books. Some of them—by Dave Marsh, Steve Erickson, Robert Christgau, Ellen Willis, and Paul Nelson—taught me how to write about rock 'n' roll, and so this book is in some ways a conversation I'm having with them.

My house has always been full of music: my three children—ages twelve to twenty-nine—all sing and play instruments and love music the way I do, and everything I write is informed by that pleasure of making and listening to music with them. This book has them as my ultimate audience.

Finally: Angel. Under skies blue and black, ever stunning, and still—*still!*—a mystery.

INTRODUCTION

WHAT JACKSON BROWNE'S HOLDING OUT FOR

THE MAN WHO DOESN'T TAKE IT EASY

The first time most people heard him was in the spring of 1972, when "Doctor My Eyes" broke into the American charts, but the song that made a much bigger splash was the Eagles' "Take It Easy," cowritten by Browne and released only weeks apart. "Take It Easy" embodied what people recognized as an "El Lay" vibe: "Drivin' down the road, tryin' to loosen my load. . . . Lighten up while you still can." In "Doctor My Eyes," Browne sang, "I want to *understand*," but the advice in "Take It Easy"—"Don't even try to understand"—hit closer to home with that big contingent of 1970s listeners suffering burnout from the decade just past and seduced by the free-flowing languor the Eagles version promised. "Take It Easy" had the fleet rhythms of a drive on a desert highway, a sing-it-with-the-top-down melody, and sun-shimmery harmonies. That laid-back tune put him on the map as a pop songwriter, and considerable monies in his pocket, but it's a terrible introduction to Jackson Browne.

Because there was nothing then, and nothing now, about Jackson Browne that takes it easy. As a young man, his looks made him a ringer for a sybaritic surfer, but his songs were troubled excursions to dark places, his own and his country's. His songs probed exactly the kinds of things that people who tell you to "take it easy" don't want to probe. He also was and remains an indefatigable workhorse, and if in more than a half century of songwriting and recording, he's released only fifteen studio albums—compare that to compatriots like Bruce Springsteen (twenty-one albums plus several box sets containing scores of previously unreleased songs) or Neil Young (as of this writing, forty-five albums plus all that side work with various combos of Crosby, Stills & Nash)—that's because his style of work is deliberate and slow: it can take him *months* to finish a song. "Take It Easy," in fact, was a song whose lyric he'd been working on so long that he finally just handed it off to his friend Glenn Frey, who dashed off the song's memorable verse about standing on a corner in Winslow, Arizona. Browne can brood for hours over single words; a perfectionist, he labors over the appropriateness of the simplest guitar riff or the ABAB rhymes of a quatrain. It's true that, except for about a fifteen-year period, from the midseventies through the late eighties, when Browne really tried to rock—and played arenas where he pulled it off—most of his music is folk-based, melodic, midtempo. But even a cursory glance at his lyrics reveals a guy who is not "mellow," "soft," or "easy," which are the adjectives streaming services tend to use to place him.

Jackson Browne's whole vision is rife with a sense of solitude, a constant, agitated struggle with himself (and his country), and an instinctive, nearly Buddhistic sense that we are all creatures of desire, and that desire gives pain. He's said it himself. "Life is full of pain," he said in 1994. "It's painful for everybody. I mean, growing is pain. And the only way through it is through it. And anything that helps is a blessing. And that's why we do what we do. That's why we do music."[1] In the realm of the personal, that leads him to a melancholic, turbulent agon with desire and mortality that reaches for something transcendent called Love, which when he was coming up—in the 1960s—possessed a spiritual meaning that went well beyond the romantic pop clichés of the 1940s and 1950s. In the domain of the political, it's a frustrated, sometimes despairing struggle for freedom, equality, justice, and environmental awareness. Sometimes—maybe not often enough—he brings those realms together and comes up with music with genuine philosophical heft: "For Everyman," "Before the Deluge," "The Fuse," "The Pretender," "Running on Empty," "Looking East," "The Long Way Around," "Downhill from Everywhere," "A Little Soon to Say." Love, and what we might call the American Ideal—understood as an idea that comes down to us from the Romantic era of poetry and revolution and gets filtered through the modern civil rights movement, the New Left's Port Huron statement, and the cultural tumult of the sixties—are what Browne is forever holding out for. He believed in these things when he was seventeen, and despite living through a history that's given him plenty of reasons to give up on them, he seems to believe these things now.

Which, to some people, including a substantial slab of rock's critical establishment, makes him a sap. Remember John Belushi in *Animal House* grabbing a folkie's lame guitar and slamming it against a wall? That was the attitude of some of the East Coast, anti-LA music critics toward Browne and his cohort of Left Coast transplants like James Taylor, Carole King, and Don Henley when they gravitated to LA around 1970. While Robert Christgau, Lester Bangs, and Richard Meltzer were busy whipping up enthusiasm for the New York Dolls, Iggy and the Stooges, Blue Oyster Cult, and (this was funny) Grand Funk Railroad, seeing them as possible avatars of a rock tradition desperate to salvage something from the waning energies of 1960s rockers, here was this whole scene full of sun-blissed hedonists hanging out on the other side of the country in a quickly mythified place called Laurel Canyon, strumming their acoustics, experimenting with "alternative lifestyles," and flirting with ideas they got from books by Kerouac, D.T. Suzuki, Carlos Castaneda, and Hermann Hesse.

Turn down any sun-dappled road in the canyon and there they were, smoking hash and dropping acid, conducting orgies in swimming pools, and (some of them) writing stupefyingly bad songs begging two girlfriends to be in a threesome (cf. David Crosby's "Triad"). Absurd to deny that the Laurel Canyon thing was substantially fired by sexual excess—almost everything was, in the late sixties—but it was also a self-protective and not entirely irrational reaction to larger events. In the wake of the twin assassinations of Martin Luther King Jr. and Robert Kennedy, violent demonstrations at the 1968 Democratic Convention, nationwide urban race riots, the Manson murders of 1969, the murder of a fan at the Rolling Stones concert at Altamont, the expansion of the Vietnam War into Laos and Cambodia in 1970, the killings at Kent State that followed, and the terrorist exploits of the Weathermen, the counterculture's political and social will had begun to implode. A light began to dawn that the utopian appeals for peace, equality, compassion, and an organic connection to the earth that the counterculture was calling for were revealed as pretty much toothless in the face of Nixon's silent majority, the military-industrial complex, and America's materialistic juggernaut. As Browne himself wrote a few years later in "Before the Deluge," in a slightly different context, the counterculture was "confused by the magnitude of [their] fury."

Thus began the rock generation's move from the political to the personal, and LA music, more acoustic, relaxed by synergies of surf, sun, sex, and cannabis, was its new soundtrack. Some of those East Coast critics, either out of envy or baked-in prejudice, scoffed at the idea that anything genuinely rocking, not to mention artful, could emerge from Southern California's warm-weather debauchery and Hollywood ambiance, and they weren't entirely wrong. Lots of SoCal-influenced music from the early 1970s really did suck: self-indulgent (again, Crosby), swamped in sentimentality about nature ("Wildfire," by Michael Murphey, or "Me and You and a Dog Named Boo," by Lobo), overly impressed with its own sensitivity (a lot of Dan Fogelberg), or self-important and superior (Stephen Stills's "Find the Cost of Freedom"). But they were wrong about Jackson Browne, whose music mostly steered clear of sentimentality, self-indulgence, or generational superiority in favor of an intelligent, dyed-in-the-wool humanism.

ABOUT THAT SINCERITY OF HIS

What some people found, and still find, unappealing, even dismissible, about Browne, is his sincerity—that serious, vulnerable openheartedness of his. In some of the hipper quadrants of pop culture, sincerity's had a bad rap for decades, so let's recall what Lionel Trilling said about it in *Sincerity and Authenticity*, his book-length excursion on the concept. For him, it's the "congruence between avowal and actual feeling," which is to say, the attempt to communicate an emotion that's honest, loyal, and "aligned" to what the self is feeling inside.[2] Trilling traces it back to Polonius's famed instruction to his son in Shakespeare's *Hamlet*:

> This above all: to thine own self be true,
> And it doth follow, as the night the day,
> Thou canst not then be false to any man.

Trilling emphasizes the last part of that quote. It's one thing, he says, to be "authentic" to yourself: to express the jumble of one's feelings outwardly. It's another to be "sincere": to feel a kind of obligation to figure out what's in your head and then to convey that truth to *others*.[3] When you're sincere, you're not merely exhibiting your authentic emotions willy-nilly—that is, spilling your guts—but communicating a comprehensible feeling *so that you are understood*. It implies a certain vulnerability and warmth on the part of the listener, too, a willingness to be touched. The very tone that sincerity imparts signals a pact between speaker and listener: I will do my best to tell you what I feel, and I will assume you will do your best to understand me in the spirit in which I've spoken.

Sincerity has a moral and social component that merely "being authentic" doesn't. To be sincere is to know that you live in a social world filled with people whose feelings are often buried and unknown to them. And since you live in that world, it helps if you are not "false to any man," that you try to understand and articulate your feelings; it not only helps you understand yourself, but it helps others understand themselves. Sincere expression, from this perspective, cares as much for the person on the other side of the communication as it does for the honesty of what's being communicated. Authenticity means expression; sincerity means responsible *connection*, one person to another. And that's what makes it a moral good.

Jackson Browne's music, whether it's his deep dives into the perils of relationships or his forays into earnest political commentary, has its roots in that sincere humanistic intention, and for some people that kind of music is smothery, sticky, or square. It lacks postmodern cool, the ironic escape clauses that help one to wiggle out of the occasional necessity to declare that one is *this* kind of person and not another, or that one is for *this* principle and against *that* one. (To be sure, sincerists like Browne can have trouble employing irony even when irony's the appropriate stance: for years, when he tried to be ironic, as in, say, "Disco Apocalypse," he had trouble pulling it off. He finally found a credible ironic voice only in the 1990s, with "My Problem Is You," but even since then, he's used it sparingly.)

The danger of sincere music, of course, is that it can slip into piousness, cross the line from moral to moralistic, and that ain't rock 'n' roll as most of us want to hear it. Browne *has* crossed that line in the pedantry of, for instance, "The Drums of War" or "Where Were You" (from 2008's *Time the Conqueror*), but when he honors his audience's intelligence and gives it emotional space, his sincerity about matters both personal and political is searing—it can burn through one's resistance. "These Days," almost the whole of *Late for the Sky*, "Those Bright Baby Blues," "I'm Alive," "Sky Blue and Black," "The Barricades of Heaven," "The Naked Ride Home," "A Human Touch": these dense explorations of internal struggle, grief, delight, and longing are triumphs of sincere personal rock 'n' roll. And if that sincerity sometimes results in embarrassing and simplistic expressions of his political commitments (antinuclear war sentiment in "Say It Isn't True," political corruption in "The Word Justice," anti–military-industrial complex in "Which Side?"), sometimes he rises above it—again by honoring his audience's intelligence—and his insights can rise to heights rarely reached by anybody writing in a rock idiom ("Before the Deluge," "The Pretender," "Looking East," "Downhill from Everywhere").

DISCOVERING JACKSON BROWNE

I myself am a long-standing appreciator of irony and the postmodern—a good part of my sensibility was shaped by pop music in the tradition that brought us Dylan in the mid-1960s, Bowie, Bryan Ferry, and Madonna;

in literature by the work of Joan Didion, Don DeLillo, and David Foster Wallace; and by the films of Hitchcock, Godard, and Paul Thomas Anderson—but I've always been drawn to Browne for his sincerity. Like many teenagers who were wedded to their transistor radios in the early 1970s, I heard "Doctor My Eyes" and caught that metaphor about seeing so much of the world that it hurt, but at the time it didn't particularly stand out from the Top 40 rotation that gave us Arlo Guthrie's "City of New Orleans," Looking Glass's "Brandy," or "Lean on Me" by Bill Withers. Again, like many of my generation, it was *Late for the Sky* that did the trick.

I was sixteen years old, beset by blunt family trauma, living in the working-class LA suburb of South Gate that was quickly turning into gang turf, and itching to get out. For me, that meant college and exposure to a wider serious culture whose waters I was just beginning to test. Reading *The Catcher in the Rye* was the beginning, and J. D. Salinger made me hungry for more of anything that could help explain my life: not just the particulars of adolescent confusion, but a loneliness that couldn't be assuaged in the usual adolescent ways. I felt a certain jittery sense of psychic isolation that manifested as dread about my future and a bottom-just-fell-out emptiness that no appeals to friends, school, sports, alcohol, pot, or sex could remedy. So on that long road trod by misunderstood adolescents everywhere, I turned to art.

I found a decrepit secondhand bookstore in town with a "classics" shelf where I could pick up paperbacks by Camus and Dostoyevsky for a quarter apiece. Urged on by my older brother, I read scraps of philosophy and plunged into existentialism, and my tiny world began to open. But the rock music I was listening to then was what everybody I knew listened to: *Goodbye Yellow Brick Road*, *Chicago VI*, Bachman-Turner Overdrive's *Not Fragile*, Cat Stevens's *Tea for the Tillerman*. I had a cool eleventh-grade-history teacher, Lou Cohan, a Jersey refugee, who tried to turn me on to a record called *The Wild, The Innocent, and the E Street Shuffle*, but I didn't know how to listen to Springsteen yet. My habit in those days was to take my earnings from a part-time job at McDonald's ($2.30/hour), head out to Licorice Pizza, and buy one record a week ($4.98 in 1974). The store had psychedelic posters on the wall—blown-up album covers of Bowie's *Aladdin Insane*, Yes's *Tales of Topographic Oceans*—and the employees burned patchouli incense. I flipped through the stacks, listened to whatever they were playing over the quadrophonic speakers, and began my rock 'n' roll education.

In among the *B*s—nestled not quite alphabetically between Bowie and James Brown—I discovered *Late for the Sky*. The front cover looked familiar—a 1950s model Chevy parked in front of a house at dusk (or maybe dawn)—but also somehow strange and surreal. The back cover listed songs that weren't playing on the radio, but I was drawn, powerfully, to the little picture of Browne: he was fragile and frankly beautiful, and his eyes were red-rimmed—he looked like he was either high or had just been crying. Whatever, there was something in that face that was intelligent, vulnerable, marked by pain, and I wanted to know that guy and be like him. Which is only to say that, at sixteen, I needed heroes, and here was a prospect. I don't know if that was why I bought *Late for the Sky* that week—by then I was reading Robert Hilburn's rock criticism in the *LA Times*, and Browne was a favorite of his—but I did buy it, and when I took it home and put it on the turntable, I got my first real sense that rock music could be as vital and mind-opening to me as *The Stranger, Notes from Underground*, or Salinger. The light really came on when I listened to "Before the Deluge" and its lyric about "the hands [that] reach for the golden ring." The image was the same one that Salinger used at the end of *The Catcher in the Rye*, when Holden Caulfield has his great insight into how it's impossible to preserve innocence. Watching his sister reach for the gold ring while she rides a merry-go-round, he worries she's going to fall off: "I was sort of afraid she'd fall off the goddamn horse, but I didn't say anything. The thing with kids is, if they want to grab for the gold ring, you have to let them do it, and not say anything. If they fall off, they fall off, but it's bad if you say anything to them."[4] Enduring the fall of innocence is one of the main themes of "Before the Deluge," too, and the song made me feel that there was nothing that literature could do that rock 'n' roll couldn't do just as well.

That was no small realization for a kid living in a ready-to-rust factory town in the 1970s. It meant that rock 'n' roll wasn't just a portal into fun and pleasure but into a world of ideas that mattered. By the time I got to college, Paul Simon's "American Tune" or Springsteen's "Born to Run" helped me understand, better than some of my professors could, what was so sad and confounding about the post-Watergate, post-Vietnam America I was growing up in—why practically everybody I knew smoked pot every day just to get by. Don Henley's lyrics in "The Last Resort" brought home to me how much the place where I grew up—Los Angeles—was wrapped up in the larger myth of Manifest Destiny and therefore of an American Dream that, despite everything, I wanted to believe in. And Browne's "Fountain of Sorrow" not only named for me something vital that I was just beginning to intuit—the labyrinthine hall of mirrors you walked into when you fell in love—but it did something more. After I listened to that song dozens of times, I realized that the chorus *doesn't* go "Fountain of sorrow

/ Fountain of *life*"—a sentiment that, in equating sadness with life itself, is straight-ahead melancholic and not particularly illuminating to someone like me, who was pretty much melancholic already. The lyrics actually read "Fountain of sorrow / Fountain of *light*." Getting that lyric right was a revelation, because to appreciate that sorrow and light flowed from the same source, and that *sorrow could lead to light*, taught me in the most intimate way the power of paradox, dissolved oppositions I thought couldn't be dissolved, and made sorrow seem productive, useful—*worth it*. It connected so many things for me, from the Crucifixion to John Keats's poetry, particularly "Ode on Melancholy," with its sublime conclusion:

> Ay, in the very temple of Delight
> Veiled Melancholy has her sovran shrine,
> Though seen of none save him whose strenuous tongue
> Can burst Joy's grape against his palate fine;
> His soul shall taste the sadness of her might,
> And be among her cloudy trophies hung.

Sorrow, I was learning, was a sort of precondition to delight and joy and, if you had the courage to experience it, could lead to a greater appreciation of what it meant to be alive. As Keats wrote in a letter, sorrow was part of the "vale of Soul-making": the power and richness of your soul largely depended upon how you responded to the sorrowful events of your life. Jackson Browne was the guy who first taught me all this. Along with much else.

WHAT THIS BOOK IS ABOUT

This book isn't a biography, though I will often enough talk about the events of Browne's life that are germane to his music and his political activism. And though it is a work of critical evaluation, I won't pretend to sober judgment. This book is about my fifty-year-long engagement with Browne's career. His music, album by album, has been a lifelong companion, a source of insight, inspiration, and delight—also frustration, irritation, impatience, even anger. No one in the sphere of popular music, aside from Dylan, Springsteen, and perhaps the band The National, has had a greater shaping influence on the way I think and experience things. Aside from his ability to chronicle what it felt like to try to find and keep love alive through the late decades of the twentieth century, I especially prize his Americanness, the way even his most personal music can be contextualized in the historical odyssey—from the sixties to the present—that we've lived through. I will appear in this book from time to time as a sort of stand-in for Browne's audience—more in the beginning than at the end. Like most of Jackson's audience, I was riveted with his music in the beginning: I was young, in love with rock 'n' roll, felt spoken to by an artist who quite obviously knew how to speak to a countercultural generation, and frankly I had the time to obsess over his records. As time went by, however, that generation disintegrated into pockets of Pretenders, Holdouts, and Lawyers in Love; my life took its own course into career and family that left less time for musing about rock music; and though I continued to follow Browne's music, he became less central to my sense of being. (I don't think that's an unusual pattern for any lover of pop music.) But he remained vital, especially as I followed the way he negotiated his own personal crises in his music, and more crucially, as I watched him respond to the calamities that typified American history of the last half century.

That common American history provides this book's backbone. Browne started out in the late 1960s as a self-conscious troubadour on a personal quest for love and experience in a post-Dylan mode, and he typified, on *Jackson Browne* (1972) and *For Everyman* (1973) a certain branch of the early 1970s counterculture: searching, traveling, experimenting, sometimes anguishing at the losses (and deaths) of the searchers, sometimes reveling "in afternoons of smoke and wine . . . [where] . . . there was nothing we could find but peace and pleasure." These albums were trying to avoid the deadening traps of what was known then as the Establishment (those conformist over-thirties who were "lost inside their houses" and living "in the mechanical city") at the same time that they were searching for a new way to be and to love, in solidarity with other questers, even amid hints of apocalypse and the rubble of the counterculture's failures. The 1974 follow-up, *Late for the Sky*, though it contained the first apotheosis of Browne's thinking about the counterculture in "Before the Deluge," was mostly an extremely personal album about a broken love relationship, but it was one that transcended the genre. Speaking in a new conversational register, free of the self-conscious poeticizing to which he'd been prone, Jackson found a way to make his own disillusionments with love rhyme with the disillusionments of a country mired in the self-doubts brought on by economic crisis, rising urban violence, Nixonian corruption, and the loss of the war in Vietnam. Director Martin Scorsese certainly noticed it, placing the love lament "Late for the Sky" on the soundtrack of a key scene in his classic modern noir of urban despair, *Taxi Driver* (1976). The gloom in the grooves of that album make it a zeitgeist record if there ever was one. The album contained no hit singles, but it attracted a large audience anyway, putting Browne at the forefront of a singer-songwriter movement alongside peers like Joni Mitchell, Paul Simon, and James Taylor.

The breakthrough to large-scale fame, long predicted by critics if not by Browne himself, came with *The Pretender* (1976). Produced by Jon Landau, who was hot off the success of producing the bulk of Springsteen's *Born to Run* and who coaxed Browne into creating a modern studio sound to complement his increasingly ambitious lyrics, *The Pretender* was a bold and unusually astute assessment of how Browne's generation was confronting the "greater awakening" that attended the shattering of its sixties hopes. At the same time, it wrestled with the loss in Browne's own life—his wife committed suicide during the making of the record. The album presaged by several years the emergence of the "yuppie"—a figure, pervasive in the 1980s, that served as a signifier for the collapse of the counterculture's idealism and its subsequent embrace of the "happy idiot[s]" of Reaganite materialism. Its platinum sales driven by two hit singles, *The Pretender* made Browne a bona fide rock star at the same time that his personal life was in utter disarray. His struggles to make love real in his life—the value his music held most dear to this point—had curdled into tragedy, and in its wake he was forced to confront that failure at the same time that he was raising his very young son.

Part strategy to avoid writing and recording a new studio record as he was dealing with his wife's death, part understandable escape to the road, *Running on Empty* (1977) somehow made Browne an even bigger star. Bookended by the opening cut's rocking meditation on a panicked rootlessness and aimlessness that amazed Browne even while he was living it ("I can't tell you all how crazy this life feels") and a sweet conclusion yoking his sincere gratitude for his life on the road with a paean to his audience ("The Load Out/Stay"), the album, almost fifty years on, remains one of the great rock 'n' roll road documents. In between there were songs, mostly written or cowritten by other people, that showed Browne loosening his control over his material and welcoming contributions from his band, particularly from David Lindley, who finally was receiving well-deserved plaudits for what he brought to Browne's music.

After that album and the international touring that followed, Browne, who had released five albums in six years, pulled back. He holed up in Los Angeles with new girlfriend Lynne Sweeney and for a while concentrated on raising his son. It also heralded a time of serious political reflection for Browne, who at the behest of friends in the Eagles had previously involved himself in Jerry Brown's quixotic presidential campaign in 1976 and found himself disillusioned by it. Now, however, he found an outlet for his political sympathies: he became a dedicated activist against nuclear power, a long-standing concern of Browne's that had prompted many of his allusions to apocalypse in his early music. That led to his helping organize, with Musicians United for Safe Energy (MUSE), the for-charity No Nukes concerts in 1979 and the subsequent live album and film that documented it. Thus began what has become a kind of second, parallel career for Browne as an activist for progressive causes.

When he got back to the recording studio, he emerged with *Hold Out* (1980) an album that explains in the plainest of terms what Browne's whole body of work has been about at the same time that it displays an uncertainty, mostly musical, that confused his fans and gave off the exhaust fumes of a man who didn't quite know where he was going. The cover itself announced a big change: discarding the subdued earth tones that color most of his first five album covers, Browne chose to be photographed against a garish neon-orange background. The cover blares that the 1960s are long gone and that this ain't even the 1970s anymore either. The sound, too, was startling for a Jackson Browne record. Here was studio-tooled rock music: big loud guitars, deeply echoed drums, quicker tempos, and the sheen of the hitmakers of the moment. And Browne's voice is bigger, more agile, and capable of holding its own against the guitars and electronic keyboards. It won't do to say that punk or New Wave had influenced him, but certainly Browne was aiming for a more intense, enveloping sound, suitable for the arenas he was now capable of filling. That helps explain guitar workouts like "Boulevard," one of the first real failures in the Browne catalog, or "Disco Apocalypse," musically dynamic if one hell of a muddle lyrically.

A song cycle about the course of a romantic relationship, the album starts with the protagonist's failure to connect with a lover in the title cut. It then journeys through songs about loneliness, temptation, short-term hookups, and the death of a friend until the protagonist declares, in the ambitious final cut, "Hold On Hold Out," that he and his new lover will forever be "holdouts," that is, people who take their stand on the ideals of the sixties, who can't and won't settle for anything less. It's disappointing, however, that the naked appeal to love that Browne makes at the album's conclusion feels forced and unconvincing. I've titled this book after this album because I think the main thrust of all Browne's music (and political activism) concerns constantly (permanently) committing and recommitting himself to the values of love, justice, and equality that he formed when he was a very young man. *Hold Out* is the clearest expression of that commitment, though it hardly contains the best musical expressions of it.

The rest of the 1980s were a hard slog for Browne. As critic Rob Sheffield has pointed out, many of the great 1960s talents—Dylan, Joni Mitchell, Van Morrison, Neil Young—did their weakest work during the 1980s, and Browne is among them.[5] That collective nadir of artistic quality might be a coincidence; a lot of their struggles were obviously personal and particular to them. Still, it's tempting to think that the 1980 election (and landslide reelection in 1984) of Ronald Reagan, which signified a wholesale rejection of the social and cultural values that sustained these artists their entire careers, threw them off in some way and forced them to reassess their music, audiences, and outlooks in ways that took them far afield from their strengths. All five of these artists lost much of their fan base during the decade, and some of them seemed to be just wandering in the wilderness.

Browne can't be said to have wandered—in fact, records like *Lives in the Balance* (1986) and *World in Motion* (1989) were maybe the most focused records he's ever made. But his dedication to public causes led him to commit himself to an explicitly political music that, to put it kindly, lacked the lyrical nuance of his previous work. At the time, especially after fact-finding trips took him to Central America in 1984 and 1985, where he witnessed firsthand the corrupt means by which the United States was attempting to subdue leftist revolutionary activity, Browne said that he "had less appetite for extreme introspection."[6] His turn toward politics was passionate and sincere, even occasionally moving, but Browne didn't have the vocal chops or musical ability to portray real rage—which was essentially the emotional response he had toward the Cold War tensions and racial antagonisms that the Reagan administration had intensified. He also didn't learn that crucial lesson that the best way to put across a political position in a pop song is not to state it outright (however sincerely) but to put it in the mouth of a character in a dramatic situation. (Emily Dickinson once advised, "Tell the truth / But tell it slant." Actually, Browne learned that lesson in "The Pretender" and then, barring a few exceptions, forgot it again.) But what is especially dispiriting about these records is that the playing and production feel like standard LA session work, expert but anonymous. *World in Motion*, in fact, bottoms out Browne's career: it's musically slick and lyrically a pedantic thud. As producer Don Was once facetiously suggested, it's like watching Browne lecturing about domestic and foreign policy with a slide projector, a pointer, and a map. At times it stumbles into agitprop, guaranteed to turn off anyone who isn't already in his camp and obvious or aesthetically oppressive to those who are.

Four years later, he came out with *I'm Alive* (1993), which astute reviewers and relieved fans saw as a "return to form"— the familiar Browne of the early to midseventies was back, the political didacticism and rock bombast of the eighties albums replaced by a modest sonic palette and songs that dealt almost exclusively with the perils of love. Browne indeed had a story to tell: he'd married Lynne Sweeney in 1982 and had a child with her, but he divorced her quickly after his romance with actress Daryl Hannah began, a relationship that would last a tumultuous nine years and include some damaging exposure in the tabloids. *I'm Alive* contains two of Browne's best songs—the title tune and the devastating and beautiful "Sky Blue and Black," along with material that delved, with convincing sympathy and anger, at a long, failed relationship. It also includes a gem called "My Problem Is You," where Browne's struggle with sensuality and the lure of beauty is more revealing than ever before and where he displays a comic irony about himself that actually works. "I don't care about the ozone layer / Just let those rays come through," he sings, kidding the political animal he was throughout the 1980s: "When I'm outside I keep my clothes on / My problem is you."

The "return to the personal" continued on the next two albums, *Looking East* (1996) and *The Naked Ride Home* (2002), but for the first time in his career he found a working balance that allowed for a full and mature airing of his social and political concerns as well. "I want to live in the world / Not inside my head," he sang in "Alive in the World," and on these albums he's fully alive in both. Songs like "The Barricades of Heaven," "The Naked Ride Home," and "My Stunning Mystery Companion" are finely etched portraits of the intimate life, as good as anything he'd ever written, while "Information Wars" and "Casino Nation" are detailed and analytically sharp state-of-the-nation addresses to an America addled by the white noise of mass media and the depredations of neoliberalism. In "Don't You Want to Be There" and "Looking East," he combines the personal and political concerns to inspiring effect. "Looking East," particularly, is maybe the most philosophically interesting song in Browne's catalog, conveying a vision of nature's power—a power that includes the animate and the inanimate, stones and seas, animals and plants, as well as the emotions of human beings—that invokes the metaphysical vastness of poems like Shelley's "Ode to the West Wind," films like Terence Malick's *The Thin Red Line*, or some of Buddha's teachings. Looking east indeed.

Both these albums, for all their intensity, are relaxed and sure of themselves, the probable result of Browne having assembled a band with whom he was to forge a long-lasting working relationship, particularly with bass player and producer Kevin McCormick. Also, and significantly, Jackson no longer seemed to care about being the rock star he was in the seventies and early eighties. He hadn't had a Top 10 hit since "Somebody's Baby" back in 1982 and, in the years since, had watched the vast rock audience move on to pop metal, grunge, hip-hop, dance music, and boy bands. Now he seemed to feel relief at dropping out of the multiplatinum success game: "I lost track of the score long ago," he sang in "Barricades." And it didn't hurt that some of Browne's political agitation had been at least partially assuaged in the nineties, as the Cold War ended and the Clinton administration's rhetoric and policies, for all their shortcomings, seemed less pernicious than those of the Reagan-Bush years. Finally, as "My Stunning Mystery Companion" makes vividly clear, Browne had found a new and very different love in Dianna Cohen, to whom he's devoted at least one song per album ever since.

Political agitation returns on the next two albums, *Time the Conqueror* (2006) and *Standing in the Breach* (2014). Leaving Asylum Records to found his own label, Inside Recordings, which from then on released and distributed his music, Browne was now free from major label commercial pressures. He used the freedom partly to release three live albums containing older, reinterpreted material, including one CD that reunited him with old sidekick David Lindley. But he also wrote music as pointedly political as anything he'd written since the 1980s, music that confronted the rightward drift of the country during the George W. Bush years and its accompanying calamities—9/11, the wars in Afghanistan and Iraq, the Citizens United Supreme Court case, the Great Recession, the Haiti earthquake, and continued environmental havoc, symbolized by the Gulf Oil Spill in 2010. Browne's political activism and charitable work, now international in scope (especially Haiti and Central America), took up much of his time during these years and became the central focus of his music once more. And again, the results are (aesthetically at least), equivocal. *Time the Conqueror* boasts two fine reminiscences of the 1960s in "Off of Wonderland" and "Giving That Heaven Away," a fascinating peek into the nature of desire in "Live Nude Cabaret," and an ambitious title track, but it's bogged down by long broadsides about the Bush administration's failure with Hurricane Katrina ("Where Were You," which goes on for almost ten minutes) the depredations and corruptions of the Iraq War ("The Drums of War," at 6:12), and the frankly tired call, in "Far from the Arms of Hunger," for the United States to "turn around" from its Ameri-centric ways.

Standing in the Breach (2014) is much better. It opens with "The Birds of St. Mark," a Dylanesque song he'd written in his late teens but never recorded, whose inventive melody and lyric rouse Browne to a strong vocal performance. Some of the record is dedicated to extended political rants ("Which Side?") but the title cut and "The Long Way Around" are profound expressions of the personal anguish involved in being a holdout for political causes. And "Walls and Doors," with its fine observation, "There can be freedom only when nobody owns it," can be rousing at a concert full of Browne-ian progressives.

Those two albums saw Jackson's fan base dwindling, however; the music that brought his fans in (the 1970s stuff and reminders of that kind of music on *I'm Alive* and *Looking East*) was largely absent, and lots of folks wondered whether Browne's muse would fully return. Which made the 2021 release of *Downhill from Everywhere* as much a relief as *I'm Alive* was after his weak 1980s stretch. Far from the downer that the title seems to imply, the album finds him energized and at the top of his game. It's full of frisky, funny pop-rock ("Cleveland Heart"), musical delight and liberation ("A Song for Barcelona"), and the finest ballad he'd written in more than two decades: the AIDS lament, "A Human Touch." Browne avoided commenting on the Trump administration—his talent, for good or ill, is too reality-based and sincere to address Trumpian levels of absurdity—but there are two songs whose intelligence and heartening strength in the face of twenty-first-century sociopolitical realities are balms for the battered souls that Browne's been appealing to for half a century. "Downhill from Everywhere," with its wide environmental scope, is as ambitious and lyrically arresting as "Looking East," and "A Little Soon to Say," which offers a slender ray of hope in the future, is as warmly poignant as anything he's ever written.

How many fifty-year careers do we have in the history of rock music that are of this sustained quality and integrity? Unlike others any of us could name—stars who extended their careers for the money or just because they were habituated to the life—Browne never stopped using music as a vehicle of existential search and social analysis. In 2004, Browne curated his own two-CD, thirty-two-song set called *The Very Best of Jackson Browne,* an exceptionally well-chosen selection of his most potent music up to that time. A 2024 update of that collection could add another fifteen songs to that list. Browne has provided a nearly fifty-classic-song legacy that chronicles his country's path through cultural revolution, economic and racial strife, political depredation, environmental devastation, and his own quest for love and the realization of the American ideal. The opening track of his most recent album is a modest little folk-rocker called "Still Looking for Something," and in its quiet way, the title says it all. Seventy-six years into his life, Jackson Browne's eyes are still smarting—just like the kid's from "Doctor My Eyes"—from seeing too much of the world. But he is *still looking.*

1

"THE BARRICADES OF HEAVEN"

It should come as a surprise to exactly nobody that Jackson Browne is prone to retrospection. He started writing "looking-back" songs (like "Looking into You") before he had that much to look back on. One of the best of them comes from 1996's *Looking East*, where after nostalgically recalling the clubs he used to play when he and his friends were just starting out in music, Browne comes at us with this:

> Better bring your own redemption when you come
> From the barricades of heaven where I'm from.

Interesting phrase: "the barricades of heaven" brings to mind "Gates of Eden," of course, Bob Dylan's psychedelic plaint from *Bringing It All Back Home*, which catalogs, in its fantastical way, the political and psychic chaos (war, the absurd, breakdowns in communication) of a modern world—the world we all know—that Dylan tells us is nowhere near the gates of paradise. Eden may exist somewhere, Dylan is saying, but who knows where it's gone—we've sure as hell been banished (presumably to Highway 61). Browne's song has less cosmic scope but is clearer and more compassionate—a not atypical contrast when comparing Dylan and Browne side by side. Both songs suggest an enduring obstacle between the idealized desires of the heart and a hard world pitilessly resistant to them. In Browne's song, however, he gives us the barricade but also a glimpse of the heaven on the other side.

The song's mostly a backward glance at Browne's teen years, but in the final verse he takes us even further back: "Childhood comes to me at night," he sings, the music quieting to a soft tremolo of guitar and a wisp of drums—and then we get a peek beyond the barricades:

Your face bathing me in light
Hope that never ends.

This is a mythical image of Mother, of course, though it's likely more than mythical: Browne's mother, Bea Amanda, had died in 1988, and these lines were surely an homage to her. The Mother's face, aglow, baths the Child in light, love, and eternal hope and gives him his first indelible sense of the possibilities for light, love, and hope in his future. So, beyond the barricades—the Primal Bliss of Mother Love. But as the Child grows, the bliss is lost, the barricades are raised, and the child becomes a man, wandering and wondering how he can recapture it. Yes, this is straight-up Freud, but sometimes straight-up Freud cuts to the chase. In any case, Jackson joins here a long history of art expressing these sentiments, from D. H. Lawrence's *Sons and Lovers* to John Lennon's radically modern "Mother" (sans the primal screaming).

That glimpse of mother love, however, is just that—a glimpse. The song is mostly about the barricades *keeping* him from that heaven, so the song is actually about living *without redemption.* I think that all his life, Browne has craved redemption from the emptiness he felt behind those barricades and that he was driven to seek that bliss again: first in music, for a time in drugs, then for the duration in sex, love, music, and communion with like-minded people whose political views aligned with his. Occasionally, he even found it—and expressed it in song. But we have to begin with those barricades—which takes us to that hard world, separating him from heaven, that Browne is "from."

WHERE JACKSON BROWNE IS "FROM"

Technically, he's from Heidelberg, Germany, where he was born Clyde Jackson Browne on October 9, 1948. (His father worked, as a civilian, for the US military paper *Stars and Stripes.*) But that doesn't tell us much, because when he was three, Browne's parents returned the family to the United States, moving back to Los Angeles and the Highland Park neighborhood where Jackson's grandfather had built a gracious Spanish-mission–style house (now called Abbey San Encino, a protected architectural site) whose interior courtyard graces the cover of *For Everyman.*[1] At the time, Highland Park was a dicey, mixed-race neighborhood, and by the age of ten, Jackson, a skinny little tough guy, was getting into scrapes with the neighborhood kids and being stopped by the LAPD, who once found chains and straight-edge razors on his person. "For two or three years before moving to Orange County," Browne remembers, "I was hanging around the public playgrounds and underneath the railroad trestle hearing tales about the California Youth Authority and the penal system. . . . I met guys all the time that probably came out of juvenile programs [and] from YA [who said that] Highland Park was almost like a no-man's land, a battleground between the Chicano gangs and the white gangs. Me and my friends were [racially] mixed, but the prevailing neighborhood style and attitudes were Chicano. We weren't gang members, but nearly everybody we knew were in gangs."[2] It was the fifties, and amid considerable talk in the national media about "juvenile delinquency"—movies like *Blackboard Jungle* and *Rebel without a Cause,* and Kerouac's sensational novel *On the Road,* were pop culture rages—Browne's parents thought it would be a good idea to remove Jackson and his two siblings from the temptations of LA's mean streets. So they moved again, in 1960, when Jackson was twelve, this time to the safe, antiseptic, and recently paved boulevards of Orange County, specifically to a new housing subdivision in Fullerton called Sunny Hills.

Jackson had loved Highland Park and later had a habit of returning to his old house, even if it meant bugging the current residents (something he recounts in "Looking into You"). He immediately found Fullerton alienating, however. In the postwar era, Fullerton, once the province of orange groves, oil fields, and cattle ranches, had welcomed in aerospace giant Hughes Aircraft and assorted other manufacturing companies, all of them eager to soak up their share of Cold War defense dollars. In the boom years of the 1950s and 1960s, unemployment barely existed in Fullerton, and the white middle class bloomed, bolstered by the GI bill, federal largesse by way of Pentagon contracts, and a thriving real estate market. The city was able to present itself as a sort of suburban paradise (West Coast, Beach Boys division), the kind now familiar from old newsreels: nuclear families (dads working, moms staying home, lots of kids) living in houses they owned, complete with TVs, backyards, and swimming pools; large parks where smartly suited-up Little Leaguers played baseball on Saturday mornings; Boys Club and Girl Scout meetings helping to sublimate all that adolescent libido; surfers heading to the beach in wood-paneled station wagons; a strong public school system filled with kids abiding by rigid codes of social conformity; and churches filled with worshippers on Sundays. Of course, de facto segregation kept whites and Hispanics (the main minority group in OC at the time) in separate schools and neighborhoods. And Fullerton, like much of Orange County, was becoming a hotbed of reactionary conservatism, providing a hospitable setting for rabidly anti-communist and racist groups like the John Birch Society.[3]

This was the context—a lily-white suburb populated with folks who could have served as precursors for "The Pretender"—in which the adolescent Jackson developed his thoughts about the larger world. Fullerton and its environs had raised its barricades against him. It was exactly the kind of place from which sensitive American dreamers drift into disillusionment—thus, despite his obvious intelligence, young Jackson's alienation and his surprisingly indifferent academic performance in high school. Though he tried to fit in—going out for football and track, surfing in Huntington Beach—he didn't, or couldn't, and found himself a loner of sorts, moody, moony, evidently constantly lovelorn, and nursing his sensitivities by writing poetry and strumming a guitar. "In the first year and a half [of high school] he was your basic squirrelly freshman," one friend noted, "running around and doing what the other guys were doing. Then, all of a sudden, he became very serious about his music."[4]

THE CRUCIBLE

What led to that sudden seriousness? It seems that during his sophomore year of high school, in the last half of 1963 and into 1964, he entered a crucible of sorts. Within the space of just a few months, a number of indelible national events occurred that critically shaped Browne and the emerging counterculture he would soon align himself with and, together with his intense anxieties about his fracturing family, changed him and gave him a focus that was to redirect his life from that time forward.

The national events are familiar and easy to enumerate, but we should try to understand how they might have affected Jackson at the impressionable age of fifteen. The first is the March on Washington for Jobs and Freedom that took place on August 28, 1963. It was here that Martin Luther King Jr. delivered his "I Have a Dream" Speech, and where, hardly coincidentally, Bob Dylan introduced himself to a national audience by singing "Only a Pawn in Their Game." King was a well-known figure by then, but to most whites—even those outside the South—he was still a troublemaker, shadowy and untrustworthy. The speech, however, was overwhelming in its impact and helped turn the tide in the civil rights struggle; it prompted even a dyed-in-the-wool Texan like Lyndon Johnson, whose political career had floated on anti-integrationist Dixiecrat support for decades, to muscle through Congress the groundbreaking Civil Rights Act of 1964 and the

Voting Rights Act of 1965. Soon after that speech, and with a little nudging from his liberal mother—Bea was an English teacher, an avid reader of the underground paper *The LA Free Press*, and a fan of left-wing radio station KPFK—fifteen-year-old Jackson enthusiastically joined the NAACP. A few years later, he even briefly participated in a civil rights action, attempting to help integrate a neighborhood, though he quickly became disenchanted with partisan politics and quit. "I was involved with the civil rights movement for a short period of time," Jackson recalled in 1976, "but that was short-lived, I became disillusioned with that. White kids with good intentions trying to see that Negroes could move in on the same block, and the fact is . . . who the fuck wants to? The real issues are whether or not they're gonna get work."[5]

The King influence on Browne, I think, was greater than the fact that King spoke to ideals of equality, justice, and freedom that smart, young white boys like Browne believed in but knew weren't real in the world they saw around them. It was also the philosophy of nonviolence behind those ideals, and behind that, the faith in the concept of love as the primary value motivating all action in the world, personal or political. King worked out these ideas in early speeches like "Facing the Challenges of a New Age" (1957) and "The Power of Nonviolence" (1958).[6] In those addresses, King Jr. pointed out the classical distinction between three kinds of love: eros, which he defined as aesthetic or romantic love (though "eros" also means sexual love, something that King, in the 1950s, didn't think it was appropriate to mention); philia, as the reciprocal love between respectful friends; and finally agape, which he defined as "the understanding, creative, redemptive goodwill for all men." Scholars of theology, King added, "would say it is the love of God working in the minds of men. It is an overflowing love which seeks nothing in return. . . . It is the type of love that stands at the center of the movement that we are trying to carry on in the Southland."[7] By 1967, in his famous "Where Do We Go from Here?" speech in Chicago, King articulated as well as he ever would the idea that love was the ultimate source and strength that supported political principle, an idea King inherited from a whole line of thinkers, among them Gandhi, Tolstoy, and Percy Shelley, but which he now saw as most relevant to the struggle for civil rights in America: "Power without love," he said, "is reckless and abusive, and . . . love without power is sentimental and anemic. *Power at its best, power at its best is love, implementing the demands of justice* [my italics], and justice at its best is love correcting everything that stands against love."[8] It was this idea that percolated slowly through Jackson's mind as a youth and eventually became fundamental to his vision of political music and activism. "When the Stone Begins to Turn" (from 1989's *World in Motion*) credits King (and Nelson Mandela) for turning the tides of history toward freedom and equality, as does "Off to Wonderland" (from 2008's *Time the Conqueror*). And in both songs, the engine of change is love.

Bob Dylan's presence at the March on Washington can't be overestimated as a critical moment for Jackson's development as well as for the counterculture generally. Dylan's topical songs like "Only a Pawn in Their Game" or "The Lonesome Death of Hattie Carroll" had revitalized a folk music movement that had largely trafficked in reinterpretations of traditional folk or dull-bladed political stabs about the contemporary situation. Dylan's songs—ballsy, alternately sensitive and nasty, incensed at the gross stupidities of leaders beholden to the death logic of a nuclear war mentality, disgusted by racial injustice, dismissive of the blancmange liberalism of his era—were bracing shots in the arm for a young generation eager to awaken from the somnolence of fifties shibboleths. It was after the March, in fact, that Browne's friends Steve Noonan and Greg Copeland formed a "protest clique" at Sunny Hills High School and began organizing hootenannies that attempted to spread the word to their high school peers about "the struggle." "Greg Copeland," Browne remembers, "was the guy who made me want to write songs. Greg and Steve Noonan."[9] Browne eagerly joined up and, in the process, his own fascination with Dylan began.[10] When Jackson had first picked up a guitar, he played the surf music popular with his brother and his friends and then moved on to the polite strains of contemporary white folk music—Pete Seeger and the Weavers, and Joan Baez. But with Bob Dylan, the floodgates were released. He became obsessed, buying Dylan's first three LPs and soaking up a whole new style of making music—of vocalizing, of lyric writing, of self-presentation in performance—that opened up worlds of possibility. In the process, he exposed himself to "protest" Dylan ("Blowin' in the Wind," "Masters of War," "A Hard Rain's Gonna Fall," "The Times They Are A-Changin'") that would initiate him to leftist politics—especially about racism, the abuse of political power, and the insanities of the nuclear arms race—that would inform his music for the rest of his life.

Less than three months after the March on Washington, John F. Kennedy was assassinated as his motorcade passed through a parade in Dallas, Texas. If there was a single event that captured the "absurdity" of the era—that sense that history's violence was purposeless, thus meaningless—it was the assassination. Albert Camus's *The Myth of Sisyphus* (translated into English in 1955) and Paul Goodman's *Growing Up Absurd* (1961) had prepped American high culture to the concept already, but Lenny Bruce's wicked standup and TV's *The Twilight Zone* (which ran from 1959 to 1964) had served as its trickle-down filter to the pop mainstream. Kennedy was a young, rich, handsome, telefriendly war hero who, in being elected president, symbolized for millions a generational transition and a new vitality in American life—and who called specifically for the young to be part of a vast and ambitious "New Frontier." Here was someone who people hoped might be able to transcend Cold War dread and the stifling conformity of the Eisenhower years. Even a cultural radical like Norman Mailer saw in the politically middle-of-the-road Kennedy the possibility of jolting the country out of its 1950s anemia.[11]

After a disastrous start to his presidency with the Bay of Pigs invasion, Kennedy proved a steady hand through the potentially apocalyptic Cuban Missile Crisis, and was resisting his generals' advice to widen US participation in the Vietnam conflict. In 1963, he was even gingerly moving toward more progressive civil rights positions, all of which felt promising to the growing contingent of liberals who had once dismissed Kennedy as an Establishment stooge. Then he was gunned down. The loss of Kennedy as a symbol of liberal hope was made manifest when his funeral procession was televised to a nation full of shocked mourners. (They made up the largest TV audience in history up to that time.) This outbreak of violence was made infinitely more appalling when Kennedy's accused murderer, Lee Harvey Oswald, was shot and killed two days later on live TV—the first ever live TV killing—by the Mafia-connected Jack Ruby, from which event conspiracy theories flourished for decades. The shock of the assassination and its aftermath to the nation's psychic life was incalculable: suddenly American trust in the strength and authority of their governmental institutions was undercut by violent psychotics and underworld figures. In fact, this undermining of authority accounts for why some historians identify the assassination as the true beginning of what we now call "The Sixties."[12]

The next year opened with a nation enthralled by the appearance of the Beatles on the *Ed Sullivan Show*. Beatlemania was real—the band's thrillingly energetic and melodic tunes injected into the national mood an irresistible mix of innocence, insouciant wit, and pent-up sexual dynamism that in many ways helped buoy the country as it worked through its mourning. Browne loved the band, too, especially John Lennon: throughout his career, in fact, he's given props to Lennon and played at charity concerts in his honor. In a 2010 interview, he said, "I've been celebrating John Lennon's [birthday] for my whole life. . . . You forget he had half a life. . . . He was so productive. The ingenuity, the bed-in, resolutely speaking out about the war, putting it all in human terms. 'Come together, over me.' That's what the Beatles always did. They were always on the forefront of everything we were discovering."[13] In a 2021 interview, when asked which artist had the greatest influence on his own ability to mix the personal with the political, Jackson replied, "John Lennon, because I grew up listening to the Beatles. And you have room on your albums to hear the most intimate song, 'She's Leaving Home,' say, as well as 'A Day in the Life.' So the breadth and the depth of the Beatles and the ability to move from a very intimate picture to a very universal one informs I think my whole life, my whole idea of music, what music is for."[14] His respect for Lennon gets enshrined in a song too. In the nostalgic "Off of Wonderland," Browne wonders if, after the sixties, "we could just believe in one another / As much as we believed in John," propping up Lennon as a kind of spiritual leader of the counterculture as well as for Browne himself. The Beatles have been a continued vital presence in his life.

The March on Washington, with the twin appearances of King and Dylan; the Kennedy assassination; the Beatles' arrival on American shores: in about four months, these events jelled and helped solidify a sense among young Americans everywhere, Jackson among them, that a change was in the air. These events would've been enough to change the perspective of any alert young kid, but for Jackson, they were occurring while his parents' marriage was falling apart.

In the fall of 1963, he began to ditch a lot of class and spend time at the Sunny Hills High School health center with the center's director, Vera Fitzgerald, who remembers a boy who quietly scribbled poetry and gradually opened up to her about "his parents' developing marital problems." "My general impression," Fitzgerald told an interviewer, "was of a rather scrawny, unattractive kid who was kind of sad, and sort of mixed up, and had to be in the nurse's room. I remember a kind of reticence to talk. Looking back, it seemed that he was a person looking for some kind of intimacy, some kind of relationship but was kind of reticent to ask for it."[15] Browne's been disinclined to talk about this part of his life, possibly because, as he revealed in a 1992 interview, he had repressed most of it: "If you ask me what kind of childhood I had, I'd say 'Normal.' Then I'd say 'I don't remember,' and that immediately makes me suspicious. . . . At one point, I realized I can't remember *anything* about my childhood." One of the things he does remember, however, was that his father was an alcoholic: "The word 'dysfunctional' gets thrown out a lot, but I don't think this was a particularly 'functional' family."[16] That his father, a frustrated jazz musician who took on jobs as a printer or teacher to support his family, was fired from his high school English teaching position after two years on the job can only have made matters worse. It's easy to imagine how a boy as emotionally sensitive as Jackson would respond to the marital discord that would, in fact, lead to his parents' separation in late 1964, a divorce in 1965, and by the end of that year, to his father leaving his family altogether to live and work in Japan. During the early to mid-sixties, divorce was by no means as common among the white middle class as it would later become, so the divorce and his father's disappearance from his life was likely a severe shock to Jackson's whole sense of the world. He reacted to it by throwing himself wholly into music. Music, to be blunt about it, was the path he took to try to redeem the emptiness created by his family's breakup and the crumbling of his country's ideals.

SIXTEEN AND ON HIS OWN

The year 1964 was the personal turning point for Browne. That's when he turned sixteen (as he says in "Barricades," "I was sixteen *and on my own*") and began building his musical skills. He became a competent acoustic guitar player, but most of his energy was directed to songwriting—and his songwriting was what first turned people's heads. Along with Noonan, Copeland, and a group of aspiring performers (which for a time included Tim Buckley), Browne started performing solo at a two-hundred-seat coffeehouse in nearby Tustin called The Paradox, where he honed his guitar picking and introduced OC folkies to his growing collection of original compositions. "These Days," a preternaturally mature song of contemplative regret about failures in love and ambition written by a high school sophomore, comes from this time. Also from this early period: "Holdin'," "Melissa," and "It's Been Raining Here in Long Beach" (recorded by the Nitty Gritty Dirt Band in 1966); "Fairest of the Season," cowritten by Copeland, and "Somewhere There's a Feather" (both recorded by Nico in 1967); "She's a Flying Thing" and "The Painter" (recorded by Noonan in 1968); "Shadow Dream Song" (recorded by Noonan as well as Tom Rush in 1968), and two dozen others, a few of which made it, sooner or later, onto other people's records, or even Browne's ("Sing My Songs to Me" eventually appeared on *For Everyman*).

That so many songs written by a high school kid were recorded by major label artists speaks to a prodigious talent, and you can hear it for yourself if you can rustle up the two-CD bootleg called *The Nina Music Demos*, which contains thirty of Browne's early songs in voice-and-acoustic-guitar demos he recorded in two sessions in New York in 1967, after he'd been hired as a songwriter by Bill James at Electra Records.[17] The demos are full of lyrics built around carefully crafted metaphors, self-consciously poetic in tone. Some are songs about the journey an innocent young man is about to embark upon, taking wand'ring steps and slow, as he leaves Eden on his solitary way. There are plenty of not-bad, sensitive, Donovanesque tunes devoted to appreciating beguiling, mysterious women. You'll hear "These Days" (when it was called "I've Been Out Walking") before Gregg Allman rewrote the melody and recorded it himself. You'll hear "Lavender Windows," whose imagery suggests that Browne was smoking a lot of marijuana, a very illegal drug in the mid-1960s. You'll hear "Shadow Dream Song," a catchy, melodically inventive tune whose line, "She's a laughing dappled shadow," was impressively Dylanish. You'll hear "The Fairest of the Seasons," even more melodically inventive and one of Browne's first attempts to put across what would become one of his specialties: the chronicling of a relationship in its death throes, when a couple, knowing things are at their end, can't quite make the final decision to end it (e.g., "My Opening Farewell," "Late for the Sky," "Miles Away," "All Good Things," lots of others). You'll hear some walkin' songs—another Browne specialty—like "4th and Main," that records a guy's impressions as he jauntily strolls through urban streets. You'll even hear some vaudeville or jazz influences that Browne tried once and would never use again.

What you won't hear is a guy who can sing. Listen to *The Nina Music Demos* closely—to the *songwriting*—and you'll know you're in the presence of a vibrant new talent brimming with lyrical and melodic invention. Listen to it casually, as you're doing the dishes, and you'll want to channel John Belushi in *Animal House* and crush Browne's guitar against a wall. It's not that Browne's voice is shallow and callow, though that's bad enough; it's that he hasn't yet learned to sing from the lungs, and so everything buzzes through his narrow voice box in a dry, croaky baritone. It's also that he sings with a sense of fake sophistication common to so many other folk artists at the time, and in a way that has no relationship at all to his natural SoCal voice and mode of articulation. (Why he didn't learn from Dylan to avoid this is a puzzle.) What's perhaps worst of all is that his strong melodies demand a voice that he just doesn't have yet. Reaching for the high notes or a tricky melodic passage, he makes you wince. To appreciate these demos, you really have to imagine somebody else singing them.

To be fair, none of this was lost on Browne. When he heard that Nina, his publishing company, had pressed a hundred copies of the demos so that they could be handed out to producers and artists who might want to cover

Browne's songs, he personally destroyed almost half of them with his bare hands.

Being a lousy singer didn't hurt him with the girls, however; his earnest demeanor, his instinctive self-confidence, and a face getting prettier by the day seemed to cover a multitude of sins. Playing at the Paradox, the Golden Bear, and other venues in OC and LA through his junior and senior years gave him a considerable popularity upgrade at Sunny Hills High. He grew his hair out to the length the Beatles sported in *A Hard Day's Night*. He paid more attention to how he dressed. The adoring looks he got from girls in the audience made him realize he was a catch, and from all indications he took full advantage. His own private sexual revolution began—a new way to try to break down the barricades of heaven. Drugs were still another way. At age sixteen, he was not just smoking pot but also dropping tabs of LSD, at the time a drug so new it wasn't even illegal yet. And by that summer, Browne was "running up 101" every chance he could get, eager to learn whatever he could from the folk-rock scene that had exploded on the Sunset Strip.

By the following summer—we're up to 1966 now—Browne managed to graduate from high school, though the last thing on his mind was academics. Aside from his music, a war was on. The United States had committed hundreds of thousands of troops to Vietnam, plunging neck-deep into a conflict that would divide the country as no other war had since the 1860s. Browne himself was drafted but managed to avoid service by taking so much methedrine in the days before his induction medical that the Army, examining his wasted body, refused to take him. (It was something that later shamed him, as he admits in the opening stanza of "For America.") A free speech movement had caught fire on college campuses, providing an activist focus for the emerging New Left. The civil rights movement was tallying its first major legislative victories. Motown's music mill had coaxed white America into an integrated love affair with black music. And Los Angeles had become the center of the folk-rock world, with the Byrds riding high with "Tambourine Man," "Turn Turn Turn," and "Eight Miles High." The Doors had just recorded "Break On Through (to the Other Side)" and would soon hit big with "Light My Fire." In the fall of 1966, there were "hippie riots" on Sunset Boulevard that inspired the Buffalo Springfield's Stephen Stills to write "For What It's Worth." Dylan's folk-rock trilogy (*Bringing It All Back Home*, *Highway 61 Revisited*, and *Blonde on Blonde*) had completely rewired rock 'n' roll circuitry, as had the Beatles with *their* trilogy (*Rubber Soul*,

Revolver, and *Sgt. Pepper's Lonely Hearts Club Band*) and Jimi Hendrix's *Are You Experienced?* The counterculture had fully arrived, and Browne was in the perfect place to receive it. In fact, he would come to embody a certain strain of it.

BROWNE AND THE MAKING OF THE COUNTERCULTURE

The counterculture of the sixties was an explosion of Dionysian energy not seen in Western culture since the late eighteenth century, when the American and French revolutions and the cultural propulsions of Romanticism (the standard bearers would be Goethe, Rousseau, and William Blake) began the long process of upending political and social orders that had been in place for centuries. The counterculture was also, of course, a specific reaction to the emotional repression, social conformity, and political quietism of the 1950s, though that repression, conformity, and quietism were themselves collective traumatic responses to the horrors of World War II, which gave us scores of millions dead across four continents, an attempt by the most culturally sophisticated country in the West to wipe an entire race off the planet, and a weapon that could incinerate seventy thousand people in seconds. (J. Oppenheimer, the man who headed up the Manhattan Project that created the bombs dropped on Hiroshima and Nagasaki, watched a test explosion of his weapon, only to remark, quoting the Bhagavad Gita, "Now I am become Death, the destroyer of worlds.")

The sixties counterculture was impulsive, often blazingly and proudly irrational; it called for an embrace of the body, the promise of the now, the flash of passion, joining a youthful disdain for a horrendous past with a patently naive hope about the future. But anyone who went through it knew where John Sebastian and his band, the Lovin' Spoonful, were coming from when they sang, "Do You Believe in Magic?"[18] Dionysian revolts are by their nature eruptions of magical thinking where one trusts one's enthusiasms (from the original Greek *en-theos*, meaning "the god within") as if they were messages from the gods. That these enthusiasms were primarily about liberation—liberation of the body, liberation from political restraints, liberation of repressed races, liberation from artistic traditions—ensured that the consequences would be profoundly messy. Watch the long traffic jam scene in Godard's *Weekend* (1968) for a great symbolic summation of the chaos the counterculture inspired.

So here was a mass, indeed international, movement, largely transmitted by mass media and manifested largely in pop culture. But the counterculture's roots lay deep in intellectual history, going back to the Greeks and European Romanticism and then forward to twentieth-century reinterpretations of those Romantic energies. Dig into the smelly canvas backpacks of hippies roaming through Morocco or Nepal, or hitchhiking on America's backroads during the 1960s, and you would find dog-eared paperbacks by Richard Brautigan, Hermann Hesse, Anais Nin, and Kurt Vonnegut Jr., all of them pressing against the barricades of propriety—literary, sexual, ideological, or otherwise—in the service of passionate if sometime hazy notions of "getting free." What was more surprising were the books, well-thumbed and highlighted, by intellectual heavyweights that the countercultural young also stashed in those backpacks: Frankfurt School veterans like Erich Fromm (*The Art of Loving, Escape from Freedom*) and Herbert Marcuse (*One-Dimensional Man*), who argued that Freud's and Marx's insights about the deeply engrained repressions of civilization called for a new order liberated by eros. And then there was Norman O. Brown, who took Marcuse's *Eros and Civilization* (1955) another step of the way and made the bold announcement in *Love's Body* (1966) that the Western world needed a full-on Dionysian revolution.

These thinkers, along with others advocating a release from societal constraints (Alan Watts's Westernized Buddhism; C. Wright Mills's analysis of the postwar American economic structure in *The Power Elite*; Eldridge Cleaver's incendiary denunciations of racism in *Soul on Ice*; Betty Friedan's and Germaine Greer's liberatory feminism), served almost as gurus to the more thoughtful elements of the counterculture and lay the groundwork for their demand for love, pleasure, and liberation as primary values.[19] Without these cultural influences (and those who later popularized their work, like Theodore Roszak in *The Making of a Counterculture* and Charles Reich in *The Greening of America*), and without Martin Luther King's example, it's doubtful that the SDS's Port Huron statement could ever have proclaimed "love" as a political goal.[20] Or that "peace and love" and "make love not war," could ever have become catchphrases of the era. Or even that a big pop hit like Jackie DeShannon's "What the World Needs Now (Is Love)" (1965) could have used the word "love" in a way that meant something quite different from the way Tin Pan Alley used it in the prerock era. Pop and rock music are frequently bullshit, of course, trafficking in barren clichés and banal sentiment, but as we all know, clichés become clichés because they originally embodied something vital, buried but broadly shared. There's a line—indirect, passing through thick skeins of cultural discourse—that connects Erich Fromm's philosophical discourse *The Art of Loving* (1941) to the Beatles' "All You Need Is Love" (1968).

Browne's place amid this early countercultural tumult? He was certainly an eager participant in the sex, drugs, and rock 'n' roll part of it: tales of orgies, LSD trips, and all-night musical bashes litter the early pages of Browne's biographies. And his music, particularly his songs that look back on the sixties from an older perspective, suggest that he gloried in its hedonism. Consider "Giving That Heaven Away" (2006), where Browne remembers a rebellious hippie girl he calls Nova, part of his group of "acid dropping, world stopping, be-bopping / Freaks." Nova was a girl with whom he spent the day rocking in a Winnebago camper, "the two of us hot as a stove / Fools for pleasure, digging for treasure." It's all a lighthearted gambol there and shows that Browne, like his countercultural compatriots, did their best, at least early on, to break through the barricades of heaven by flying the flag of the god of wine and frenzy.

But bacchic frenzy is hardly what we think of when we think of Browne's relationship to women, sex, love—or life itself. The part of the counterculture that Browne embodied was a Dionysianism tempered by studied reflection, self-control, and empathy. There's a wide streak in Browne that hems in his excesses and indulgences, that yearns for control, order, sensibleness, *reason*. (That's particularly true of his politics.) We only know a few of the books that were in *his* canvas backpack during the sixties, but he was always an avid reader who soaked up the zeitgeist around him. We know that he thought of himself as part of a generation that believed in "the idea that we could reconstruct things, we had a responsibility to change the world for the better, to look at what was wrong and change it."[21] (Another thing we know is that he valued lucidity of mind: he gave up marijuana early on, once he discovered it made him lazy, unproductive, and mentally confused.) And going back to the songs on the Nina demos, we know that Browne thought of sex less as a mere indulgence in pleasure than as a deep challenge to the self, a possible route to connect one soul to another, a foray into his deepest hopes and fears. And he seemed to know, early on, the pain of failure. In "These Days," he says, "I had a lover / It's so hard to risk another." Browne's Dionysian urgencies were always controlled by sympathy for the other, by the knowledge of how easily love and sex could hurt not just yourself but the girl in the bed with you. Love was never just eros to him; agape and philia were always a part of his makeup.

BIDING HIS TIME

Jackson's journey to free himself from the barricades started long before he graduated from Sunny Hills High in the late spring of 1966—it started when he first picked up a guitar—but graduating at least released him from Orange County. Though he briefly became a member of the Long Beach–based Nitty Gritty Dirt Band, their Dylan-meets-jugband music was hardly his style, and he began to spend much of his time up in LA, playing clubs, making connections, and eventually moving to his mother's apartment in LA's Echo Park, just a few minutes by freeway from his grandfather's Highland Park Abbey. His connections got him a songwriting contract with Bill James and Electra Records, complete with a $500 signing bonus that he had to use in order to get out of a marijuana possession rap. (Browne's day in court turned out to be an early lesson in white privilege and structural racism. "The summer I was out of school I got busted for pot," he said a few years later. "But I got out of it because I paid a lawyer to tell the judge that I was a nice boy and that this was the first and the last time I would ever be in trouble. I had this $500 publishing advance from Electra's publishing company, Nina Music, and it was all used up to buy off some smarmy judge who had the same twinkle in his eye as my lawyer. There were 200 black and Chicano kids in court that day, and it was an inescapable fact that they were all going to 'the slammer' while the other three or four clean-cut kids like me, whose parents had paid a lawyer to stand up and say how 'upright' we were—well, you just knew we weren't going to jail. I mean, I was glad not to be going to jail, but it was pretty obvious that whoever had the bread was gonna be all right."[22])

He also began to travel. One of his trips took him and his friend Steve Noonan cross-country to New York, where he played his first out-of-state gig, opening for Steve and Tim Buckley. And then a weird break: Buckley, who was supposed to play guitar behind Nico at her gigs at Andy Warhol's Dom club in Greenwich Village, backed out, and Nico, hearing the very shy but eye-catching Jackson play electric guitar, hired him to fill in and then took him to her St. Marks apartment building to initiate him into her mysteries. Nico and Jackson were a match made in hell: she, a postmodern German chanteuse who emanated a weary Weimar ironic cool, was the reigning queen of Warhol's Factory; he was an unworldly eighteen-year-old kid from the Coast who'd literally never been inside a bar. Their affair was brief and intense and did not end well: during a show, Nico publicly accused him of making lewd phone calls to her, and Jackson, stunned, put down his guitar and walked offstage. The Warholian corner of the counterculture—disaffected and decadent, where sincerity was a joke and surface was everything—was not for him. "I was so fucking naive in those days," he told an interviewer about those weeks in New York. "I was just waltzing through a very decadent scene . . . and it was real obvious that I had no idea what was going on around me."[23] He did get a song out of it, though: "The Birds of St. Mark" is about his Nico episode. Written in the tradition of Dylan songs about women who are false in love—though, typical of Browne, replacing rancor with pathos—and full of images of queens and castles and birds symbolically flying into the distance, it was probably his most accomplished song to that point. He didn't record a version for release for until a half century later, however, when he made it the glistening opening track of *Standing in the Breach.*

Returning, a bit chastened, to LA, Jackson got back to writing songs, performing, and slowly expanding his web of musical connections, which eventually took in Pamela Polland, David Crosby, Linda Ronstadt, and Joni Mitchell, as well as Glenn Frey and J. D. Souther, who shared an apartment upstairs from his in Echo Park. He began to hang out, like everybody else, at the Troubadour rock club, the pumping heart of LA's folk-rock scene. His lyrics were quoted in a national magazine. Crosby said of him in *Rolling Stone*: "One of the probably 10 best songwriters around . . . he's got songs that'll make your hair stand on end, he's incredible."[24] A bevy of performers, including Nico, Gregg Allman, Tom Rush, Steve Noonan, and Ronstadt, covered his work on record, and the pressure began to build on Jackson to make his own. But he knew he wasn't ready. For one thing, there was that voice of his. Taking voice lessons helped—eventually they helped a lot—but then there was that side of him that needed to control things. Seeing how albums by his friends Steve Noonan and Pamela Polland didn't turn out as planned (and bombed commercially) made Jackson wary of launching himself too soon. After a number of aborted projects, including one where he was teamed up with the future members of Blue Oyster Cult(!), he finally signed on with one of the great hustlers of the business, David Geffen, as his manager.

It might be apocryphal, but the story is that Jackson sent in a tape and an eight-by-ten glossy of himself to Geffen's office, which Geffen threw out without even listening to the tape. But lured by Jackson's pretty photo, his secretary retrieved it from the trash, took it home, listened to the tape, and came back the next day raving to Geffen about the new kid in town. Geffen gave it another listen, saw the potential, and signed him. He then shepherded Browne to all the major record companies in search of a deal, but everyone passed. It was Ahmet Urtegun, president of Atlantic Records, who prodded Geffen to start his own record company and sign the wunderkind Jackson to it. Geffen finally set up Asylum records, with Browne the first artist on his list. But even then Jackson hesitated, worried that a record of his would be unduly influenced by a producer and wouldn't reflect his exacting standards. His didn't enter a recording studio to make his debut until 1971.

2

"WHERE DO YOU HAVE LEFT BUT TO GO IN?"

The hippie musicians who made LA's Laurel Canyon enclave famous settled there in the mid- to late 1960s, thinking it the best of both worlds. A quick drive down the hill brought them to the heart of Hollywood, to the clubs, bars, and coffee shops where they gathered with other musicians to play, drink, and talk shop. Then back up the hill, where the winding roads and deep green shades screened them from the intrusions of what Browne came to call "the mechanical city," and allowed them to feel those midsixties vibes that gave us sweet paeans to the Canyon like the Mamas and the Papas' "Twelve Thirty." It was here that Mama Cass Elliot held her 24/7 music 'n' drugs salons and Crosby, Stills & Nash harmonized for the first time. It was here where Monkee Peter Tork hosted his swimming pool orgies, Joni Mitchell served as leading Lady of the Canyon, and Jackson honed his musical chops. By the turn of the decade, Laurel Canyon, tucked into a rustic corner of the Hollywood Hills and far from the madding crowd, symbolized West Coast sixties hedonism but also the counterculture's *retreat* from urban strife and political engagement. It was places like this where the counterculture began its fabled "turn inward" and "return to nature." The political values for which Jackson Browne has been a permanent holdout were forged during this period, so it might help to remind ourselves of what he and his country were going through during those years.

THE RETREAT

The year 1968 was a cultural linchpin. Until then, the counterculture felt little need to retreat. Since the midsixties, it had been buoyed by an explosive pop revolution, lifted by Dylan, the Beatles, the Rolling Stones, Jimi

Hendrix, and major music scenes in Detroit (Motown), San Francisco (the Grateful Dead, Jefferson Airplane, Janis Joplin), and LA (the Byrds, Buffalo Springfield). The music was challenging but largely celebratory, stoked by dreams of a utopian future, soaring with excitement, experimentation, and the prospects of bacchic ecstasy. There was a coalescence of musical styles and audiences that gave the impression that certain boundaries—musical, cultural, racial—were on the cusp of being magically overcome. "Magical," in fact, was a sort of byword of the times. The summer of 1967 brought thousands of young people to San Francisco for a "summer of love": *Sgt Pepper* and "White Rabbit" flowed out of apartment windows in the Haight, and be-ins, love-ins, and acid tests proliferated. The promise of sex was everywhere. For sure, it was "irresponsible"—there was rampant venereal disease as well as countless bad trips, overdoses, drug deaths—but for a lot of people, the flood of Dionysian energy was genuinely transformative and couldn't be dismissed as fashionable grooviness. Throughout the country, middle-class morality (competitiveness, the success myth, "plastic" culture) was being questioned, its repressive conformity slowly lifting. The civil rights movement was tallying legislative victories, and Martin Luther King Jr. had boldly expanded his critique of American society to target poverty and the Vietnam War. Large anti-war demonstrations were having their effect: polls showed more and more Americans wanted the Johnson administration to bring the boys home. The Beatles' "All You Need Is Love" went to number one, and a lot of good people believed the message.

But 1968 was catastrophic. In January, the North Vietnamese and Vietcong mounted the Tet Offensive, which caught the American military off guard and gave the lie to government propaganda that the war was being successfully prosecuted. TV showed video of the fighting every night on the *CBS Evening News with Walter Cronkite*. American soldiers were dying at the rate of three hundred every week—estimates of weekly deaths of Vietnamese ran into the thousands—and the end of the conflict was nowhere in sight. Then in April, King was assassinated by a white man in Memphis, Tennessee, simultaneously outraging and deflating the civil rights movement and setting off a wave of race riots in 130 cities over the spring and summer. In June, the anti-war movement's best hope, Robert F. Kennedy, was shot and killed right after a primary victory in California that had catapulted him into major contention for the Democratic Party's nomination. America's young Left, which since the Port Huron Statement had insisted on a strategy of nonviolent confrontation, broke down into chaos, rioting at the Democratic Convention and alienating the white, middle-class "Silent Majority" who watched the bedlam unfold on television.

As for the Republicans, they nominated Richard Nixon, a shrewd if widely reviled politician with a history of Red-baiting that made him a longtime bête noire of liberals. Despite all this, the Left almost pulled off a victory. Hubert Humphrey, an old-school liberal who had a late-inning conversion to the anti-war cause, lost to Nixon in a half-million-vote squeaker. The closeness of the election made it all the more dispiriting. In a single year, the counterculture lost its two most inspiring leaders and spokesmen, squandered its reputation as agents of nonviolent change, watched helplessly as Nixon (who was more than willing to exploit racial and cultural divisions) took over the reins of power, and seemed unable to pick up the pieces. If ever W. B. Yeats's visionary prophecy of cultural breakdown seemed applicable to America—

> Things fall apart; the centre cannot hold;
> Mere anarchy is loosed upon the world,
> The blood-dimmed tide is loosed, and everywhere
> The ceremony of innocence is drowned;
> The best lack all conviction, while the worst
> Are full of passionate intensity.

—it was that year.[1]

And then things got even worse. In November 1969, journalist Seymour Hersh published a report saying that a year earlier, American forces had massacred upward of four hundred Vietnamese villagers at My Lai and that the army had covered it up. Subsequent investigations determined that the villagers, which included old men and women, children, and even infants, were often gruesomely mutilated or raped before being killed. A war that had already outraged half the population began to seem not just untenable but literally unbelievable, and lots of American GIs, upon coming home, found themselves called "baby killers," further dividing the country. In August, Charles Manson, an acid-crazed hippie on the fringes of the California music scene (he cowrote a song that ended up on the flip side of a Beach Boys single) amassed a cult "family" that, doing his bidding, murdered nine people, many from the entertainment industry, in a series of attacks that made SoCal musicians paranoid and convinced a broad swath of the American public that hippie culture—tolerable as long as it stuck to tie-dyed shirts and peace signs—had become a true threat to the republic. In December, following the relative peace at the Woodstock music festival, the Rolling Stones hosted a free concert festival in Altamont, California, during which the crowd passed bad acid around like it was candy and four people died. Three succumbed to overdoses, while one was beaten to death by security men (actually Hell's Angels members) wielding pool cues right in front of the stage, in full view of Mick Jagger and the band as they played "Under My Thumb." (The beating is captured in the concert film *Gimme Shelter.*)

The bad vibes gathered to an apex in May 1970. Though in 1968 Nixon had run on a platform of the "Vietnamization of the War"—the slow handing off of combat responsibilities to South Vietnam and our eventual withdrawal—by 1970 he had actually *expanded* the war into Laos and Cambodia, first by secretly bombing these countries and then, in May, by invading Cambodia in a misguided effort to subdue Vietcong military units hiding out there. The anti-war movement's response was immediate and massive: hundreds of college campuses erupted in huge demonstrations of protest. On one of those campuses, Kent State in Ohio, four demonstrators were shot and killed by National Guardsmen in a shocking display of state-sanctioned violence. (Eleven days later, two black students at Jackson State, in Mississippi, were killed by police after a racially charged confrontation.) Again, the country reeled from the news: the authorities were now firing on and killing American students for protesting against war or racism. Parents across the land called their children on college campuses and demanded they come home. Dozens of universities canceled final weeks of classes and closed down their campuses. And the more radical political wing of the counterculture staggered: unable to affect change through nonviolent means, their frustrations boiled over into violence and even terrorist activity—some SDS members splintered off into the Weather Underground and started bombing selected government and business targets.

Many young people—scared or exhausted by the turmoil—regarded Kent State as the final straw: in-the-streets political activism dwindled, seen now not only as dangerous but futile. What it taught them was that they had failed, and the Man had prevailed; there seemed little more, at least politically, to be done. "The world had become so mysterious from the vantage point of the '70s," Joni Mitchell said in a 1985 interview. "The disillusionment, the killing of the president, the stain of the Vietnamese war. It was a natural thing for people to look into themselves. That period was one of soul searching. The dream, everything that America stood for, was broken, and the people break a little with the dream. Where do you have left but to go in?"[2] The turn inward, and with that, the "return to nature"—Mitchell's call in "Woodstock" to go "back to the garden"—now beckoned. And the young Jackson Browne followed.

GOING "IN"

While Browne and his cohorts were processing the dark days of 1968 to 1970, they were also trying *not* to process them. Browne wrote a song that he gave to the Eagles (for their first album) called "Nightingale." It's a deceptively upbeat country-tinged rocker extolling the "light and joy" and "peace of mind" that a girl gives him, but the protagonist is only celebrating because she helps him deal with his frankly apocalyptic fears about the world (his head is filled with a "devastation trail" where "the fires burn and . . . the floods return"). "Don't let me see that morning paper," the singer warns, "'cause I don't need those dues."

Browne is just as eager to keep the morning paper at bay on his own debut album's "Something Fine," his gorgeous encomium to warm, lazy sex in the afternoon:

> The papers lie there helplessly in a pile outside the door
> I've tried and tried, but I just can't remember what they're for.

He makes a good case—the "something fine" he's got going with his lover convincingly blots out "the world . . . tugging at my sleeve." Yet the world still tugs, and Browne's protagonist still needs a girl there to blot it out. He won't always be able to keep the world at bay—neither the world nor the girl will always cooperate—but by the early 1970s, Browne, like the counterculture he belonged to, was trying to forge an uneasy truce with a world that was much more powerful and adversarial than he'd bet on. That's what "Doctor My Eyes," with its singer bemoaning "the slow parade of fears" that the papers are talking about every day, is really about. How do we live with "the evil and the good without hiding"?

For Jackson and the counterculture as the new decade began, there was more hiding than confronting, a lot of Mitchell's going "in," a conscious effort to address what was in one's control rather than what wasn't. If, after Kent State—"we're finally on our own," as Neil Young put it in "Ohio"—the counterculture's values having been violently put down, the next step was to make a separate peace. That meant, for a lot of people, "getting in touch with the self," the existential, spiritual reckoning with the inner life. It wasn't exactly a new project for the counterculture, of course: the sexual revolution, now in full swing, was always about getting in touch with the body and the desires that the older generation seemed afraid to face. But the counterculture's liberation project had its spiritual counterpart: the paperbacks that the hippies continued to haul around in their backpacks, like Hesse's *Siddhartha*, Kerouac's *The Dharma Bums*, or Alan Watts's *The Book*, were all about facing down Western assumptions and embracing new spiritual values, often from Hindu or Buddhist sources. The films that were turn-ons for the young—*Bonnie and Clyde, The Graduate, Easy Rider*, and foreign films by the likes of Antonioni, Godard, and Fellini—offered harsh critiques of the Establishment while dramatizing the exciting if indeterminate journeys young seekers were taking.

And then there were the drugs, especially meditative or mind-expanding ones like marijuana or LSD. The countercultural desire for mind-expansion penetrated commercial radio on the sly, in the Electric Prunes' "I Had Too Much to Dream Last Night," the Airplane's "White Rabbit," or Hendrix's "Are You Experienced?" but it's perhaps captured best typified in the Beatles' astonishing slice of psychedelia, "Tomorrow Never Knows." "Turn off your mind, relax and float downstream," the song begins, and everyone knew that that meant lighting up a joint or laying the tab on the tongue. The point of it all, at least for the spiritually adventurous, was so "that you may see the meaning within." What was the meaning? "It is *be-ing*" itself, Lennon suggested, and then he tells us what "being" means: "Love is all and love is everyone." As cynical as post-sixties generations have been about it, for many in the counterculture, drugs really were experiments in metaphysical exploration, offering the opportunity to open "the doors of perception" that Jim Morrison alluded to when he titled his band and which he got from reading Aldous Huxley and William Blake.[3] For a generation that had been psychically hemmed in by what America was in the 1950s, mind expansion was not a joke.

But getting in touch with the self also meant getting in touch with the natural world. When Canned Heat released its commune manifesto "Goin' Up the Country" (a week after Nixon's election in November 1968), it sparked a flame. Social consciousness about the human relationship to the natural world had been growing slowly since at least the late 1950s, when Barry Commoner, one of the fathers of the environmental movement, called for a nuclear test ban, citing the ravages of poisonous radioactive fallout on the environment. Rachel Carson's 1961 book *Silent Spring* alerted the world to the dangers of inorganic pesticides that industrial farmers had been inundating our soil, air, and food with for decades. Though Congress passed a heavily compromised Clean Air Act in 1967, the dangers of air and water pollution were more and more filling the pages of those newspapers that Browne's eyes were getting too pained to read. In early 1969, an oil rig platform operated by Union Oil leaked up to one hundred thousand gallons of crude onto the shoreline near Santa Barbara, killing birds and marine life, befouling hundreds of miles of coastline, and appalling surfers like Browne, who had always thought of the ocean as a watery refuge. (I often vacation in the central California seaside town of Cambria, 125 miles north of Santa Barbara, and I still find black dabs of oil on the shoreline, more than fifty years later.) It was, at the time, the largest oil spill in American history. In June of that year, Ohio's Cuyahoga river, astonishingly, caught fire—*water was on fire*—the result of tons of industrial sewage dumped into the river. (Randy Newman's "Burn On" [1972] was a brutal, understated satire on the event.) The oil spill and river fire catalyzed the ecology movement of the early 1970s and dovetailed with the counterculture's increasing distaste for the "unnatural"—synthetic clothes and makeup, processed foods, and plastic. (The very word "plastic" had become a metaphor for Establishment phoniness, as a famous scene in *The Graduate* makes clear.)

It was a quiet, less centralized revolution, this turning inward to the psychological, the spiritual, and the natural. It didn't try to levitate Pentagons, end a war, overthrow a repressive economic regime, or solve inequalities of race or class. Its aims were suitably modest for a time that so closely followed the enormous violence, literal and psychic, that was visited upon the country in the late 1960s. It had its own excesses—among them the tendency for psychological introspection to curdle into an omphalos-gazing narcissism that Tom Wolfe would say transformed the 1970s into the Me Decade.[4] But it probably had a greater long-term effect on the culture than all the louder manifestations of the sixties did. And it's the context that sets us up to understand the values Browne developed and then held out for his whole life, as well as to appreciate what Browne accomplished on his first two albums.

"THERE'S A WORLD, YOU KNOW"

Jackson Browne (1972) has a palpable feel for the hazy deceptive indolence of Los Angeles circa the early seventies, at least the Laurel Canyon corner of it. It was a place populated by transients who seemed ready to leave almost as soon as they arrived, lovers stoned on erotic pursuit, ambitious dreamers stalled by inner turmoil, oddball imports from all over whose ground was shaking beneath their feet (literally: the deadly Sylmar earthquake of 1971 is alluded to twice on the album) and so clung to the western edge of a country and a national dream, both of which, by the turn of the decade, seemed to be on life support. "Tip the world on its side and everything loose will fall into Los Angeles," Frank Lloyd Wright once quipped. This is an album about those who've been tipped loose into LA and its fallen sky, unsure about where they've been or where they're going, free but more desperate than they'd admit, and lonelier too. It's also a hippie album in many ways, where friends laze through "afternoons of smoke and wine . . . peace and pleasure," where nobody's yet locked into career or routine—that will wait till *The Pretender*—and where everyone seems so bruised by the events of the late 1960s that life becomes a sort of shell-shocked experiment into realms of the new and untested—realms of the mind, travel, friendship, sex, and love.

Browne had been writing songs for the album for at least three years before he went into the studio—none of the Nina recordings made the cut—and once he started recording, first in London and then in LA, he kept at it for six long months (a lot of it spent rerecording his vocals, which Browne knew needed work). He was a perfectionist and a control freak, and producer-engineer Richard Sanford Orshoff gingerly guided him through the process. The recording, anchored by the subdued drums and bass of Russell Kunkel and Leland Sklar—Browne at first aimed for the minimalist sound of Dylan's *John Wesley Harding*—was given tasty assists from Albert Lee and Jesse Davis on electric guitar and David Campbell's crucial viola on "A Song for Adam." But the mood of reflective melancholy is provided mostly by the natural, "organic" sounds of acoustic guitar and piano that had been de rigeur among LA's folk rockers since Joni Mitchell's *Ladies of the Canyon* and Carole King's *Tapestry*. Browne's voice, though still thin and unresonant (listen to "I Thought I Was a Child") is getting better: his singing voice sounds like the natural extension of his speaking voice (something he may have learned from James Taylor, whom he got to know well before making the album), and so he's better able to put across the subtleties of the lyrics and the inventive, hummable melodies. Critics still harped on the voice—he did still have a long way to go—but they heaped praise on the songwriting, which was, of course, the main attraction.

Every song is in first person—the go-to singer-songwriter perspective—centered in a consciousness that would become familiar to his fans: intelligent, questioning, alert, beset by a pervasive loneliness; an innocent who knows full well he's tumbling headlong into a post-sixties world of painful experience; sensitive as a Richter scale to the emotional trembling in himself and others; hungry in body and soul but tentative because, being fundamentally melancholic, he's attuned to a sadness and a dark void at the center of his life. The Browne character makes his baldest appearance in "Doctor My Eyes," where he wonders whether his awakening from a world of adolescent dreams, his exposure to the world of "the evil and the good," has frozen him and made it impossible anymore to "see the sky" (in Browne's music, "sky" almost always signifies hope, promise, the blessings of a free imagination). The song feels full of fear, propelled musically by an incessant quarter-note left-hand piano pulse that conveys urgency but also anxiety. There's a panic beneath the song's lively melodic kick, and it beautifully explains why most of the rest of the album retreats to the realm of the private and the intimate. It feels like the only way not to go blind.

I count five songs of retreat on the album, beginning with "A Child in These Hills." Marred by a weak vocal and dabbling in the pretentious poeticizing and self-conscious mythmaking common to his early efforts, it nonetheless gives us a clear view of our Brownian protagonist. In these hills—Jackson has said they aren't the Sunny Hills of his adolescence or the Hollywood Hills of his apprentice years but the hills of upstate New York, where he wrote the song in 1968—he's isolated: "away" and "alone," he "chooses to be gone / From the house of my father." In his seclusion, he's searching for someone who will "ask me my name"—who will, presumably, validate an identity that he's only now beginning to discover. "Child," the earliest of the songs Browne wrote for the album, starts the journey of the album's protagonist.

In three of the songs, the identity he's discovering emerges from being in a bed with a woman. Actually, in "Jamaica Say You Will," it's not in bed but in the "tall grass" where he spends long, shady afternoons hidden away with his lover. At first the song seems like some sort of warm Caribbean idyll, a tropical pastoral that aims to get back to a version of Joni Mitchell's "garden," away from anything having to do with industrial war-torn America and all its bad news. And the music certainly pours down slow, sweet, and sensuous. The love Jamaica offers the protagonist is restorative, less sex than "a comfort and a mercy." Still, he keeps insisting that she fill his "empty hours" and his "lifeless sails." Why is this young man with his willing island lover feeling so empty? We're not told. His emptiness is a given, as if Browne assumes we're all existentialists, that we know that life is meaningless "these days," at least without the saving grace of an unspoiled girl from the tropics. His attempt to fill that void is what actually gives the song its drama, far more than the conventional conclusion that Jackson gives it, in which Jamaica's father takes her away to sea, leaving him bereft.

The protagonist finds himself in a more conventional bed in "Under the Falling Sky," the album's most overt sex song. "I've got lightning in my pocket / I got thunder in my shoes" makes his original intentions clear, and the arrangement, with its bouncy organ, bongos, and some fleet-fingered guitar at the end, tries to work up some sensual intensity. But the song points up his early limitations. It's supposed to be a seduction song—"Easily we will lie while I bring it to you"—but it doesn't come off. Browne sings in a flat low register that doesn't convey much intensity; the song includes the album's most shopworn lyric: "If for only one stolen moment we will live forever"; most crucially, Jackson's protagonist can't seek sex without betraying the reason he seeks it: because of the void within. "Your bright fields" is how he describes the woman's body, but he describes his own as "this prison." And then this whole song about connecting through sex takes place "under the *falling* sky," which evokes either some postlapsarian state of loneliness and exile or a world where a hard rain's gonna fall. Again, the protagonist's desires for love and sex are desperate appeals to fill his own emptiness, and his retreat reveals dread more than anything else.

"Something Fine" is the best of the bed songs, unagitated by loneliness or despair. Written after a brief romantic interlude with a woman while he was in London—"one of those magic times that you knew wasn't going to last forever," he remembers[5]—the song centers itself in a single bedroom, outside of which are piled those newspapers that he refuses to read—if he does, he knows they'll kill his buzz. The song evokes in its pretty acoustic guitar figures the sunny, unhurried pleasures of secluded lovers that poets have written about since Shakespeare wrote his sonnets or John Donne his "The Sun Rising." Here, in this room, he and this sister of the sun are going to rock on the water, contemplating past and future, memories of California and Morocco, under no falling sky but amid the "something fine" they have created together. Browne's protagonists are usually too preoccupied by the void to dissolve into the "love's body" that Norman O. Brown talked about, but here he manages to dispel the emptiness for once. "Something Fine" is a song that presents the retreating counterculture as it most liked to see itself: self-sufficient, indolently erotic, tolerant and free from possessiveness, able to love, able to leave, confident that love endures as a principle even if it's fleeting in the moment.

The last of the retreat songs, "Looking into You," takes place not in a bed but in the mind of Browne's protagonist as he contemplates, from a secure psychic space, his past. It's the first of his ruminations on time, a minigenre that will include "Farther On," "Running on Empty," "The Barricades of Heaven," and "Time the Conqueror." Browne plays piano on the song, thick, warm major chords that are church-like in tone, grounding the plaintive retrospection of the vocal. The first few verses are about an adolescent Browne visiting the house he once lived in—presumably his grandfather's Highland Park Abbey—out of some impulse to connect with his early youth, only to realize that all the certainties he grew up with have disappeared. Then the prototypical Romantic insight occurs: he realizes he really is *on his own.* Life is "a hotel at best, you're here as a guest," Browne sings—an only slightly more comforting version of Dylan's caustic "you're on your own / with no direction home." He's going to have to get used to a sense of homelessness.

At this point an inner voice asks him if he's "ready to fly" into that homeless future. He has no choice, of course, but where to go? He considers "the dream of the millions"—the ideal American dream as his countercultural generation conceived it—only to realize that that dream no longer feels real or graspable—after the 1960s, how could it? And so he ends up "here . . . at the edge of my embattled illusions." As arty and mythopoeic as this line is, it establishes the image and theme that will run through his first three albums at least: that of a Romantic seeker battling innocent illusions but unwilling to give up on them, earnestly holding out for the possibility that he can make those ideal visions real.

The lyric also serves to distinguish him from Bob Dylan, whose influence he addresses in the next verse. Dylan as truth teller, Dylan as prophet: the protagonist admits that, at first, that's how he saw Dylan—until he realized he'd have to forge his own path and look "for a truth that is my own." The very way Browne couches his break from his precursor suggests that the influence can't have been that strong to begin with. Dylan was always way too disillusioned to adopt the Romantic tropes that Browne prefers: the journey myth, the move from innocence to experience, seeing someone as a prophet who tells the "truth." (Compare this song to Dylan's song to his great influence, Woody Guthrie, in "Song to Woody." That song is respectful but casual, and nowhere suggests that Guthrie—or anyone—was worthy of hero worship.) In interviews, Browne has always pointed to Dylan as the man who set him on his path as a songwriter—he calls him one of the "great people." With Dylan, "you get what you can get—not to sound like him but to allow his music to take you somewhere."[6] Precisely: what Dylan did for him was simply swing the doors of songwriting possibility wide open. What Browne learned from Dylan's early records (besides a progressive political sensibility that he stuck with long after Dylan abandoned it) was that songwriting was as personal and open-ended a form as any in modern art. Once you learned that, you were free to follow where your instincts took you.

The five songs of retreat are complemented by two songs—"From Silver Lake" and "Song for Adam"—about the literal desire for travel on the open road. These are the two most counterculturally evocative songs, where friends replace family and characters are itching with wanderlust. "From

Silver Lake" brings within the Browne protagonist's orbit two friends, a man and a woman (whom, in true early-1970s argot, the protagonist calls "our brother" and "his lady"). It's one of Browne's first story songs, about the man, unable to breathe in "the mechanical city," coming over to tell the protagonist that despite "the peace and pleasure" he's had with him and his own lady, he's leaving for a place "across the sea." As the song proceeds, his itch to travel becomes contagious, catching both the lady and the protagonist, so by the end all three are "bound to go" on some unspecified journey. The music nicely conveys the sense of freedom and mystery that travel offers, buoyed by some lovely counterpoint by Leah Kunkel, Browne's own confident vocal, and an elegantly structured piano-and-guitar arrangement.

"Song for Adam" is even stronger, often singled out by other songwriters as an example of Browne's craft. Another song about friends and wanderlust, this one tells the story of Adam Saylor, a real-life friend of Browne's who, after leaving Browne and a friend behind on a road trip, ended up committing suicide by jumping off a building.[7] It's a stately elegy, with a sad viola weaving in and out of Browne's warm guitar figures and bravely unsentimental vocal. The four line verses all rhyme AAAA—hard to do without butchering syntax—and Browne provides a smooth and clear narrative, emphasizing throughout that though Adam was a friend of his, "I did not know him well." That detail ensures that the song won't overdose on sentiment and provides the protagonist with the distance he needs to express what the song is really getting at: confronting death's mystery. In the chorus, Browne introduces the striking metaphor of his protagonist sitting before a candle, which provides "so little light to find my way," and in getting shorter by the hour, reminds him of himself—of the limits of time and of his own eventual death. Of all the songs on the first album, this song reads the best on the page—not exactly a poem, but close. But what's most impressive is Browne's mature and subtle handling of the theme: there's a compassion and sympathy in the vocal and arrangement that radiates, which has a lot to do with the enthusiastic reception the album got when it was released.

After all that existential exploration and "going in," Browne's protagonist returns, in "Rock Me on the Water," to the wider world that threatened to blind him in "Doctor My Eyes." "Rock Me" is the album's best song, with as soulful a vocal Browne has, to this point, laid down, instantly hummable gospel melodies on both verse and chorus, a rocking piano, and fine harmonies provided by David Crosby that open the song out to the celebratory conclusion it deserves. It provides the release that the album's tensions have so far held back. Not that it's all release—in fact, it starts out pretty dark and dyspeptic. It's dismissive of the Establishment—"You're lost inside your houses / There's no time to find you now"—and suffused with the apocalyptic imagery that will pepper Browne's lyrics on all his early 1970s releases. The glowing spirit of the song comes from the singer seeking solidarity with others—presumably the remnants of the counterculture—who will help him down to the sea and the sisters of the sun who will give him solace from "the fires burning hotter and hotter." (Those fires may refer to the race rioting that was rife in the late 1960s. Jackson has recalled that "I read *Soul On Ice*"—the disturbing and electrifying book by Black Power writer Eldridge Cleaver—"when I was writing 'Rock Me on the Water.'"[8]) Those sisters stand for the same hope that the singer sees when he looks up—"a seabird gliding in one place / like Jesus in the sky." The Christian imagery is mere allusion—Browne is not a Christian, but like the good humanist he is, he borrows from its mythology to reinforce his spiritual intimations. The title metaphor, like so much rock music inspired by gospel, is both sexual and spiritual, and the music, with those pounding ascending piano chords at the end, reinforces that redemption can come from either source. After an album full of tentative retreats from a dispiriting world, here at last Browne's protagonist embraces it.

Jackson Browne's coda, "My Opening Farewell," is a song about a romantic relationship that's become intractable—not a bed song but a song about a door someone is about to walk out of. The couple know they can't stay together, but they can't seem to break up either—they're almost exaggeratedly kind and attentive to each other as they draw out their leave-taking. Browne will write a lot of songs about the final scene between lovers, but never with this timorous sensitivity. Browne's reputation for writing sympathetic portraits of women, vulnerable in love, probably starts here. But what interests me most is how the song concludes. These lovers are the flip side of those in "Something Fine," just as secluded but no longer nourished by passion. The protagonist, realizing that the seclusion and retreat are debilitating, suggests that outside "there's a world, you know," with trains going "either way," providing options to help both of them regain their footing and a sense of vitality. Like "Rock Me on the Water," the album's closer opens up to the world, demonstrating that retreat and "going in" are strategies that entail just as many perils—and can be just as blinding—as opening them to the parade of fears in the outer world.

***

David Geffen held onto the album for months before having Asylum release it in January 1974, not wanting it to get lost in the Christmas rush. Knowing that a debut album wouldn't sell without a hit single, he had "Doctor My Eyes" remixed to give it a bit more brightness and rhythmic heft, and he was rewarded when the single landed with a bullet on the *Billboard* charts. It climbed steadily till it hit the Top 10 during the spring, pulling the album up with it. The album reached number 53, which was enough to put Browne on the map as a singer and performer, not just as a songwriter. The reviews were mostly sterling: typical was Bud Scoppa, in *Rolling Stone*, who said that the record by itself placed Browne "among the first rank of recording artists" and compared it to Van Morrison's *Astral Weeks* and Neil Young's *After the Gold Rush.*[9] Even the self-appointed "dean of rock critics," Robert Christgau, struggling mightily against his instincts, squeezed out a backhanded compliment—"Many people I like like Browne. Me, I don't dislike him"—before casting him as bland and inconsequential.[10] Browne went on a four-month-long tour, opening for Joni Mitchell—with whom he had a brief relationship that was clouded, his friend Pamela Polland said, by his own sense of competitiveness: "It became too heavy for Jackson to be with someone who was so much more prolific than he. She was so creative in so many ways, and it came out of her so easily, that to face his own struggle with his craft, his own slowness with his craft—to have those two mirrored against each other—I think was very painful for him"[11]—and exposing himself to an audience that was perfect for him. He returned to LA after the tour, and, like every other artist in those days, was pressured to get a new record out ASAP.

WAITING FOR EVERYMAN

Putting out an album per year, as Browne was pressured to do in his early career, was a challenge. Dylan could record three albums (one a double) in eighteen months during the genius days of *Bringing It All Back Home*, *Highway 61 Revisited*, and *Blonde on Blonde*, but Browne was more like Paul Simon, obsessing over every song—writing and rewriting for months before recording and rerecording till he got it right. Browne, like Simon, has never left anything "in the vaults"—there are virtually no outtakes or previously unreleased tracks at hand ready to fill out deluxe rereleases on CD or for streaming services. So when he got back from opening the Joni Mitchell tour—they were an item until he met Phyllis Major—and reentered the studio for his second album in the fall of 1972, he reached into his back catalog for three songs: the previously unrecorded "Colors of the Sun" and two Nina demos—"These Days," which had been recorded by, among others, Duane Allman and Nico, along with the near-fragment "Sing My Songs to Me." He also decided to record "Take It Easy," which had been a huge hit for the Eagles just a year before. Recording was even slower and more painstaking than with the first record but, given his newfound commercial success, he was able to draw on name musicians and singers to help out, among them Elton John, Bonnie Raitt, Mitchell, Don Henley, and Glenn Frey, though no one put as great a musical stamp on the record as Browne's new guitar and fiddle player, David Lindley.

If Browne's first record touched on some of the counterculture's anxieties as the sixties closed out, the year 1972, between the first and second albums, only engraved those anxieties deeper. In 1972, Richard Nixon was reelected, crushing the Left's choice, George McGovern, in a humiliating landslide. Nixon had campaigned on the theme of "peace with honor," arguing that the United States could hand over the reins of combat to South Vietnam and withdraw, despite clearly not winning the original goal—to drive North Vietnam out of the South. Most of America bought his line and by then were so sick of the war that it had in many ways tuned out. As a recent book argues, news "coverage of political unrest, the civil rights movement, and the war was vastly reduced" in the early 1970s: "People had almost forgotten about Vietnam (although Americans continued to die there for five more years)."[12] Nixon's victory was even more dispiriting to the Left because in June 1972, news emerged that Nixon's own campaign had broken into the offices of the Democratic National Committee at the Watergate apartment complex, and that fact seemed to make nary a ripple among most voters. (It would take more than a year into his second term before Watergate began to matter, and a year after that before Nixon resigned because of the deep corruption that the Watergate investigations revealed.) By 1973, the American Left was practically a ghost, a battered ideology in search of a constituency. Much of the disintegrating counterculture began to treat the whole realm of the political like toxic waste. And so it's fascinating that Browne, who had gone along with the countercultural retreat on his first album, now had his doubts, and on the album's best song—the best song he'd written so far in his life—was seeking engagement again.

The themes of *For Everyman* are similar to those on *Jackson Browne*, but the tone and the emphases have decidedly shifted. It may come down to this: if on the first album, Browne sings that "I am a child in these hills," on this one he only "*thought* I was a child" and realizes he isn't anymore. There's still some retreat, and there's still the preoccupation with the personal, but there are no more complaints about how hard the world has been on his eyes. He knows the world's not going away and has got to be faced. Browne's protagonists display a new confidence too, born perhaps from simply growing older—"Ready or Not" is about moving in with a woman who's going to have his child—and a newly sprung sense of humor that's frankly cheering for a singer so typically drawn to the Slough of Despond. The music contains his first balls-out rocker, "Redneck Friend," and in "For Everyman," insists that "sooner or later you'll have to take a stand" in a song that's filled with a New Left compassion and commitment to participatory democracy that most of his generation had by now forgone.

"Take It Easy" sits atop the record as a sort of prologue, a hint that *For Everyone* will be more energetic and fun than *Jackson Browne*, though it's debatable whether his version is different enough from the Eagles' hit to warrant its inclusion except as a commercial gambit. What it does have is Sneaky Pete Kleinow, the former Flying Burrito Brothers guitar player, on pedal steel, and David Lindley on electric guitar, who circle and entwine their riffs around each other in a way that evokes the atmosphere of desert highway driving (almost) as well as the Eagles' arrangement does. Browne's baritone aims for a casual hedonism, but he can't pull off the seductive, self-satisfied narcissism that Glenn Frey's breezy tenor brings to the song. Jackson's version, despite Frey's sly Winslow, Arizona, verse, can't quite throw off the suspicion that the song is more about "a world of trouble on my mind" than it is about getting the girl to climb aboard his Ford.

Lindley and Sneaky Pete's guitars cruise lazily down the highway for a bit before the song segues into "Our Lady of the Well." Set in rural Mexico—Browne has suggested as much in concert[13]—among "families who work the land as they have always done" in harmony with the natural world, the protagonist contrasts it with the "cruel and senseless hand" that has cast its shadow across his "home," that is, America. That hand is everything that Browne's counterculture found abhorrent: America's disconnect from the rhythms of nature, the pile-driving materialism that buries any sense of enduring "love and truth." The protagonist would love to draw water from Maria's well, the Lady of the title (water always means "life" for a surfer like Browne), but he understands that his responsibility is with his own people. This a song about deciding *not* to retreat and foreshadows Jackson's commitment to his country's precarious ideals that we'll hear in "For Everyman."

Private rumination and the demands of the intimate life nonetheless continue to exert a strong pull on Browne's imagination. *For Everyman* has its bed song in "The Times You've Come" and swirling introspection in

"Colors of the Sun" and "These Days." "The Times You've Come," built around a sleepy acoustic guitar and a wistful, feminine harmony vocal from Bonnie Raitt, works around a sexual pun—the protagonist's partner is both visiting him and having an orgasm—but Browne, to his credit, doesn't snigger. I can think of no other song in the history of pop music that gives the idea of sexual climax this degree of dignity and seriousness. The couple here aren't quite a couple: they come and go, they find and lose each other, but each time that they return to each other, "lying here / in the ruins of our pleasure," he affirms, "I've loved these times you've come." It's that rare song that underlines, without any coarseness, what a powerful and necessary thing good sex is to a relationship.

"Colors of the Sun," a gathering of abstractions that Browne plucked from his adolescent songbook, is too in love with its own image-conjuring. The melody's pretty, but the piano is portentous without having anything to be portentous about, and a cannabis aroma clings to the lyrics. The protagonist trips on surface impressions and flashes of light reflecting off the ocean and insists that others "leave me where I am." The music is slow, creamy, and dreamy, with Lindley's guitar lifting the song above lyrics that flirt with solipsism, but the song's a dead end, stuck inside a mind that's too estranged from the world outside to fully connect with the listener.

Not so "These Days." Anchored in a descending chord progression familiar from the Band's "The Weight" and the Grateful Dead's "Friend of the Devil," and featuring Browne at his most confessional, the song is not only impressively vulnerable but—Browne's been singing it for fifty years—serves as a shifting commentary on his long journey as songwriter and man. The Nina tapes version, "I've Been Out Walking," provides the lyrical template: at bottom it's a simple song of regret about things that the protagonist "forgot to do—for you," and in the song's conclusion, he begs the listener, "Don't confront me with my failures / I had not forgotten them." The critical take on "These Days" has always been that these lines are pretty astonishing coming from the sixteen-year-old kid who wrote them, and that's true enough. What's worth underlining, though, is how the protagonist's mistakes have made him shy away from life, no longer willing to "risk another" lover, or to ramble and gamble, dream and scheme, as he used to. Failures in love are a pop lyric staple, and it's not uncommon for a song to locate the source of the failure (of nerve or sympathy) in the protagonist himself, but "These Days" distills the lover's guilt and sorrow into a form—an intense display of sincerely expressed emotional pain and exhaustion—that few performers can pull off. Elvis Costello, who famously (and hilariously) dismissed "the 'fuck me—I'm so sensitive' Jackson Browne school of seduction," could very well have been talking about this song, but he was wrong: he couldn't see that "These Days" and Jackson's other relationship songs have little to do with seduction. There are no ulterior motives operating here, just a naked honesty that you either accept as existential revelation, or don't.[14] I very much do.

The version that's on *For Everyman* evolved considerably from the one on the Nina demos. Nico gave the song exposure on her *Chelsea Girl* album (1967), mostly copying Browne's melody line but larding on a stiff chamber music string arrangement to sweeten the Teutonic gloom. Gregg Allman recast the vocal melody on his version from *Laid Back* (1973), dragging it out of Nico's *Weltschmerz*. He also cut some of Browne's more despairing lyrics and added a line—"and now I believe I want to see myself again"—that opens the song to a glimmer of hope. Browne loved Allman's track, and he ended up borrowing much of Allman's arrangement for his version. He may also have seen value in Allman's brightening up of the lyrics, because when he recorded it, he added the lines "I'll keep on moving / Things are bound to be improving."

But what makes "These Days" soar on *For Everyman* is David Lindley. The song clocks in at 4:45, and Lindley's slide is everywhere, weaving in and out of Browne's affecting vocal harmonies with bassist Doug Heywood. Twice he simply takes over the song in lengthy solos. His playing, aching but uplifting, patiently rising up the scale against the descending piano chord motif, is a powerful complement to the song's despondency, and it's a credit to Browne that he allowed Lindley to transform the song from one of earnest vulnerability to something that enters the realm of the beautiful.

The song's had a long afterlife, with more than a dozen versions recorded by other artists. In recent years, Browne's restored some of the details of his Nina demo in concert, and reincluded the darker intimations of how he's "stopped my dreaming" that aren't on his studio version. That inclusion makes the final lines about not wanting to be confronted with his failures (because, decades later, they're still around to haunt him) more poignant than ever. When the song—and Browne—were young, we could marvel at the protagonist's knowingness and maturity; now it sounds like it comes from a man who knows his failures—our failures—are endemic: he's never going to get over them, and facing *that* is its own kind of remarkable.

Side two—we can pretend we're listening to the long-playing record as fans did in 1973—radically shifts emotional registers, opening with the raucous "Redneck Friend," Browne's first comic gesture and his first danceable song. Propelled by Lindley's ubiquitous slide, a rhythm section that finally lets loose, and Elton John's best Little Richard imitation (the liner notes credit piano to "Rockaway Johnnie"), Browne's protagonist urges a girl to dump her dull, controlling parents and head off with him. "I may not have an answer but I believe I got a plan," he tells her—the plan being to introduce her to his "redneck friend." The song's so well crafted—the lyrical details concise, Browne's vocal strong and unironized—that it may elude first-time listeners that the song is about the protagonist's penis. (It eluded Browne's friend, Duane Allman, who for a long time thought the song was playful nod toward him, a redneck Southerner.) Once you get past the ooh-gross image that the title calls up, the song's a riot, and it forces you to reconsider Browne's whole persona to this point. Jackson Browne calls his cock his red neck friend? Whoa Nelly. It's a glimpse into a side of Jackson we haven't seen and which he'll rarely reveal again. Whatever: it's a welcome addition to the Browne canon and certainly jacks up the excitement quotient at his shows.

"Ready or Not," about the beginning of his relationship with Phyllis Major, has a similar good-natured vibe, with Lindley's lively fiddle nicely complementing Browne's country narrative about getting into a brawl while "defending [the] dignity" of a lady in a bar, and then bragging that "that girl came home with me." Like "Redneck Friend," the lyrics are pure realism, avoiding psychology and poetic imagery in favor of colloquial language and outward-facing storytelling, as good country songs do. It's another welcome development in Browne's songwriting—he realizes that lyrics don't need to prettify themselves with diction borrowed from (usually premodern) poetry, and we'll soon see how this recognition will help Browne when he creates his first real apotheosis as a songwriter, *Late for the Sky*. For now, suffice it to say that "Ready or Not" pinpoints the precarious moment when impending fatherhood inspires both jangled nerves and happy excitement.

The album concludes with "Sing My Songs to Me," a keyboard-heavy near-fragment (Joni Mitchell contributes almost invisible electric piano) that segues into the title track. "Sing" traffics in the kind of gossamer imagery (sunlight, shadows, dreams, etc.) that isn't long for the Browne songbook and is the weakest cut on the album. It does, however, supply the meditative two-chord instrumental intro for the album's strongest and boldest song.

"For Everyman" was written in dialogue with two other songs: Crosby, Stills & Nash's "Wooden Ships," and Browne's own "Rock Me on the Water." The impetus for "For Everyman" seems to have come from a discussion Browne had with David Crosby about "Wooden Ships," an ambitious but, to Browne, cynical post–nuclear-war fantasy in which a few survivors, boarding some wooden ships, say good riddance to the remnants of a wrecked civilization: "We are leaving / You don't need us." According to a CSN biographer, Browne, having listened to the song, asked Crosby, "What about the guys who can't escape?" That is, was Crosby really disclaiming any responsibility for those who are unhip enough not to be among the countercultural "us"? Aren't we all responsible to the civilization made by the Establishment? Crosby's answer—"Fuck 'em"—evidently got Browne started on "For Everyman."[15] But "Rock Me on the Water" must have been in the back of his mind, too, since Browne's gospel tune reiterates the hell-with-other-people sensibility of "Wooden Ships" in a way that might have been a little too close for comfort. After all, "I'm going to leave you here / and get down to the sea somehow" sounds a lot like "We are leaving / You don't need us." "For Everyman" is Browne's corrective to his own song as well as to the counterculture's capitulation to quietism and retreat after Kent State.

From the beginning, the song acknowledges the desire to escape, "to give up the race and find something better." The protagonist admits, too, that he's come up with "well-thought-out schemes" to escape with a few of his friends to some hazy "motherland" of the counterculture's dreams. And he knows that he's not the only one: everyone he talks to has the same fantasy, and he sees them all "standing alone / each with his own ticket in his hand." But the picture in his mind of individual members of his generation "standing alone" makes him long for the solidarity that was an ideal of the old counterculture. So he revives that solidarity, saying that now all his hopes (for his generation and his country) "have all eventually come down to waiting for everyman."

The waiting means a responsibility to leave no one behind and implies an understanding of democracy that goes back to Walt Whitman, where one identifies one's very self with America and the destiny of its people. The song is a burst of post-countercultural moral activism, and its diffidence ("I'm not saying that I've seen the plan / Turn and walk away if you think I am,") makes it all the more palatable. He's not going to abandon his people, his land, his country; he's going to wait for them to come around so they can together face the fragile future. It's Browne's longest song to date—more than six minutes—and Browne gives over the last two minutes to his band, with no one instrument—drums, bass, organ, piano, or guitars—dominating. Each one takes its turn in the limelight and then subsides to support the others in a gentle aural democracy that ends the album on a strong, hopeful note.

★ ★ ★

For Everyman avoided the dreaded sophomore slump. Though its singles didn't click—"Redneck Friend" stalled at number 85 on *Billboard*, and "Take It Easy" didn't chart at all—the album rose ten spots higher than the debut, topping out at number 43. (It went gold in 1975.) The critics were generally appreciative: Christgau, in the *Village Voice*, reluctantly coughed up a *B* grade in his capsule review, but Janet Maslin's rave in *Rolling Stone* made great claims for Browne as a "purebreed seventies intelligence" and was the first to state what I have in many ways tried to elucidate in this book: "He is the first major songwriter to have emerged with the knowledge that the battles Bob Dylan depicted a decade ago are either over or too ambiguous to be worth fighting any more. But unlike most older writers, he is not yet ready to retreat into merely mining the realm of private problems for subject matter. He has internalized the remains of those larger struggles and still dares to hope for solutions."[16]

Browne didn't immediately tour in support of the album. Major gave birth to their son, Ethan Zane, just weeks after the album's release, and, ready or not, Browne and his new family moved into his grandfather's Abbey in Highland Park. There he found himself closing a circle of sorts. The child in these hills had birthed a child of his own, and both were now nestled in the longtime family home. The stage was set for a period of calm and stability. But it wasn't to be. "I had a relationship and a kid all at once," he told Ronald Brownstein, "and in the time it took to have the baby and to be moved into this old family house of mine, I sequestered . . . I mean all kinds of things happened in my life that I wasn't . . . paying enough attention to."[17] From the evidence of the music that would eventually turn up on *Late for the Sky*, he had found himself, at age twenty-five and seemingly for the first time, in a deep chasm of life-and-death turmoil.

3

LATE FOR THE SKY

Everyone says *Late for the Sky* is Jackson Browne's "masterpiece"—that's what Bruce Springsteen called it when he inducted his friend into the Rock & Roll Hall of Fame—but what's masterful about it? Listen to the album after spending time with his first two records and you realize that, first of all, something has happened to his voice. It's not, however, a matter of his voice having gotten "better" (though it had). What you hear on the third album is the voice of a man who's been deeply scarred. He sang about "my lifeless sails" in "Jamaica Say You Will," or about how "I've been losing so long" in "These Days," but there's a depth of sadness in *Late for the Sky* that's of another order altogether and makes his previous allusions to sorrow seem almost like posturing. What comes through in the voice is that here's a man who's come to some kind of *knowledge*—of what sorrow is, and means, and how you live through it. Browne's songs are often called "philosophical," but it's not because he sprinkles allusions to Hegel into the mix. It's because his songs are patient about suffering; he dwells in it because he knows it has something to teach. His songs integrate the depth of what gives pain into a larger vision that expresses, as he puts it in "For a Dancer," "a reason you were alive / that you'll never know." A fountain of sorrow *gushes* on this record, and the beauty of it is that he gathers it all up in the strong light of his compassion and renders up a fountain of light.

THE SECOND CRUCIBLE

What did Jackson go through that made *Late for the Sky* possible? The most at-hand answer is that his partner (later his wife), Phyllis Major, had given birth to his first child, that he was now a father living with his new family in the Abbey San Encino house where he grew up, and that despite what would seem like positive developments in his life, he was living "through the romantic tumult that he'd experienced with . . . Phyllis Major, and the personal and social upheaval that seemed to dog him at every step." As the album's coproducer, Al Schmidt, remembers, "I think it was a tribute album to try to get his relationship back on the track again. His wife came by the sessions and I know he was madly in love with her and striving to get this thing to work, but I know there was some turmoil there."[1] There's nothing in Browne's biography that he's been more private about than his relationship with Major—in a long interview with Bud Scoppa, he alludes only briefly to a "split with his wife"[2] during this period—but from the scant evidence available, and certainly from the music itself, it seems that the two of them were deeply enmeshed and troubled, and that the jauntiness of the relationship described in "Ready or Not" didn't last long. His turmoil was exacerbated by the sudden death of a friend who Browne looked up to as full of life and creativity, as well as the general freefall of the country in the early 1970s. In other words, Browne was forced to radically reassess, in his real life, ideas of love, death, and his generation's place in history that he had been harboring since he picked up a guitar.

When Jackson met her, Phyllis was a worldly, adventurous but quite fragile young woman who had lived in Greece (where she knew Leonard Cohen), Switzerland, and France, dabbled in poetry and songwriting (two of her songs were recorded by Al Kooper), hobnobbed with rock 'n' roll royalty, had an affair with Keith Richards, sustained a successful career as a model, and passionately loved rock 'n' roll. She also had taken her share of drugs, was subject to deep bouts of depression, and had a history of emotional instability—she'd attempted suicide after her affair with Richards ended.[3] The songs about her on *Late for the Sky* are agonized. That their love—precarious and distressed, ultimately tragic—was of a different kind than any romantic relationship he'd had before is self-evident; Browne had been singing about love since he started, but these songs open up to a passion (Latin root *passio*, meaning "suffering") that is brand new in his work. That that relationship was supposed to be the solid bedrock beneath the life of their newborn son could only have made things more difficult. (When Phyllis and their one-year-old accompanied Browne on the tour for *Late for the Sky*, she ended up leaving Browne—and the baby—behind. "After Phyllis saw that life on the road wasn't as glamorous as she might have imagined, she flew home, while Ethan stayed with Jackson," one biographer wrote.[4] That a new mother would leave her infant child on a raucous, drug-fueled rock 'n' roll tour with a father who was consumed with the business of travel and performance is striking and suggests a disturbance in their relationship that foretells their later difficulties.) Finally, that this new family was living in the house where Browne spent his early childhood years might have echoed back to the troubled marriage of his parents, which would eventually end and abandon Browne to the crucible of his teen years.

Now he was entering a second crucible. Listen to the way he sings the "how long" choruses in "Late for the Sky," or the lines "while the loneliness springs from your life / like a fountain from a pool" from "Fountain of Sorrow," or the lines about the angels and the light of the past in "Farther On." This is a man whose life has been scarred and scorched—but, crucially and finally, *burnished* by the experience of love, romantic and familial. He comes out of it still having "faith in the distance" and able to write a rousing "prayer for the human race": a testament to a remarkable strength of soul. And it all begins with the voice.

Then there's the songcraft, which takes a leap forward on this record; the songwriting practically comprises a clinic on how to create tight, consistent rhyme structures, lucid images, colloquial poetry, and thematically unified statements. This is also the first record where Browne assembled a true band to make an entire album. He was now successful enough not to have to hire studio session players but to pay four musicians—Lindley on guitars and fiddle, Doug Heywood on bass, Larry Zack on drums, and Jai Winding on keyboards—to stick around long enough to create a cohesive sound (some of them also toured with him when the record was done). Rehearsals were conducted at the Abbey: "We rehearsed everything in a room in my house," Jackson recalled, "the house I grew up in, which my grandfather had built. This room we were working in had stained glass windows, a pipe organ and a choir loft, high ceilings. It was a little like being in a church. It might have been one reason the songs sound kind of churchy."[5] And when they went into the studio, things went quickly: the album was recorded in six weeks (as opposed to *For Everyman*'s six months). The result is a record with a remarkable aural unity that possesses a distinctive church-like solemnity. It's mostly piano-based, backed by Jai Winding's hyperresponsive organ, bass, and drums that are reserved and functional, and by the deeply emotional coloring of Lindley's guitars and violin. The opening four songs, comprising side one of the LP, feel very much like a suite, and the album closer, "Before the Deluge," brings the whole thing together, demonstrating that the record's sound—forged to support the most personal of observations about love and sorrow—was just as appropriate for an elegy on the fate of the counterculture, not to mention the fate of the planet.

THE DEPRESSION OF 1974

The album was released in November 1974, and if its somberness beautifully captured the gravity of his personal struggles, the record did a pretty good job of seizing the larger zeitgeist of that dismal year too. American news was dominated by the deepening of the oil crisis that began in 1973: gas prices jumped 35 percent in a single year, paralyzing an oil-dominated American economy already beginning to suffer from an unprecedented combination of inflation and recession that would come to have a new name—"stagflation." The gasoline rationing, rising unemployment, and high prices were bad enough, but the oil crisis signified something bigger: that the United States no longer seemed to be in control of its own destiny. The global superpower that had triumphantly strode through the "American century," conquering fascist dictators and world markets alike, was being brought to its knees by a group of Middle Eastern oil barons calling themselves OPEC. As one writer put it, the 1970s constituted "the first great crisis of postwar U.S. power."[6] Already suffering a deep loss of prestige from its failures in Vietnam, the United States was wallowing in what President Jimmy Carter, a few years later, would call a "crisis of confidence" in which there was a "growing doubt about the meaning of our own lives and . . . the loss of a unity of purpose for our nation."[7]

And then there was Watergate, a two-year-long soap opera cum political tragedy in which, for the first time in the country's history, a president resigned from office in the face of evidence of rampant corruption and abuse of power. (Nixon's own vice president, Spiro Agnew, had resigned from office the year before for an unrelated corruption scandal, thus elevating Speaker of the House Gerald Ford to the vice presidency. When Nixon resigned, Ford took his place, and, again, for the first time in history, the occupant of the White House was a man the country had never voted for.) The two years of investigation, the daily drip-drip-drip of evidence of the administration's spectacular corruption, depredations, and lies, was psychically debilitating to the whole country. Trust in government, the military, the corporate establishment, religious and educational institutions, authority of all kinds—they all plummeted, and young people, especially, felt disenchanted and directionless.

I remember those times well myself. I was sixteen and set to graduate high school that school year. I waited in long lines that coiled around the block to pump two dollars of gas—all I could afford—into my dad's Chevy Impala, then had to do it all over again a few days later. I watched Sam Ervin's Watergate Committee on TV relentlessly chip away at the idea that the American presidency was an office worthy of respect. In loud dinner arguments that rivaled those of the Bunkers in *All in the Family*, my father, a Romanian immigrant and a staunch anti-communist Republican, defended Nixon to the end, but that stopped making sense to me and my brothers, who were seeing movies like *The Conversation* and *The Parallax View* that introduced doubts and conspiracies that made us paranoid about any and all authority.

To many of my peers, the success track that we were taught in school and on television—high school, college, career, marriage, kids, the suburbs, and so forth—had been discredited by, well, *events*, not to mention the counterculture's biting criticisms of the Establishment, but by now the counterculture—young people perhaps five or ten years older than us—seemed discredited too. They seemed defeated and lost. At the time, I saw the straggling hippies that roamed through the streets of my town as pathetic, reeking of pot, their faces shadowed by the knowledge that they had actually become adults and were going to have to *make a living* in a system they deplored but didn't understand, though they often affected a self-protective sense of righteousness and moral superiority that I could see right through, even as a kid. I remember touring a college campus as a high school senior and talking to a philosophy professor who bemoaned the careerism and absence of social conscience in her current students, though they were only a few years younger than the firebrands she taught in the late 1960s. Nobody wanted to talk about politics—it was an affront to even bring it up, just as it was an affront to your dignity to have to sit in a line of cars for ninety minutes to get gas.

Like a lot of people, for years I thought of the early 1970s as a "sixties hangover," but it was no more a hangover than the sixties were a drinking party that got a little out of control. The early 1970s felt like a time of a plague of the spirit, depression on a societal level, presenting many of the classic symptoms of depression but experienced culture-wide: pervasive anxiety (and often paranoia), disappointment cratering into inertia, frustrated anger, massive fatigue, an inability to focus, and an escape into sex and/or drugs (though the drug of choice shifted from meditational marijuana to mind-frazzling, up-all-night cocaine). It's there in the high literature of the early 1970s, for instance, in the reactionary hysteria of

Rabbit Redux (1971) by John Updike, a writer who before the sixties had been pretty much unflappable. It filtered into pop culture too, in films like *McCabe and Mrs. Miller*, *The Godfather* movies, *Mean Streets*, or foreign films by Antonioni (*Zabriskie Point*) or Godard (*Weekend*) that young Americans had made their own. Even TV had caught on: watch an early 1970s TV show—say, *Mod Squad*, *Mannix*, or *M.A.S.H.*—on one of the nostalgia cable channels and you'll feel it: an enveloping unease, characters blurred out of the conventional categories of hero or villain, disquieting soundtracks, "existential" endings, values so up for grabs it showed in everything from the frantic camera movements (lots of bad zoom shots) to the way nobody knew how to dress or wear their mustaches.

Music in 1974 was in similarly dire straits. In the sixties, rock 'n' roll, for all its variety, was a unifying force for the young, but now that the rock audience encompassed three generations of listeners, it was fragmenting. (Robert Christgau explored this in his great essay from 1977, "How the Rock Audience Got to Be Too Big for Its Own Good."[8]) Browne lucked into an era where his kind of music prevailed in the marketplace—Carole King's *Tapestry* was, for years, the best-selling album in history—but now all sorts of music was being made by people who wouldn't be caught dead listening to *Sweet Baby James* or *For the Roses*. Bands like Black Sabbath, Uriah Heep, and Deep Purple, which had followed in Led Zeppelin's heavy metal wake, bled the blues down to cartoon satanism or stoned boogying, but dug deep into the culture, so influential that they inspired everything from the hilarious satire *This Is Spinal Tap* to the great portrait of a 1970s "wastoid" in David Foster Wallace's *Something Having to Do with Attention*. Insipid pop by the likes of Olivia Newton-John or the Captain and Tennille dominated radio, prompting pronouncements that "rock is dead." Rock pros like Elton John or Paul McCartney, as entertaining as they were, lacked ballast, singing silly love songs and seemingly going out of their way to dissuade listeners from thinking actual thoughts. There was more splintering: the prog rock of Yes or Emerson, Lake, and Palmer, or the glam of David Bowie or Queen, sold well but to more and more exclusive niches of the audience. Soul and R & B continued to soar artistically, with Marvin Gaye, Aretha Franklin, and Al Green at the top of their games, but they were appealing, especially in their live shows, more and more to a restricted black audience.

Then disco showed up, doing for Lycra spandex and polyester what the Laurel Canyon troubadours had done for natural fibers. Disco inspired some hateful rhetoric—often racist or homophobic—that was inexcusable, but to many counterculture survivors, the new dance music promoted a tawdry, coked-up hollowness of spirit, a meretricious glamour that reinscribed elitism into a sixties rock culture that had worked hard to eradicate it, and glorified material excess and an in-your-face fakeness/performative quality that mocked the very sincerity and desire for meaning that audiences of performers like Browne valued most in music. "Disco Sucks!" bumper stickers were plastered on every fifth AMC Pacer or Ford Pinto sputtering down the boulevards of my hometown, and though some of the anger was, again, racist or homophobic, some of it wasn't: disco seemed to say that everything about the sixties (aside from the sex and the drugs, which remained near and dear to the disco ethos) was dead and in the ground, and for many (including me), that was a depressing thing to be dancing about. It's no wonder, then, that Jackson Browne's most confusing song, ever, is his celebration/critique of the movement in "Disco Apocalypse."

THE SIDE ONE SUITE

As I got used to the gas lines and, through a thickening pot haze, adjusted to Gerald Ford and a new and depressing conception of what it meant to live in this country, I sat in my bedroom and listened to side one of *Late for the Sky* on an old, banged-up stereo that a friend had given me. You could stack up to four albums on the spindle, and once you pushed the auto button, it would plop a record onto the turntable, play the side, pull back the tone arm, and plop down another record. You could play almost two continuous hours of music that way. But I never stacked *Late for the Sky* with my other records. It didn't work on me as a rock record among other rock records. Every time I played it, in fact, I had the strange sensation that when each song ended, the whole side was over. "Late for the Sky," the opening track, was five and a half minutes long, but by the time the song faded out, it felt like a half hour had gone by: it took me through a world of emotion. When the next song, "Fountain of Sorrow," started—this one almost seven minutes long—it was like I hadn't processed what the first song had done to me yet. When "Fountain of Sorrow" ended, I felt the same sensation. I wasn't ready for the next song. It flooded me with feeling and, together with "Late for the Sky," it all began to back up in me so that I would sometimes have to stop the album before continuing with "Farther On" and then "The Late Show." At the same time, the songs begged to be heard in succession, as a single artistic unit. I've been listening to rock albums for half a century, and I've never had that experience with any other record.

Much of my response was of course personal—the way Browne sang "while the loneliness seems to spring from your life / like a fountain from a pool" did what so much good art does: it pulls out of the ferment of your being emotions you didn't know were there and gives them a name, gleaming and indelible. But it wasn't just me, obviously. When I finally saw Browne in concert, that was clear enough. Here we were, I thought, his fans, each in their own way, "standing alone / standing with his own ticket in his hand" ("For Everyman"), together in a communal recognition that loneliness was legion, and that it was a good thing to recognize that communally.

It was a brave decision to start the record with "Late for the Sky," which sounds so exhausted that at first it's hard to imagine Browne and his protagonist having the energy to bring the song, not to mention the album, to any conclusion. But Browne has an unusual verve to explore intractable situations, and here he investigates "the end / of the feeling we've known" with an unswerving patience. It's another of his bed songs—obviously about he and Major—that is so vulnerably and sincerely sung that it stands as a test case for anyone who wants to know if Browne is for them or not. And like "My Opening Farewell," it takes up a relationship that is in its end stages. The lovers lie together, having said everything there is to say, but the protagonist, looking at his lover, is shocked to learn that "there was nobody I'd ever known," which sends him off on a wailing lament about the delusions that got them here. Eventually, he realizes they are "late for the sky"—that is, *too* late for their lost love to be part of the openness, freedom, and spiritual regeneration he knows is possible in life (which is what the sky stands for in Browne's music). The tempo is slow and patient, Browne's piano laying down an elegiac foundation over which Lindley's guitar comments with enormous compassion. The lyrics, colloquial and drained of the self-conscious poetic imagery of his earlier stuff—are set down in a series of tercets that rhyme ABB until they burst out in the "how long" choruses, where the rhyme scheme expands to an ABBB quatrain. By the time it ends, the song's enormous passion and formal restraint is held in such balance that it feels almost Wordsworthian: powerful emotion recollected in tranquility.

The song's power actually overflows itself, broadening its meaning from mourning the end of a love affair to something that stands in for a more universal confusion and sadness. The last ninety seconds of the song appear in Martin Scorsese's seminal 1970s film *Taxi Driver*, in a scene where Travis Bickle, the Dostoyevskian antiheroic everyman, is driven to violence by his disgust with New York's urban chaos and his own loneliness and resentment. Travis, watching dancers on the show *Soul Train* on the television in his apartment, holds a revolver in his hand, occasionally pointing it at the screen but usually close to his head: suicide is obviously on his mind. In the scene immediately preceding this one, Travis had shot a black man who was holding up a bodega he happened to be in. Browne's lyrics, "how long have I been sleeping / how long have I been drifting through the night," sound over Travis's face, and the song is transformed from love lament to a grieving commentary on the free-floating despair that so many associated with life in the 1970s.

"Fountain of Sorrow" is, if anything, even more powerful. The tempo picks up a little, but the emotional ground tone and themes are similar: "When you see through love's illusions, there lies the danger / And your perfect lover just looks like a perfect fool." There is the same careful lyrical craftsmanship—here we have ABAB quatrains blooming into a finale where each of the last ten lines rhyme. There is the painstaking analysis of self-delusion, of the protagonist's own romantic dodginess and foolishness, and the same recognition that, as John Irving put it a few years later in the novel *The Hotel New Hampshire*, "sorrow floats." Listening to "Fountain of Sorrow" can work on you like a good therapy session. But it's a song, with a strong appealing melody and Lindley's remarkable translations of Browne's vocal tenderness. Crucially, the song finds in its own depths reason for optimism. The last line, "but you go on smiling so clear and so bright," would seem tacked on and unconvincing if it weren't for the song's grounding metaphor. The water from the fountain of sorrow springs from "loneliness"—loneliness is the fundamental human condition on this album—but accepting that loneliness brings a clarity and a freedom that allows you to have compassion toward others and yourself. German philosopher Artur Schopenhauer used to say that when we come upon a fellow human, we ought to greet them by saying, "Hail, fellow sufferer!" "Fountain of Sorrow" hails the listener in that way.

"Farther On" and "The Late Show" play variations on the themes that side one's suite has already developed. "Farther On," a retrospective on Browne's early years that recalls "Looking into You" (Browne claimed it was "the exact same song,"[9] though it isn't) pits the isolation of his youth ("adrift on an ocean of loneliness") against the dreams that allowed him to rise above it, dreams inspired by "book and films and songs." But the loneliness is winning out: halfway through, the song nearly comes to a halt, with him admitting "I'm not sure what I'm trying to say." But then he comes upon a metaphor—of angels—that buoys the rest of the song (Browne will come back to the metaphor over and over the rest of his writing life.). Here, the angels are like those in Wim Wenders's great film, *Wings of Desire*: mute seraphic witnesses to human sorrow and struggle, standing beside or behind us, invisible but close, reminders of "the vision of the paradise" that we carry around within us and which Romantics like Browne can't help but try to make real. Those angels allow the protagonist to affirm his "faith in the distance / Moving farther on."

"The Late Show," the suite's closer, hearkens back to the opener. Similar in pace and its tone of subdued desperation, it expands on the same wrangling and intractability of a struggling relationship that we get in "Late for the Sky" ("I'm so tired of all this circling / and all these glimpses of the end") and again painfully dramatizes the Romantic theme: the great distance between what we want and what we have. Lyrically, it's all over the place: it conjures various scenarios of lovers, finds solace in the idea of friendship, expresses frustration that "no one ever talks about their feelings anyway." The connections between ideas aren't quite as logical as Browne's usually are, and the song actually threatens to fall apart thematically near the end before Browne rescues it. Summoning all instruments to go quiet, the protagonist addresses his lover directly: "Listen," he begins, and tells his lover he's sitting in his car outside her house waiting for her. "Go pack your sorrow, trash man comes tomorrow / Leave it at the curb and we'll just roll away." Which is to say, essentially, "Fuck it, forget all this tired circling, let's turn our sorrow into light by sheer force of desire." Browne borrows a classic 1950s teen romance scenario but uses it to deploy the protagonist's existential choice: he chooses spontaneous trust in passion over the endless meditative ambivalence that characterizes most of the rest of side one's suite. If you want to know what "faith in the distance" means, here it is.

THE OPEN SKY

Nowadays, we don't think about the "sides" of albums; in the streaming age, most people don't even think in terms of albums, not to mention albums as artistic wholes. But in the halcyon days of analog, people saw a side of an album as something that you listened to from beginning to end, unless you were willing to get up from wherever you were, walk to the turntable, pick up the needle ("dude, don't scratch the grooves!") and either skip a song or play it over again. In any case, side two would in a sense "start over," often with a different feel. Side two of *Late for the Sky* is like that. Though the opening track, "The Road and the Sky," is a narrative continuation of "The Late Show"—the guy now has the girl in his Chevy and is rolling down the highway—Jackson is done for the moment with solemn meditations on love and sorrow. Instead, we're presented with Browne's attempt at a rocker, a track replete with Jai Winding's 1950s-style piano pounding, chunky rhythm guitar, buckets of slide guitar from Jackson himself, and two great lines: "Get a little higher / see if I can hotwire re-al-i-*teeeee*!" Along with "Walking Slow," the other rock track on side two, "Road" is Browne trying to (temporarily) lighten his/our load because, obviously, he's still got a world of trouble on his mind. Neither song holds up to the rest of the record, though, and Browne knows it. Decades later, he told an interviewer: "The biggest problem I had with this record is I didn't know how to make rock 'n' roll happen. . . . I was far outstripped in that area by The Eagles and Little Feat. I couldn't find my way into that kind of playing."[10] It wasn't just a problem of technique though: both songs try too hard to be "up" on a record whose domain is the depths.

"For a Dancer" plunges us right back into them. It's the album's most direct song—all about death and how we face it. The title refers to an acquaintance of Browne's named Scott Runyon, a talented dancer who, after an illness, had to give up dancing, and in recompense went all-in on other creative enterprises: clothing design, photography, rock music. Though operating on the fringes of Browne's life, Runyon's wild spirit captivated him, and so when Runyon died in a Hollywood bathhouse fire, Browne wrote a song for him. As in "Song for Adam," Browne uses the death of his subject to meditate on the mystery of mortality, and ends up writing what amounts to a kind of prayer, one that urges the listener to "keep a fire in your eye / pay attention to the open sky." There is a desire here to attend, vigilantly, to something *in existence itself*, to the "fire" and spirit of a life force within and without us, that is crucial to everything in Browne's maturing vision. It's what connects him to a Romantic tradition going back to Shelley's West Wind or those crucial lines in Wordsworth's "Tintern Abbey":

> And I have felt
> A presence that disturbs me with the joy
> Of elevated thoughts; a sense sublime
> Of something far more deeply interfused,
> Whose dwelling is the light of setting suns,
> And the round ocean and the living air,
> And the blue sky, and in the mind of man:
> A motion and a spirit, that impels
> All thinking things, all objects of all thought,
> And rolls through all things.

This faith in a sublime presence in existence that we can feel in us and around us, that rolls through all things like a gentle breeze, is, for Romantics, what gives them a sense that the earth is both our natural and spiritual home, that we humans belong here, and Browne's sharing in that faith is I think what critics really mean when they call Browne a "Romantic." The open sky's mysteries, that fire in the eye, are the things that give him the strength and faith to transform the fountain of sorrow into a fountain of light. It's the spirit of the angels in "Farther On." It's what gives him the courage, in this song, to make a "joyful sound" despite the uncertainties of life and love and the certainty of death. It is what he has instead of God. Of course, for this to mean anything, that fire and attentiveness to the open sky has to be conveyed musically, and the triumph of "For a Dancer" is that it all comes across with a beautiful tenderness and clarity. You hear it in Browne's soulful, utterly earnest singing. You hear it in the craft of lyrics that consist of a series of octets consistently rhyming AABCCBBB, but whose rhymes feel so unforced they sound like real speech. And you hear it in Lindley's eloquent violin solo, both funereal and celebratory, that follows after Browne sings "in the end there is one dance you'll do alone."

If this sounds too literary or overwrought, recall that Kendrick Lamar's Pulitzer, or Dylan's Nobel, were awarded partly for the way these artists participated in and extended what are essentially literary traditions. And Browne is doing no more than that. The album's culminating track, "Before the Deluge" is, if anything, even more elevated in tone than "For a Dancer" and participates just as much in its visionary Romanticism. When Browne sings the song's final line: "When the light that's lost within us reaches the sky," he's speaking of that "presence" again, imaged again as "light," that rises into the sky from our battered souls and reconnects us to the universals of life, love, spirit, and possibility.

Browne has said that the inspiration for "Before the Deluge" came from two books.[11] The first is Otto Friedrich's *Before the Deluge*, which, surprisingly, is about the cultural and political ferment in Weimar Germany in the decade and a half that followed World War I. Friedrich describes with novelistic skill that extraordinary combination of political and economic chaos, wildly original cultural production (Bertolt Brecht's plays, Mann's *The Magic Mountain*, George Grosz's expressionistic paintings, architecture's Bauhaus movement, films like *The Cabinet of Dr. Caligari*, Isadora Duncan's dance) and moral/sexual decadence that characterizes Germany in the years before "the deluge" of Hitler's Third Reich. In a 1995 preface to a new edition, Friedrich says the book "did not and does not attempt to demonstrate parallels between Berlin of the 1920s and America of the 1970s . . . but I nonetheless had that possibility much in mind when I wrote it."[12] Certainly Browne felt the parallels, too, because he swiped Friedrich's title to write a song about a generation deeply wounded by war (Vietnam), experiencing chaos in the political/economic sphere, and in the midst of a cultural revolution that portended future devastation.

The other book that Browne said influenced "Before the Deluge" was a collection of essays called *Eco-Catastrophe*, put out by the editors of the leftist journal *Ramparts* in 1970.[13] The book as a whole comprises a systematic analysis of mid-century American capitalism as the primary culprit behind the emerging worldwide environmental crisis. According to the foreword, it identifies "the root of the ecological crisis in the very structure of American society, and [points] to the necessity of a revolutionary reconstruction of that social order as a precondition for any practical and effective reform." It contains articles on the Santa Barbara oil spill, the harrowing Rocky Flats nuclear accident of May 1969, and an unflattering assessment of the country's tepid "conservation movement": "Today's big business conservation is not interested in preserving the earth; it is rationally re-organizing for a more efficient rape of resources (e.g., the export of chemical-intensive agribusiness) and the production of an even grosser national product."[14] It includes an examination of the "eco-establishment," the quiet covenant between government and corporate interests to nudge the country toward (a mostly rhetorical) environmentalism without actually hurting business interests. It even anticipates the debate on global warming: "We must drastically revise our traditional notions of what constitutes an environmental 'pollution.' A few decades ago it would have been absurd to describe carbon dioxide and heat as 'pollutants' in the customary sense of the term. Yet in both cases they may well rank among the most serious source of future ecological imbalance and pose major threats to the viability of the planet."[15] This, in 1970! Overall, the book is a post-Marxist broadside—"Propertied society, domination, hierarchy, and the state, in all their forms, are utterly compatible with the survival of the biosphere"[16]—that anticipates by fifty years the alarm sounded by recent books like Naomi Klein's *This Changes Everything*, and must have been intellectually bracing to a young autodidact like Browne, who used it as a kind of urtext for a political vision that would, in future years, become more and more comprehensively progressive.[17]

All that reading, and all the personal strife of the preceding seven songs on the album, get absorbed into a tale of countercultural failure, grief, and fear on "Before the Deluge." Browne's own personal doubts crisscross with the social doubts of his entire generation, enhance each other, and make everything so dire that Browne ends up prophesying apocalypse. David Lindley's stately violin intro establishes a dignified tragic tone for a narrative that, in classic Romantic fashion, traces the counterculture's journey from innocence to disillusioned experience. Starting out with "the energy of the innocent" and a desire to go "back to nature," Browne's generation starts out strong and unified, but the longer they fly on "the brave and crazy wings of youth," the more their feathers grow "torn and tattered," until ultimately they trade their dreams "for the resignation that living brings" and exchange their hopes for love "for the glitter and the rouge." The metaphors here are as precise and evocative as any the counterculture came up with to describe its general disillusionment as it faced its failures to transform the Establishment. The third verse introduces the specifics of the counterculture's struggle to preserve the environment against "the men who learned how to forge her beauty into power." The "men" here likely refers to those in the eco-establishment who were thrusting the world further and further into a dangerous reliance on nuclear power, but more generally, it's about an entire economic ethos that looks at nature as what philosopher Martin Heidegger called "a standing reserve"—that is, as simply products designed for our exploitation, as a living forest can be seen as nothing but potential stacks of lumber. Browne pushes the pessimism to the point where he envisions a deluge even more destructive than the one Hitler ultimately unleashed in Friedrich's book—a nuclear accident that leaves only a few survivors.

How "Before the Deluge" peeks into apocalypse would be a devastating way to end the record, but Browne is determined to be redemptive, just as he was in "For a Dancer" or "Fountain of Sorrow." "Before the Deluge" is another prayer—secular and humanist—that asks the listener, even among the ruins, to "let creation reveal its secrets by and by." Which is to say, "pay attention to the open sky" because that's where "the light that's lost within us" has gone—and where it may be recaptured. The counterculture may have lost hope, but hope, like sorrow, floats, and so may be recaptured, even "after the deluge." "Let the music keep our spirits high," Browne sings, and to emphasize the point, Lindley comes in at the end with a spirited bit of bluegrass, calm but celebratory, a hint of renewed faith.

Late for the Sky is steeped in sorrow but meets it with a soulful strength and compassion that resonates far beyond the personal and familial struggles Browne was dealing with at the time. It's his first great album. It was also his most commercially successful record to date, going gold even without the benefit of a hit single. Though the *Village Voice*'s Christgau was splenetic—"his linguistic gentility is inappropriate, his millenarianism is self-indulgent, and only if he sang as well as good as Dylan Thomas would I change my mind"[18]—for *Rolling Stone*, the *New York Times*, and the *LA Times*, the album made good on the promise Browne had been exhibiting for years, and it placed him atop the heap of the singer-songwriter movement. In the years since, it's become the standard by which the rest of his albums have been assessed. It's his *Highway 61 Revisited*, his *Born to Run*, fated to be shorthand for what people think of when they think of a Jackson Browne record. Inevitably, it'll be the album most noted in his obituaries, though he would go on to write at least two dozen more songs that will match it in emotional intelligence, passionate insight, and beauty. It's both his gleaming achievement and his albatross.

4

THE DELUGE

The shadow of Phyllis Major's suicide hangs dark and heavy over the two albums that made Jackson Browne a household name. That an artist's private pain sometimes translates into mass public acclaim is one of those ironies pop musicians learn to live with. But unlike the 2020s, when so many pop artists revel in 24/7 social media exposure, in the 1970s some semblance of celebrity privacy still existed, and Browne insisted on maintaining it. In interviews during the 1970s, he kept a tight seal of silence around the circumstances of his wife's death and his reaction to it, and he's never really addressed it in song directly, though allusions to their fateful marriage are there for anyone to hear. There are strands of regret, longing, sorrow, guilt, and anger in "Your Bright Baby Blues," "The Only Child," "Here Come Those Tears Again," "Sleep's Dark and Silent Gate," "Running on Empty," and, probing just a little, in "The Fuse" and in any number of the on-the-road tracks from *Running on Empty*. On *The Pretender*, especially, Browne conflates the private deluge of his catastrophic marriage with the death of the counterculture in a way that's similar to how F. Scott Fitzgerald equated his wife's mental breakdown with the death of his Jazz Age generation in *Tender Is the Night* (which title Browne will steal for a song on *Lawyers in Love*). Browne's mid- to late 1970s albums put a period to the first phase of Browne's life as an artist—they're the apotheosis of his talent as a singer-songwriter, a confirmation of the relevance of his music to a mass audience, his funeral dirge for the sixties, and a door into the confusions—personal, political, musical—that he would grapple with in the 1980s.

TRAUMA AND REACTION

The *Late for the Sky* tour was Browne's longest to date—a six-month campaign that started in the fall of 1974 and went well into the spring of 1975—and for the first time featured Browne as exclusive headliner playing 3,000-seat halls. When he returned to LA, he quickly jumped into the producer's chair for his friend Warren Zevon, whom Jackson was instrumental in getting signed to Asylum. The resulting album, *Warren Zevon* (1976), got buried commercially under the avalanche of prominent West Coast albums of the time (Linda Ronstadt's *Hasten Down the Wind*, the Eagles' era-defining *Hotel California*), but it's one of the best-ever albums about Los Angeles. ("Desperados under the Eaves" could have been slipped onto *Hotel California* and made it a better record. Indeed, Frey and Henley sang background vocals on it.) Browne's clean production, together with his ability to bring in members of the *Late for the Sky* band, LA session whizzes (Waddy Wachtel, Gary Mallaber), and his musician buddies (such as Bonnie Raitt) are hardly incidental to the album's stellar reputation today. Browne was involved in every aspect of the project, from corralling a rowdy group of cocaine-fueled musicians into focused and subtle performances to turning the knobs, playing piano, and singing backup vocals. He finished up on Leap Year Day 1976—February 29—and the very next day slipped into Electra Sound Recorders to start laying down backing tracks for *The Pretender*.

During the making of *Warren Zevon*, he and Phyllis married (in December), but Jackson's hectic schedule—he was producing Zevon and writing the songs for *The Pretender* at the same time—left little time for the couple to address their own difficulties. Major was eager to resume her modeling career, but this creative woman, neurasthenic and fragile, found it difficult to be stuck home with a baby. She felt stymied when her manager quit his job without notifying her, which evidently tipped her into a steep depressive cycle. She spiraled down until the night of March 24, when she overdosed on sleeping pills. (Ethan was with a nanny at the time.) Browne came home after a night in the studio and found her body. She was buried three days later after a funeral in Santa Barbara, and Jackson took about six weeks off from recording to grieve and be with his son. He returned to the studio on May 6.

These are the bare facts. The rest is silence, from Browne anyway. Friends and acquaintances of the time fill in some blanks: according to one, after the suicide Browne seemed "absolutely rigid, trying to hang on in the world." His old Fullerton friend Steve Noonan remembers that Browne was quiet and depressed when they met soon after the death, with Jackson finally saying, "I just have to keep working . . . I have to keep moving. Keep myself working." Pamela Polland, Jackson's friend from his first years in LA, recalls that when she met him soon after the suicide, "I remember this shattered sense of him. . . . It was like a cloud that hung over the whole meeting the whole time."[1] Years later, Browne admitted to considerable chemical assistance during that period: "I used to do a lot of coke," he said. "It was in the wake of my wife's death."[2] Trauma and reaction: the death of his wife, the terse decision to keep busy, moving, working, distracting. The songs will have to tell the story.

Unfair, and inaccurate, though, to say that *The Pretender* is *about* Phyllis Major's suicide. "The perception was that I wrote the album about my wife's death, which was not true," Browne said more than a decade later, "because the album was pretty much written before she died."[3] Fairer to suggest, as Jackson did soon after the album's release, that "*The Pretender* depicts the last couple years of my life. . . . The nature of my music has to do with dealing with very fundamental things by depicting my own experience. That's the way it is, and I guess it's okay. I mean, the truly personal and private things are not in there."[4] The marriage and Phyllis's death, then, provide the salient emotional context for the album's songs, but they're not everything; in fact, the album for Browne was living proof of his *surviving* the trauma. "I think that [the album] was basically about going forward and still living in the world—just the act of finishing the record."[5] Furthermore, as autobiographical a songwriter as Browne is reputed to be, his songs rarely take up his life straight up. They fictionalize: grounding facts are shaped and addressed from different angles in order to make for better art. In any case, *The Pretender*'s concerns extend far beyond the tragedy of his marriage: "The Fuse" is about time, meaning, and notions of the spirit, expressed in metaphor and philosophical abstraction; "Daddy's Tune" is about his relationship to his father; and "The Pretender" is the next chapter in Browne's ongoing rumination on the fate of his generation.

Again, that generation of his: that massive cohort of boomers—seventy-six million strong—whose most influential spokespeople strode through the second half of the American century believing it was their job to shape the future in the most idealistic of ways, only to discover that the economic, military, and political power that America had amassed on its way to postwar hegemony was hardly going to be dislodged by something as fragile and airy as youthful demands for equality, justice, and allegiance to Mother Earth.

The years 1975 and 1976 were woeful extensions of the mass cultural depression that characterized the early 1970s. The United States' participation in the Vietnam War came to a pathetic end, with TV images of the last US helicopters rising from Saigon's airport, desperate Vietnamese literally hanging from the skids of the landing gear. This was followed, humiliatingly, by North Vietnam quickly overrunning the South and sealing the inarguable fact that the decade-long US venture to save South Vietnam from communism was an abject failure. Nixon was gone, and his successor Gerald Ford pardoned the disgraced president to rid the country of having to deal with the consequences of his corruption, but Ford's attempts to restore American patriotism—Whip Inflation Now lapel buttons, or a campaign to celebrate the nation's bicentennial at a time when the country could hardly have been less proud of itself—felt not just ill-timed but, to many of us, dumb: inappropriate, irrelevant, *lame.*

A sliver of pop culture potency was supplied by a new late-night TV satire called *Saturday Night Live*. Bruce Springsteen, with *Born to Run* (1975) had revived the hope that rock music could emerge from its 1970s doldrums, and Bob Dylan regained his footing with the *Before the Flood* tour and the genius *Blood on the Tracks* (1975), but I remember little else on the pop culture scene that conducted anything like the charge of 1960s music. I was a college freshman in 1975, a scholarship student who'd escaped my hometown and found myself plopped down among a lot of affluent kids at a very good private college, and my head was wide open to my course syllabuses: there seemed no end to what Plato's *Apology*, Freud's *Civilization and Its Discontents*, and *The Federalist Papers* could teach me. Wildly excited by the new world I was entering, I expected revelation from books, films, and music. And music gushed, as did plenty of pot smoke, from the open doors of my dormitory mates: Fleetwood Mac's self-titled album (the one with "Rhiannon" on it), Queen's freaky "Bohemian Rhapsody," "Fame" by David Bowie. In 1976, you couldn't cross campus without hearing *Frampton Comes Alive*, Boz Scaggs's *Silk Degrees*, or the Ohio Players' "Fire" blasting from somebody's window. Then there were the rock perennials of 1970s dorm life: *Who's Next*, *Moondance*, *Court and Spark*, and *Dark Side of the Moon*. On the black cover sleeve of this last one, we poured cheap Mexican shake out of plastic baggies, plucked out the seeds and rolled joints that gave us both highs and headaches. Occasionally, you would hear "Blitzkrieg Pop" on late-night pirate radio or read in *Creem* or *Crawdaddy* about Joy Division or some punk thing brewing in London. One guy down the hall was a football player who played nothing—nothing—but Led Zeppelin, and since *Physical Graffiti* had just come out, "Kashmir" started entering my dreams.

I liked all this stuff, but just liking stuff didn't cut it. *Late for the Sky* taught me to expect experiences with records that would affect me the way great books or films did, and in order to get that I had to go back a few years, to Van Morrison's *Astral Weeks* (1968), midsixties Dylan, or Springsteen, who I was now getting to appreciate. I had a small group of friends who felt the way I did, but most of my classmates were work-hard/play-hard preppie types, econ and poli-sci majors who knew how to ace exams and get *A*s but saved their enthusiasm for Saturday night keggers that they would wax nostalgic about for decades (if the "Class of '79 Notes" of my college's alumni magazine are any indication). They openly admitted that these were the best years of their lives, and that after college, they'd go to law school or enter daddy's business and submit to a way of life that they themselves mocked as phony every time we watched *The Graduate* on late-night TV. I puzzled over this, intimidated by their monied savoir-faire but quietly suspected they were in for massive disappointments down the line. And then halfway through my sophomore year, just days before Americans would slough off the political dirt of the past decade by electing a born-again Georgian peanut farmer to the presidency, *The Pretender* came out. Obsessed by the title track, I marveled that it seemed to nail the lives of half the people around me. My mind opened wider.

THE PRETENDER

On the back cover of *The Pretender*, Browne printed Pablo Neruda's "Brown and Agile Child" (translated by Kenneth Rexroth) alongside a photo of his two-year-old son Ethan cavorting naked on the California shore. The poem's speaker isn't explicitly named as the father to the child of the title, but the implication's obvious. It's a love poem to the child and its connection to—its identification with—Nature itself:

> You are the delirious youth of the bee.
> The drunkenness of the wave, the power in the wheat.

The boy, that is, is still part of Nature's primal energy. He hasn't yet grown up to find himself, through self-consciousness, separated from it. Yet the speaker/father, for all his sweet appreciation of the child, knows that he himself *has* made the separation that constitutes adulthood, and so "nothing draws me to you / Everything pulls away from me here in the noon"—noon, the time of shadowless, merciless sunlight, when there's no hiding from the adult truth that the child will someday grow up and lose his innocence and connection to Nature, just as the speaker has. Still, the speaker's "somber heart seeks you always," desiring the love of the child's primal purity even as he knows he'll never fully experience it again. This is undiluted Romanticism, and that Browne prints the poem on the back of the album is probably one reason why Paul Nelson, Browne's most avid critical supporter in the 1970s, called him "our greatest practicing romantic."[6] The language of the poem is pure Neruda: simple and rooted in the primordial elements, calmly poised between a desire to transcend human limits and a realization that you can't always get what you want.

The poem's appropriate for *The Pretender*, and not just because it links to "The Only Child," Browne's tender song of paternal advice to his son. It also suggests a Romantic metaphysics that Browne began to outline in *Late for the Sky*, that he develops further on this album, and will later elaborate in "Looking East," which will steal Neruda's phrase "power in the wheat" and serve as Browne's most complete expression of his own defiant Romanticism. "For a Dancer" and "Before the Deluge" both hint that there's a sublime unifying presence in existence itself that, if we can tap into it (usually through the experience of love, be it agape or eros), can give us a sense of belonging to the world as well as a sense of responsibility to be good stewards of the earth. *The Pretender* will explore that idea, crucially, on the opening track, "The Fuse."

Which is where Jon Landau comes in. Landau was a producer and rock critic who famously announced, in 1974, that Bruce Springsteen was "rock and roll future" and then tried to make the slogan stick by helping produce the Boss's breakthrough *Born to Run*. Landau was one of the few critics Browne read and respected, and he had given Browne some pointers on producing Zevon's album (Landau is credited with "shadowboxing" on that LP). Browne was sensitive to complaints from critics and fellow musicians that his first three albums, all of which he at least coproduced, suffered from subpar sound. Dave Mason, the singer-songwriter from Traffic who was building a solo career at the time, told Jackson, after listening to *Late for the Sky*, "[You've written] a great bunch of songs, but somebody needs to produce you."[7] When Browne met with Landau, they agreed they wanted to make a rock album with the best LA session musicians available and to "produce a record with punchy musicianship and singing, but more than that, with a musical *pulse—no dead time.* At one point or another those previous LPs had lost that pulse. This one wouldn't."[8]

Landau's production showcases everything that makes *The Pretender* different from the previous albums, and we sense it immediately in "The Fuse," whose music reinforces the lyrics in ways no previous Browne song has. The fuse of the title is an image of time burning up, second by second.

Now, any serious song about time is really about death: when we genuinely experience time's passage—when we feel that the fuse is burning right now and always—we can't help but sense that we are losing the past as we slip into the present, and that the present is taking us inevitably to our deaths. (This is straight-up Heidegger, for the philosophically inclined.) What makes the song new in the Browne catalog is that the meaning comes through in the sound: the burning fuse comes through in the sizzle of cymbals throughout the song, the eerie long sustains and harmonics on Lindley's slide, and Craig Doerge's tick-tock piano, which sounds miles away from Jackson's usual calm, thick chording. This is the first Jackson Browne song where you don't really have to listen to the lyrics to know what it's about.

The experience of feeling the inevitability of death *in* the passage of time is what prompts the protagonist to feel the "fear of living for nothing." Yet the speaker's idealism saves him: after a long instrumental section in the middle of the song that prepares us, he comes out with it—a statement of Romantic faith:

> There's a part of me that speaks to the heart of me . . .
> Alive in eternity that nothing can kill.

This goes beyond the prayer (i.e., the hope) in "For a Dancer" to keep a fire burning in one's heart and to pay attention to the promise of the open sky. This song says that there's something in us that's eternal, that we participate in something—call it Spirit, Being, God, what you will—that's alive in us, and which we share with the rest of creation. This is the "fire high in the empty sky" that the speaker senses at the beginning of the song. It's also what the speaker celebrates so optimistically at song's end: "I will tune my spirit to the gentle sound . . . of the waters lapping on a higher ground." Lyrically, "The Fuse" is central to what we call Browne's whole perspective on the world that he'll work to affirm for the rest of his career.

Landau's production proves more problematic on two of the weaker songs on the album. "Linda Paloma" contains a searching lyric that explores a romantic relationship whose love is "slipping away" because it resides not in "the heart" but "in the shadows preferred by the mind" (Jackson's indicated that the woman in the song is based on Phyllis[9]). But the music is overbearing. Browne learned, in future records, to explore Mexican and Spanish music with subtlety, but Landau just piles it on here: a lute-like Spanish instrument called the *vijuella*, a *guitarrón*, a ranchero-inspired violin, mariachi background vocals that you might hear in just about any LA

Mexican restaurant, and a harp so loud and far out in front of the mix that it coats the song in treacle. "Daddy's Tune," a song Browne had been writing off and on since 1968, reaches out to Jackson's father, who was a jazz musician and aims to close the distance between them. But it's unconvincing lyrically and musically: "Make room for my forty-fives / Along beside your seventy-eights" is slight and sentimental, and the horns that try to lift the song into festiveness at song's end sound like they were cadged from a Chicago album (not a compliment). More forced buoyancy. Browne's attempt through "Daddy's Tune" to reconnect with his father doesn't work, which suggests a chasm between them that could hardly be bridged by a song. Indeed, in a 1992 interview, Browne admitted that he had been so estranged from his father that he couldn't remember the year of his death: "'Five or six or seven . . . he might've died ten years ago. I should know the date, but. . . . ,' Browne's voice trails off again. 'When he died, I didn't stop my tour to come back or anything.'"[10]

"The Only Child," Jackson's song to his shore-frolicking son on the back cover, is so intimate and sincere that it does an end-around critical analysis: you can carp at the forced rhymes, or the too-sweet background vocals, but Lindley's violin provides lovely instrumental counterpoint, the paternal advice is considered and loving, and the repeated counsel to "take good care of your mother" takes on extra pathos when we realize that by the time the song came out, there was no mother for the boy to take care of.

Three songs on the album most obviously address the Browne-Major predicament. "Here Come Those Tears Again," cowritten with Phyllis's mother, Nancy Farnsworth, gave Jackson his first hit since "Doctor My Eyes" (it reached number 23 on *Billboard* and charted in Canada and Australia as well) and certainly helped push the album into platinum territory, but it's not the record's strongest song. The woman in the song is indeed fascinating: devoted to flighty impulses, she leaves the speaker at one point only to return to him later to gloat about "how [she has] grown." The speaker, though, confused, abandoned, and still very much beholden to her, can respond only with "tears" and thus comes off as a bit of a lovelorn dishrag. (One of the weaknesses of Browne's songwriting is his overreliance on words like "tears," "crying," "smile," and "laughter" to denote emotion, and the twelve repetitions of the title phrase here don't help.) It's a rock song, though, with a sturdy piano-pounding beat, a melody that sticks in your head whether you like it or not, and strong backing vocals from Bonnie Raitt and Rosemary Butler, and so the fact that it was a radio hit isn't surprising. But it pales beside the album's central song about Major: "Your Bright Baby Blues."

"Baby Blues" is one of Browne's best songs, as complex and moving a study of romantic torment as most of the stuff Bob Dylan laid down for *his* marital breakdown album, *Blood on the Tracks*—and more emotionally clarifying. Written before Major's death but recorded afterward, it sets off sparks that light up the before and after of Jackson's grief. Featuring a confident, cathartic, melodically inventive vocal that attains a gospel-like ache and power, its six-plus minutes patiently build (thanks largely to a soft bed of Billy Payne's wistful organ) to a summit of tension where love and desperation, tenderness and anger, become indistinguishable, and then it melts all its ambiguities in a slide guitar denouement that is as beautiful as anything Lindley has ever played for Browne.

The song begins on an open, empty highway—the landscape of the West—and brings to mind "the long distance loneliness rolling out over the desert floor" ("The Fuse") along with intimations of transience and journeys where there's plenty of time to get "lost in the mysteries" and to ponder how to justify one's life. The protagonist here desperately wants to lose himself but can't ("No matter how fast I run / I can't never seem to get away from me") and so decides to return to his woman in the hope that she can free him with her "sweet tenderness." But the woman is more complicated than the capricious lover from "Here Come Those Tears Again," her tenderness buried deep beneath layers of defensiveness, distraction, cynicism, brittle confusion. The fourth verse, beginning with "Well I can see it in your eyes," is probably the most penetrating and concise portrait of Phyllis Major that Browne has written, and despite the speaker knowing that his portrait seems "cruel," he still longs for her. That longing comes out in Lindley's beautifully tentative slide solo that immediately follows. But the solo ends not with connection between speaker and woman but more loneliness. The next verse is about the speaker taking a drug—seemingly peyote—that, far from delivering him from his loneliness, makes it clearer than ever how desperate he is. The song ends with his pleading with her to pull him through "the hole in your garden wall"—out of the desert wilderness and into the Edenic tenderness he knows is in her—but nothing in the song suggests that that's going to happen. "Your Bright Baby Blues" is a clear-eyed portrait of the longing and limits of a marriage in deep crisis, and like "The Only Child," its pathos is all the greater for how we know that marriage ended.

"Sleep's Dark and Silent Gate," the only *Pretender* song that Jackson wrote after Phyllis's death, is, like "The Fuse," about time, death, and love, but it's underdeveloped, nearly a fragment (and at 2:35, the shortest track he's ever recorded). Until the third verse, it's a half-baked meditation on the marriage and a too-obviously "poetic" title metaphor. Only when the counterpoint comes in does the song soar: the melody is gorgeous and culminates in Browne's open wound of a line—"Oh *God* this is some shape I'm in"—which basically sums up Jackson's state during the making of the entire album.

The Pretender is the third album in a row that concludes with a song that gathers all the personal themes of the preceding songs and consolidates them into a commentary of the body politic. If "For Everyman" tried to reassert the counterculture's values of compassion and solidarity just as they were falling apart, and "Before the Deluge" elegized his generation's political failures while praying that its holdouts cleave to its values anyway, "The Pretender" buries the counterculture's Romantic ideals for good, hoping that the shock of the death ignites something greater than a capitulation to 1970s malaise and cynicism. It's fully worked out thematically, opening out to a trapped-in-the-American-dream vision that's as persuasively detailed as anything in a John Cheever or Ann Beattie story of suburban ennui. As "aware of the time going by" as the speaker in "The Fuse," here is exuberance clashing with resignation, panic with exhaustion, sympathy with moral critique, all hovering over a darkness that seems to call for satire. But Browne, too much of a humanist for that, opts for sympathy and pathos instead.

Scrupulously produced, tightly structured, and robustly melodic, the thematic power of "The Pretender" comes largely from the fact that Browne wrote it from the perspective of a persona with whom he empathizes but who's clearly not him. (Would that he had used the same strategy in his more explicitly political music of the 1980s and beyond.) The Pretender *has* capitulated: he's given up on believing in "the changes / we waited for love to bring"—that is, on the counterculture's hopes that love as a social principle could be transformational, and that there is something "alive in eternity / that nothing can kill." He's forsaken personal love too; he won't look his lover in the eye but makes love with his dark glasses on. He's going to be "a happy idiot / and struggle for the legal tender." Yet he *knows* he's capitulated: he has Browne's intelligence without his will to resist the blandishments of American materialism. The "ads [have taken] aim and lay their claim" on him, heart and soul, so by song's end, he's asking us to pray for him because he doesn't have the will to pray for himself. As the song fades, Browne throws out a kicker: "Are you prepared for the Pretender?" suggesting that the future better be ready for more of this character, which was prescient indeed. "Young urban professionals"—yuppies, unapologetic "greed-is-good" lawyers in love (cf. the 1987 film *Wall Street*) who turned their backs on precisely the countercultural values they grew up with—would stalk the steel-and-glass canyons of America's downtowns in the 1980s, getting and spending in a frenzy and making sure that Reagan got and kept power throughout that long and rapacious decade. Here's Jackson's own take on the song: "'The Pretender' is about 1960s idealism, the idea of life being about love and brotherhood, justice, social change and enlightenment, those concepts we were flooded with as our generation hit its stride; and how, later, we settled for something quite different."[11]

Selling more than two million copies, *The Pretender* elevated Jackson Browne to the big time in the United States and broke him as an international star. West Coast critics like the *LA Times*'s Robert Hilburn were buoyant. East Coast stalwart Dave Marsh, who had long dismissed "El Lay" rock as dull and enervated, wrote a *Rolling Stone* review that castigated parts of it ("much of this album is the mellow California rock of which the Eagles are the alternate prototype. If Browne's music has more backbone than the rest, the genre itself is not very challenging") while admitting that his "songs really do merge poetic vision and rock."[12] (Marsh would eventually come fully around to Jackson's music—Browne invited him to write the fine liner notes to *The Best of Jackson Browne*.) The record clearly got under Robert Christgau's skin: "This is an impressive record, but a lot of the time I hate it."[13] Also under Richard Meltzer's, the gonzo rock critic who had been one of Jackson's early supporters but had since soured on him. Though his piece for the *Village Voice* never got published, he summarized it with this cheap shot: "There was no kid left in him. It really felt to me [that he had become] a late-night DJ reading *The Prophet* to thirteen-year-olds."[14] (Sincerity of Jackson's variety can do this to cynics ashamed of their former idealism.) But most of the reviews were extremely positive: Sam Sutherland wrote one of the most penetrating, noting that Browne was "pitting an unflinching, almost pitiless candor against his richest and most adventurous melodic ideas," and that "at the heart of his writing is an ongoing dialogue with the self that translates even the simplest lines into potential questions: intimations of mortality, premonitions of apocalypse, meditations on meaning itself are root forms drawn from an existential base line."[15] Paul Nelson, for his part, called Jackson "the only Seventies hero who can match Springsteen. . . . Browne is our finest, most consistent and most thoughtful singer/songwriter."[16] While reviews piled up—the lion's share enthusiastic—Browne, clearly needing to keep moving, took off on the first of two extensive tours that would provide him the material—and the distractions—that would show up a year later on *Running on Empty*.

"KEEP MOVING"

> "You can only be lonely for so long, you can only feel unhappy for a while . . . the next album will be easier, happier."[17]

Here's what Jackson Browne did to keep moving after he finished *The Pretender*: He embarked on the widest-ranging tour of his life, spanning three continents (Europe, Oceania, Asia) starting in the late fall of 1976 and going into the spring of 1977. He met, in Brisbane, Australia, a young woman named Lynne Sweeney who would in a few years become his second wife and the mother of his second child. After touring, he holed up for four months in the studio producing Warren Zevon's career-making *Excitable Boy*, this one breaking through with the bizarro noir classic "Werewolves of London" and including their writing collaboration "Tenderness on the Block." ("Tenderness" is catchy piano pop that would never fit on a Jackson Browne album: it's terminally winsome, and only works on Zevon's album because its innocence is sweet relief from the nightcrawlers, mercenaries, and murderers that crowd the rest of the record.) While in the studio, he laid out plans for a double-LP live album of his own—since *Frampton Comes Alive* became a megaseller in 1976, double lives were cropping up everywhere—but this one would be especially ambitious. It would be a true chronicle of a rock 'n' roll tour, featuring live versions of Browne classics (he thought many of his studio recordings were inferior to the stage versions and wanted to correct for that); new songs recorded onstage, backstage, or in hotel rooms; collaborations with other writers; and snippets of talk backstage, in hotels, or on the bus from musicians and crew. He was aiming for an honest audio documentary that would demystify the whole idea of rock 'n' roll touring, which by the mid-1970s clearly needed demystifying. When Zevon's album was done, he went on *another* tour, this one a two-month jaunt through the United States to make the documentary, for which he hired the Section (Leland Sklar, Russell Kunkel, Craig Doerge, Danny Kortchmar, and Lindley) to back him up, and where the idea of an ambitious double live album got whittled down to a single disc. He saw a lot of country from the windows of a Continental Silver Eagle bus. He did his share of cocaine. He played lots of shows and supervised the recording of them. When the tour was over, he compiled, edited, and produced the tracks that would make up *Running on Empty*, which was released in late December 1977 to great acclaim, all of which was crowned by his sold-out New Year's Eve performance at LA's Fabulous Forum, at the time the West Coast's go-to venue for superstar rockers. And, lest we forget, he wrote and delivered what was probably the best song of his life. How's that for "keep moving"?

Running on Empty is, for sure, "easier, happier" than any record he'd made before (or since). Except for the title track, it's no great shakes in terms of songwriting, but for the first time, songwriting wasn't the real point. Of the ten tracks on the record, Jackson wrote only two of them himself; four are cowritten affairs; and four are by other songwriters. This checked a number of boxes. It allowed him to release an album without having to write a full slate of compositions (for Jackson, that usually meant eight to ten songs), thereby placating Asylum, which wanted a follow-up to *The Pretender*. It also forced him to loosen up, to *collaborate*, something this control freak had just begun to learn to do on *The Pretender*, where he allowed himself a cowriter on "Hear Come Those Tears Again" and handed over the producing reins to Landau.

Finally, it served the concept of rock 'n' roll demystification. By the mid-1970s, acts like the Eagles, Led Zeppelin, Rod Stewart, and the Rolling Stones were hauling in millions on massive tours, traveling on private jets, disfiguring hotel rooms, hoovering lines of coke off the bellies of groupies, indulging in excesses that would have made Caligula blush. But *Running on Empty* is about a bunch of mere mortal musicians on a tour bus, doing journeyman road songs like "Shaky Town" (by Kortchmar), "The Road" (by Danny Keefe), or "Nothing but Time" (Browne and tour manager Howard Burke), which are decent and detailed and easily relatable in their everydayness. It's full of clichés that Browne would have edited out if they were all his own songs. It's about passing the time reading magazines and watching Richard Pryor on video, or laughing like doofuses while snorting lines backstage. It's about the sound man meeting a sweet girl at a show but ending up alone, beating off in his room at night when "the drummer swept that girl away." It's about killing time "in our hotel rooms, and wandering round backstage," and it's about how, ultimately, it's not about the sex or the drugs, it's about the rock 'n' roll—by and for everyman. The songs don't try too hard: they're funny, they're not slickly produced, they're convivial and familial. All in all, they do the job: they convey an honest sense of what it means—despite the boredom, the long separation from loved ones, and the routine of it all—to play music you love, night after night, for people who appreciate you. (Contrast *Running on Empty* to the gargantuan rock 'n' roll mystification of Zeppelin's concert film and album, *The Song Remains the Same*, released a year earlier.) *Running on Empty* is Jackson holding out for rock 'n' roll sincerity.

"Love Needs a Heart," cowritten with Lowell George and Valerie Carter, is the closest thing to a solo Browne composition. Though there are lines here that are hard to imagine Jackson writing ("Love won't come near me. . . . It walks past my vacancy sign"), it's an affecting breakup song that resonates with the Phyllis Major material on *Late for the Sky*. "Cocaine," with its snorting/hyena-laughing audio at the end, feels necessary as a documentary matter, given the drug's ubiquity on the tour, though Browne, after giving up all drugs in the early 1980s, downplayed the humor. On subsequent tours, he included a lyric that said, "Sitting here thinking about way back when / Everybody was my best friend . . . dead and gone." Still later, he just dropped it from the set. "At the end of the song," Jackson said in a 1983 interview, "there's a bit where David did his Strother Martin voice and said, 'It takes a clear mind to make it.' I was high, doing coke, and David was trying to tell us, 'Look, making music in front of tape recorders is best done when you've had some sleep and you know what you're doing.' Trying to tell us he was not having a great time. I'm glad that's on there, because, in a way, it's like a little disclaimer. At that time, I think I must have sounded like an ad for coke. So a couple of years ago, we said: 'What is this, a song or a cheer?' And we stopped doing it. . . . And when I listen back, David was right: it does take a clear mind to make it."[18] "You Love the Thunder," Browne's own tune, is a strong companion piece to "Your Bright Baby Blues" and "Here Come Those Tears Again" and feels like another characterization of a typical Browne relationship—either with Phyllis or with new love Lynne Sweeney—one that's filled with a fire and hunger and a "crazy longing that time will never tame."

Which leaves us with the album's bookends, the title track and the show closer, "The Load-Out/Stay." The closer is Jackson's valentine to his band, his roadies, his audience, to the very idea of the communion between performer and audience that rock music, at its best, makes possible. The lines, "People, you've got the power over what we do / You can sit there and wait or you can pull us through" makes explicit the ideal that rock shows had held out from the beginning: that performer and audience aren't fundamentally different, that they need each other, that they create the show together, urging each other to heighten the passion, meaning, and delight of the music. "The Load-Out" does this in a humble and intimate way, and its segue into Maurice Williams's "Stay," just turns it all into a revel. Rosemary Butler belts out her verse with startling gusto, and Lindley's falsetto is so funny that you imagine the whole crowd leaving with happy grins on their faces.

"Running on Empty" may be Browne's quintessential song. It's the rockingest song he had written to date, the most confessional and autobiographical, the most "LA," the most openly desperate, and I'm guessing the one that has been the most cathartic for him to sing. Again using the road as symbol of the journey into time and life's possibilities, it looks back at the past in wonder, faces the present with impressive honesty, and has no idea where the hell the future will take him. It's the song that most challenges Browne's own Romanticism, his "faith in the distance" or of a redeeming "fire high in the empty sky." If in "The Fuse" Browne committed himself to "tuning his spirit . . . to the waters lapping on a higher ground," in "Running on Empty" all metaphysical bets are off. "I don't know how to tell you all how crazy this life feels," he wails. And later: "I don't even know what I'm hoping to find." But, like so many of rock's greatest songs, the expressive force of its despair gives it a power that's alchemical: Browne's naked vocal delivery, combined with the simplicity of the music (the now classic three-note, two-chord piano motif, the Section locked into a relentless groove), overrides its own confusion and ends up affirming what the lyrics seem to be denying: in the end, the song transforms itself into a celebration of a soul's endurance. I can think of no other song that conveys how jarring Phyllis Major's life, love, and death must have been to Browne's sensibility. The song is the musical deluge that best represents the deluge of the life he'd been living the last few years. And in so doing, he managed to universalize his own experience in a song that provided an indelible stamp on the despair and confusions so many of us were feeling in the dark directionless days of the mid-1970s.

NO NUKES

And then, the plunge into politics.

As we've seen, Jackson Browne has always been a political animal. A male mentor named John Menesees made him sensitive to the plight of Native Americans when he was a young boy, and decades later he recalled that mentoring as the "beginning of my political education."[19] His mother introduced him to leftist thinking in his teens, and he joined the NAACP at fifteen. His musician friend J. D. Souther said Jackson "always had that edge of socialism about him."[20] Some of the best songs on his first five albums constitute an incomplete but fairly considered politics, mostly inherited from the countercultural critique of 1950s America as a misguided and overly militaristic culture obsessed with material wealth, blind to economic and racial inequities, and more and more alien to vaunted American ideals and its relationship to nature. When he began his career, he did benefits for Native American schools or for sacred lands in Arizona, but he stayed away from any sustained political activism. That began to change during his Deluge period.

During the 1976 presidential campaign, Eagle Don Henley roped Jackson into a benefit for Jerry Brown, the young governor of California and upstart presidential candidate. Jackson was intrigued by Brown's progressive platform, which called for radical campaign reform to make politicians less beholden to corporate contributors, as well as an ahead-of-its-time "small is beautiful" philosophy that envisioned economic policy based not on ever-increasing "growth" (and ever-increasing depletion of the environment and its natural resources) but on principles of economic and environmental sustainability. Browne performed at the benefit, but after getting exposed to the inner workings of the campaign, he was turned off. "I regretted having supported Brown," he said. "I think there's a sort of hybrid lifetime politician ethic which I don't find attractive."[21] He was particularly disappointed that Brown refused to support California's Proposition 15, which would have prohibited the construction of new nuclear power plants in the state and curtailed the use of current ones. (Jackson ended up doing a benefit for Prop 15, but the measure failed at the polls by a more than two-to-one margin.) The reading Jackson did before writing "Before the Deluge" had made him a staunch opponent of nuclear power, and so when he was introduced to activist groups (like Tom Campbell's Pacific Alliance) that were waging campaigns against nuclear power, Browne got on board. He did some benefit shows for the Alliance, including a few to stop the Diablo Canyon nuclear power plant in January 1978.

Soon after that, John Hall, a member of the pop group Orleans who had befriended Browne when they had toured together a few years back, started his own grassroots antinukes campaign. He invited a number of artists, including James Taylor and Bonnie Raitt, to play a benefit concert in New York City for the family of Karen Silkwood, a nuclear plant worker and antinuclear activist who had died from radiation poisoning and become a kind of martyr to the movement. (Mike Nichols had made the film *Silkwood* about her, starring Meryl Streep.) Following the success of that benefit, Hall came to California in November and proposed to Browne and Graham Nash that they start an organization called Musicians United for Safe Energy (MUSE) that would perform benefits to support antinuke and alternative energy groups and fund an education campaign. The three men ended up proposing the group sponsor two nights of shows at Madison

Square Garden to kick off the project, followed by a film and a multialbum soundtrack of the performances.

At the time, Browne was home in California, finally getting a rest after more than five years on the write-record-tour treadmill and beginning to regain his footing after the trauma of Major's suicide. Though eager for some downtime with his son and girlfriend Sweeney, he couldn't resist the opportunity. He was a big star now—*Running on Empty* sold three million copies and he was now a huge concert draw, one of the most respected rock artists of his generation, with a measure of power and influence, and as he approached the age of thirty, he was ready to wield it. He dove into benefit planning, soliciting the participation of some of the biggest names in the business at the time, including the Doobie Brothers, Crosby, Stills & Nash, James Taylor, and Bruce Springsteen.

In March 1979, while Hall, Browne, Bonnie Raitt, and Nash were drumming up support and awareness for the antinuke cause, a high-profile Hollywood film called *The China Syndrome* came out that depicted a near-meltdown at a nuclear power plant. Twelve days later, a genuine nuclear accident occurred at the Three Mile Island nuclear plant in Pennsylvania, which caused a partial meltdown and the release of radioactive material into the atmosphere. For months afterward, the nation's public discourse focused heavily on the dangers of nuclear power and consequently raised MUSE's profile. Browne was an unusually articulate advocate for the cause in interviews and press conferences—he even appeared on the popular daytime talk show *Dinah!* to talk about it—and for many inside the group he became MUSE's "spiritual center."[22] At a MUSE press conference, Browne deadpanned, "The government has not found it in its interest to fund, research or subsidize private enterprise that's working to develop solar energy. The most obvious reason is that there's not a great deal of profit to be made from harnessing the sun."[23] In a 1979 *Rolling Stone* profile, Browne linked up the nuclear energy industry's greed to the larger afflictions of America's deluded and narcissistic materialism. "The threat is real," he said, "being victimized is real, the need for change is real. . . . The 'need' for nuclear power is not true, and their success lies in the fact that it takes so much money and energy to perpetrate. Their thing is based on selling something to somebody that they don't need. That's Madison Avenue. That's Jiffy Pop. That's hair dryers. New and more expensive ways of using power for the aggrandizement of oneself. It's been sold like a drug. Like a mirror that will lie to you."[24] Browne was now making some of the same arguments that the essays in *Eco-Catastrophe* had, making an explicit link between corporate capitalism, environmental degradation, and consumer consciousness. He was beginning to develop a coherent political point of view.

At Madison Square Garden, Jackson's set included "Before the Deluge" (containing a fiery violin solo by Lindley) as well as Sydney Carter's brooding folk tune from 1963, "The Crow and the Cradle," about looming dangers (the crow) hanging over the young generation (the cradle) and whose connection to the nuclear issue could hardly be missed by the crowd. Late in the show, Browne was called back to the stage by Springsteen and invited to sing his big hit, "Stay." The proceeds from the show, the film "No Nukes," and the three-album set of the same name were less than anticipated, given the exorbitant up-front costs to make the film, but it whet Jackson's appetite and set him on a passionate path of social and political activism he'd follow the rest of his career.

5

TROUBLE IN THE 1980S

Was there anybody in America who was sad to see the 1970s go? As the decade wound down, the economy got worse, the political situation more fraught, the cultural depression more depressing, the fashions more hideous, the general cynicism more pronounced, and—except for some promising buds of change—the rock 'n' roll more than ever aimed at dollar signs. The New Year's Eve party on December 31, 1979, I attended was dedicated to ritualistically burying the whole thing. We dug a hole in somebody's backyard and threw in the single for "My Sharona," a coy slice of fake punk by The Knack that went to number 1 that year. In went the soundtrack to *Sgt. Pepper's Lonely Hearts Club Band*, that abomination of a movie starring Peter Frampton and Bee Gee Barry Gibb. We threw in a *Time* magazine story on EST, the most infamous of the "personal growth seminars" that were all the rage then and which curdled the middle class's new interest in psychology into cringeworthy displays of unabashed narcissism. (EST was one of the big reasons Tom Wolfe called the 1970s the Me Decade.) Someone floated into the hole a diaphanous synthetic shawl of some kind, meant to be flaunted while disco dancing. Also lobbed into the depths was the well-nigh ubiquitous poster of Farrah Fawcett, she of the blond tresses, pearly whites, and aroused nipple. If any of us had owned them, we would have buried a leisure suit or a pair of platform shoes too.

There was good reason for our distaste, but a pop culture that sucked was, as my Marxist philosophy professor liked to say, just epiphenomena, cultural effluvia that reflected entrenched structural troubles of society. The late 1970s was a time when the US economy was literally out of control; Nobel economists and Fed chairmen alike were flummoxed trying to find ways to pull the country out of a stubborn recession: a staggering combination of huge government budget deficits, inflation that exceeded 13 percent, unemployment that wavered between 6 percent and 8 percent, and prime interest rates that by the end of the decade skyrocketed to 20 percent. The Vietnam debacle led to Pentagon panic that the US military was "weak," which led to jacked-up defense budgets and macho military posturing, especially in Central America. All this led to pullbacks on Great Society social programs (to compensate budgetarily), which led to higher rates of poverty, particularly among minority groups and children. Despite President Carter's egalitarian rhetoric and attention to human rights, his administration in fact embraced what came to be called neoliberalism, a philosophy that was neither particularly new nor particularly liberal, which said that the free market, privatized and deregulated and as free of trade barriers as possible, was the ultimate panacea for the world's economic (and ultimately social) ills. Much of what will trouble Jackson Browne's music in the later 1980s will have to do with those two interlinked subjects—America's post-Vietnam military adventurism and its new love affair with a "free market," which disguised the most aggressive capitalism of the postwar period.

Meanwhile, a sea change was occurring among a restless and wayward populace. The still waters of conservative discontent had been running deep among the Silent Majority all through the countercultural years, and those waters seemed to rise to the surface all at once, in November 1979, when the American embassy in Tehran, Iran, was overrun by militants who took sixty-six Americans hostages and paraded them through the streets (and before cameras) in a brazen attempt to humiliate the United States. It worked. Though the hostage takers, loyal to the Ayatollah Khomeini, the Supreme Leader of the fundamentalist Islamic movement in Iran, released the female and African American hostages later that month, fifty-three white males were imprisoned for 444 days, prompting a bitter anti-Muslim backlash in the States and a surge of populist aggression. "Bomb Iran" bumper stickers appeared everywhere, quickly followed by the more flagrant "Fuck Iran." (A novelty song called "Bomb Iran," parodying the Beach Boys' "Barbara Ann," got surprising amounts of mainstream radio airplay.) I attended a rally at the Los Angeles Coliseum soon after the hostage crisis began, innocently thinking that it would be a kind of large-scale teach-in. It was not. It was a flag-waving, rage-filled, race-baiting demonstration where the demagoguery flowed and the aggression was palpable: several fistfights broke out in the stands. In April 1980, a flailing Carter administration, sensitive to popular sentiment that it was wimping out, attempted a bold rescue mission called Operation Eagle Claw that failed spectacularly.

US helicopters crashed in the Iranian desert, eight Americans died, and no hostages were rescued.

When you put all that together with its piloting of a floundering economy, the Carter presidency looked hapless, which opened the door to Ronald Reagan to win the 1980 election in a landslide. His actorly delivery of a throwback patriotic optimism was simplistic, but it seemed to be exactly what a weary electorate wanted. Calling America a "shining city on a hill" served as a nostalgic balm against the cultural gloom of the last decade, and an exhausted citizenry was eager to apply it. His election set the stage for what we now think of as "the eighties."

BROWNE AND THE ANTINUKE MOVEMENT

Jackson Browne's response to the convulsions of the late 1970s was at first fairly tentative, but his success with MUSE and the No Nukes shows convinced him to throw himself more fully into politics, first as an advocate for the anti–nuclear power cause and then for other issues. In 1981, at the "Survival Sunday" benefit at the Hollywood Bowl, put on by the Southern California Alliance for Survival, he made an impassioned speech:

> I want to sing a song for the Nuclear Regulatory Commission. I was up at San Luis Obispo [near the Diablo Canyon nuclear power plant] and they had these hearings. And for all the information that was presented to them, all the people talking about safety, the only thing that was really obvious was that these gray-flannel-suit heads *were not listening*. They had already made up their minds before the information was presented. I think if you put up a nuclear power plant on top of an earthquake fault right next to where you live, they'll put one up anywhere. On the other hand if you shut it down they'll stop putting them up anywhere. This song goes out for them and for the people of San Luis Obispo who need our support when they blockade that plant.[1]

He and his band went into "Whole Lotta Shakin' Goin' On," and he slipped in these lines: "We don't need Diablo, we got the power of the sun." That summer, he put his body where his mouth was, participating in the human blockade at the Diablo Canyon plant, and getting himself arrested.

He followed this up with an appearance at Peace Sunday at Pasadena's Rose Bowl in early June 1982, where he played second to last (only behind Tom Petty) on a long and impressive bill that included Linda Ronstadt, Stevie Wonder, Crosby, Stills & Nash, Joan Baez, and Bob Dylan. This charity concert protested not nuclear power plants but the proliferation of nuclear weapons, a concern made more urgent when, in the late 1970s, the Soviet Union and NATO began upgrading their nuclear arsenals in Europe, thereby elevating the possibility of a nuclear confrontation. President Reagan's decision to drastically increase the US defense budget, and his bellicose rhetoric (calling the Soviet Union "the evil empire"), raised tensions all the more. "We are entering the most dangerous decade in human history," read a statement by the European Nuclear Disarmament Appeal, which helped initiate the 1980s anti-proliferation movement. "A third world war is not merely possible but increasingly likely. . . . The remedy lies in our own hands. . . . We must learn to be loyal, not to 'East' or 'West,' but to each other, and we must disregard the prohibitions and limitations imposed by any national state."[2] The anti-proliferation movement's goals and rhetoric were fully in line with Browne's politics (and his fears), and so he eagerly joined up. In fact, a week after Peace Sunday, he crossed the continent to play at the Concert for Nuclear Disarmament in Long Island's Nassau Stadium. A few days after that, he made a prominent appearance at a rally in Central Park, where an estimated one million people gathered to call for a nuclear arms freeze.[3] The Central Park rally was attended by anti-nuke activists as well as those in the growing antiwar movement, which had sprouted up after Reagan's aggressive moves in El Salvador and Nicaragua. Jackson's exposure to these activists got him thinking about American involvement in Central America and would soon become a central focus of his albums of the late 1980s.

HOLD OUT

Browne's political activism was more pronounced as the country lurched into the 1980s, but his lyrical concerns, with an exception or two, stayed away from the political or from large-scale pronouncement about America à la "Before the Deluge" or "The Pretender." Musically though, major changes were afoot. Jackson, who, aside from the help that Jon Landau had provided him, had long kept his own counsel when it came to how he wanted his music to sound, was now holding his finger up to the winds, noting the fast-changing dynamics of the pop landscape and feeling the need to adapt. He had no truck with punk rock, whose volcanic anger and crude musicianship didn't at all jibe with his sensibility (though by the end of the 1980s, he would sense punk's importance: "I didn't really understand during the late '70s and early '80s to what extent the punk movement was an expression of no faith in the status quo," he admitted. "It was a reaction against complacency.")[4] Disco he loved and would try his hand at it, as we shall see. New wave influenced him less for its insouciance and danceability than for its use of synthesizers, which Browne adopted for the first time during his performance of "Running on Empty" at the No Nukes shows (it's in the movie, not on the soundtrack) and would incorporate into all his 1980s albums. But what probably affected him musically more than anything was his own stardom. He was now performing in ten-thousand-plus–seat arenas, and his fans expected him to rock like a rocker.

If you listen to the No Nukes shows from 1979 (the movie and the album), and put aside the few affecting performances (Browne's "For the Deluge," James Taylor's poignant "Captain Jim's Drunken Dream," Springsteen's "The River"), it's pretty clear that most of the show is tedious, driven by tame 1970s folk- and jazz-influenced rock played by complacent if expert musicians breezing through their set lists and clinging to past glories. The whole production suggests that mellow 1970s rock had reached its endgame.

Though you'd hardly know it if you went to the No Nukes shows, mainstream rock was by 1979 experiencing a transformation, though it wasn't punk, disco, or new wave that was its prime instigator. It was the fact that while rock rocked harder than ever before, as a business, it had succumbed utterly to corporatization—it had lost all resistance that its countercultural forebears of the 1960s might have harbored to cold capitalist logic. The major labels, having had a couple of decades to adapt, had learned how to corral the feral energies of rock musicians so that they would yield up reliable, and sometimes gargantuan, revenue streams. Some records, like the Eagles' *Greatest Hits*, Fleetwood Mac's *Rumours*, or the *Saturday Night Fever* soundtrack, were selling upward of *ten* million units. The movie industry had accomplished the same trick: having survived the death of the studio system and the rise of the New Hollywood (where truculent hippies like Dennis Hopper could make counterculture megahits like *Easy Rider*, while traditional big budget vehicles like *Dr. Doolittle* bombed), they discovered a new generation of filmmakers like George Lucas and Steven Spielberg whose movie instincts—nostalgic and childlike—and technical mastery meshed precisely with the corporate mandate to exploit the youth market for maximal profits.

The music business, now routinized and professionalized to serve the burgeoning rock audience, was signing up a new generation of musicians who, raised on rock, were shrewdly aware of how to exploit its commercial potential and more than eager to do what the suits asked of them. Boston's

"More Than a Feeling" (1976) was a perfect example: technically proficient, its meticulous production shaved off every bit of roughness and spontaneity to reveal the smooth crunch of that most basic of rock pleasures—the four-chord riff. The band threw on top of that a white vocalist's startlingly good simulation of R & B passion, lyrics that expressed a vague yearning, and a catchy-as-hell melody. The result was a gleaming slice of what came to be called "corporate rock"—record label honchos couldn't have dreamed up a more commercial shtick. The guys in Boston were as anonymous and studied about their work as Wall Street investment bankers planning a corporate takeover, which is basically what they accomplished. The only good thing was that it was an improvement over Pablo Cruise or Ambrosia.

Browne was not immune to the pressures of this new environment. His friends in the Eagles, thanks to *Hotel California*, were rock dynasts, and Jackson, in those years, was, as he put it in his Hall of Fame acceptance speech, "a little bit competitive." (He was still "among those there [the Hollywood rock scene] to test their fortunes and their will.") But there was also something else going on in late-1970s rock: the Bruce Springsteen effect. Springsteen, with *Born to Run* (1975), *Darkness on the Edge of Town* (1978), and a long trail of legendary concerts already behind him, had revived the myth of the romantic working-class, guitar-wielding poet as rock hero and gave a commercial kick in the pants to "heartland rock"—music deeply versed in rock tradition (Bob Seger, John Cougar Mellencamp, Tom Petty) which yoked rock power to lyrics as personal and sometimes as poetic as what Browne and the singer-songwriters had been doing.

Jackson was especially drawn to Springsteen. They had known each other since the early seventies, when they were both starting out, and Browne had been overwhelmed and intimidated by Springsteen's three-hour shows, which were part James Brown extravaganza, part Rolling Stone relentlessness, part Dylan introspection. "I feel sheepish about going onstage in a town where he's appeared recently," Browne told a radio interviewer in 1978. "There's nothing to compare to what he's doing. He's the best show in rock 'n' roll." When asked if Bruce was influencing him to play harder rock 'n' roll, he said. "Yeah, I suppose so. I get a lot from seeing Bruce."[5] (Tracks like "Boulevard" from *Hold Out*, "Downtown" from *Lawyers in Love*, and "For America" from *Lives in the Balance* are especially indebted to Springsteen and, frankly, suffer for it.) Still, though Jackson would never be a showman, in "Running on Empty," "The Road and the Sky," and "The Fuse," he and his band had learned to ignite a full-throttle style of rock 'n' roll without sacrificing lyrical substance or subtlety. This commitment to being a modern rocker, as opposed to a folkish singer-songwriter dabbling in rock idioms, is what distinguishes Browne's early 1980s records.

Which can be a bit jarring when one first hears *Hold Out*. Lyrically the album is a culmination of his commitment to the social and personal values he has been developing since he started out—love, justice, equality—but musically *Hold Out* shows Jackson stretching to find a relevant place in the new rock landscape, and he's stepped out of his comfort zone. His attempt to stretch is admirable (and no doubt necessary for him as an artist); the results, not so much. "Boulevard," the album's most obvious attempt to rock, was a Top 20 hit in the States, but it's almost embarrassingly trite. Trying to portray life "on the streets," it comes off as a suburban kid's slumming on Hollywood Boulevard; compare it to the street songs on, say, Springsteen's *Darkness on the Edge of Town* or Lou Reed's *Street Hassle* (1979) and *New York* (1989), albums by guys who knew intimately of what they spoke, and Jackson sounds studied and distant. Plus the guitar riff, grating, repetitive, and drowning in reverb, just too blatantly announces itself as the work of a man trying to prove his rock bona fides.

"Disco Apocalypse" is just as jarring—though a more interesting kind of failure. Jackson's voice is in fine fettle—your hear it in his wail in the first line ("Down the *SIDE*-walks on the avenue")—and Browne's band, mostly composed of the musicians from *Running on Empty*, deliver a competent disco bounce. But the song's surge and energy are confused. In interviews, Jackson said he loved disco: "It's totally infectious. It's a wonderful place to go. It's the one form I'm most interested in now."[6] But he also hedged: he called the song "a parody. That's better than calling it a joke. It was meant to be a sort of self-mocking parody. The title still makes people smile. But right away, I became interested in the possibilities of what the song would actually say. I got 'serious' about it in spite of myself. Or maybe because of myself."[7] This explanation is itself confusing, so it's not surprising that the results are muddy. He'd been obsessed with the idea of apocalypse since "Rock Me on the Water," but why was he yoking it to disco? In the late 1970s, there was some flaccid cultural chatter that disco's decadence and narcissism betrayed a fuck-civilization-it's-going-to-hell-anyway attitude, but that didn't deserve more than the sly cunning of Prince's brilliant "1999" (which came out two years later, in 1982). Browne's protagonist portrays discos as places where desperate folk go to wash off the boredom of their everyday lives. The dance music churns, "The skies awaken / Through the wind and the fire," but does the protagonist mean it, or is this just the hyperbole of a dancer who's snorted too many lines? When he whispers the word "apocalypse," is he joking or serious? I don't think Browne knows, and the ambiguity ends up cheapening the serious and untrendy concern with widespread disaster that Browne had shown throughout his career, and which his antinuke activism was suggesting was dangerous and real.

Another issue concerns synthesizers, which Jackson uses for the first time on record here. Mainstream rockers had been integrating synthesizers into rock contexts for a while (some highlights: Stevie Wonder's "Superstition," The Who's "Baba O'Reilly," Peter Gabriel's "Solsbury Hill"), and, of course, they were central to new wave, but Browne had avoided using them so far; they were still associated with spacey prog rock, and their sonic textures seemed antithetical to the warm organic quality that defined his early music. Craig Doerge's string synthesizer is tasteful on *Hold Out*; still, it feels like it was layered in as a concession to modern rock and doesn't seem organically integrated. Their use on *Hold Out* contributes to the album's nagging sense of unease.

If Jackson wasn't clear on the album's musical direction, lyrically he had a solid sense of what he was doing—it's just that his ambitious plans outstripped the flawed results. Paul Nelson, in his revealing *Rolling Stone* interview on the eve of the album's release, outlined what he thought of as the album's concept—a song cycle about Jackson's relationship with Lynn Sweeney, dramatized as one man's journey from romantic alienation to commitment, from being a solitary failure at love to being a "hold out" not just for love of a woman but for a communal sense of love for whole "human race." Here's Nelson:

> I hear the new LP as a love story between two people—you and Lynne—who have difficulty coming together because the man at first doesn't want to make a commitment. That's clear enough in "Hold Out." But by the end of the record, he's changed his mind and tells the woman that he loves her in "Hold on Hold Out." And the transitional song is "Call It a Loan." All this is set against the gritty urban background of "Boulevard" (Hollywood Boulevard, obviously). "That Girl Could Sing"—a song that's not about Lynne, I would guess—and "Disco Apocalypse."

When Nelson is done, he asks, "Is that an accurate summation?" and Jackson affirms, "Yeah."[8] And it is accurate, as far as it goes. The opener "Disco Apocalypse" sets the scene by describing a social world that is fervent, desperate, and lonely. It's followed by "Hold Out," in which the protagonist, in a promising relationship with a woman who deserves better, admits he's been unfaithful ("You wish that I'd been true / Darlin' so do I") and backs out of the relationship, urging her, however, to "hold out" for real love (while he relegates himself to stalking through a world of faithless passion, taking "what love I can find"). In "That Girl Could Sing," a charged rocker that's underprized among Browne fans, the protagonist does exactly that, finding a temporary lover who's exciting and mercurial but who soon disappears on him, leaving him to celebrate/regret the episode. (The song contains one of Browne's—one of rock's—wittiest and most inspired lines honoring the beauty of the female form: "Talk about celestial bodies.") Dumped on the streets, he finds himself back on the "Boulevard."

Still alone, he confronts the death of a good friend—Lowell George—and gets outside his own concerns enough to console his daughter ("Of Missing Persons"). Then we get the superb "Call It a Loan," which Nelson calls "transitional" because it's the song where the protagonist, thinking that he's still taking "what love I can find," discovers that he's found a woman with whom he's really falling in love. All of which culminates in "Hold On Hold Out," where the protagonist discovers that the encouragement he offered to the woman in "Hold Out"—to hold out for genuine love—now applies to him too: "You're a hold out / Well I'm a hold out too," he realizes, and not just a hold out for personal love but for love for the "human race."

That's the cycle. As concepts go, it's a good one: it shows Browne urging himself (and his fellow counterculture survivors) not to give up, despite the temptations to give in to the compromised life of the Pretender or the endless escapes of running on empty. The problem is that he can't artistically pull it off. "Hold Out," "That Girl Could Sing," and especially "Call It a Loan" are strong songs, up to the standards of his past, but that's only three out of seven tracks. "Of Missing Persons," while an OK goodbye to Lowell George, one of his musical mentors, is flabby compared to elegies like "For a Dancer" or "Adam's Song." "Boulevard" is a full-on failure, "Disco Apocalypse" awash in crossed purposes. And "Hold On Hold Out," the most ambitious song Browne had written to date (it's more than eight minutes long), fails in a way his fans could hardly have imagined: on a song that needs him to be as vulnerably intimate as he's ever been, he sounds strained and inauthentic.

Being the Jackson Browne partisan that I was (and still am), I wanted to love "Hold On Hold Out" when I first heard it forty-something years ago. I still admire its impressive scale, its striving to say something bold and big. I like how it breaks out of the verse-verse-chorus structure of the rest of the album, and how it changes dynamics (loud to soft and back, fast to slow and back) to emphasize different emotional tones. I appreciate how much momentum Craig Doerge generates out of his piano riffs (he gets cowriting credit) and the way Jackson phrases the lyrics around a flurry of syncopated chording. I especially admire how Browne links the commitment to personal love to a wider love for "the human race." "Give up your heart and you find yourself / Living for something in somebody else" is one of those Browne-ian couplets that pithily enshrines a hard-won romantic verity, but it's not just romantic love he's talking about. To "live for something in somebody else" can be applied to a political or social commitment to a group, a cause, a country. When the protagonist sings about being a hold out "for the countless souls beaten by their goals," or "the ones betrayed by the deals they made," he's talking about all the Pretenders out there, and the song becomes part of a series—"For Everyman," "For a Dancer," "Before the Deluge"—in which Browne recommits himself to a morality grounded in sympathetic love for his fellow humans. Such sentiments, coming at the end of a forsaken decade and the cusp of a new one, were, for the twenty-one-year-old I was at the time, more than welcome: they gave me encouragement and a sense of renewal.

At least, the first five minutes of the song did. The last three minutes of the song are crucial to Jackson's intentions, but to me—again, someone who wanted the song to work—they're a disaster. Jackson stops singing and starts talking. He drops the mask that artists use to transmute their personal feelings into art and starts speaking in his own voice to his lover, Lynne Sweeney (to whom he dedicates the album). What he starts saying ("Will love be true? Can it pull you through?") is clichéd even if spoken in a private context, one lover whispering to another; as song lyrics they're just mawkish—there are limits, after all, to how sincerity can function in art. Browne seems to be trying for a kind of direct communication with his lover that would essentially erase the entire context *as* song. But it *is* a song, after all, not a personal conversation; he's talking into a microphone in a recording studio and not in the ear of his lover; and the listener isn't just Ms. Sweeney but millions of his fans spread all over the planet. These contexts matter, and we assume them whenever we listen to a song, no matter how personal and sincere the song is: they allow us the distance to hear a song not as overheard intimacy but as works of art we can relate to on our own terms. The "I love you" Jackson utters near song's end might be openhearted and boyishly awkward—I don't doubt he means it—but instead of being those things, it comes off like a *pose* of openhearted, boyish awkwardness. It's embarrassing, is what it is, and one of the biggest miscalculations in Browne's career as a songwriter. (And this is the most uncomfortable paragraph I've had to write for this book.)

By 1980, Browne was such a big star that the generally poor reviews the album received did little to slow sales. Robert Christgau's gleeful I-told-you-he-sucked review in the *Village Voice* was atypical only in its urbane nastiness: "Never hep to his jive, I'm less than shocked by the generalized sentimentality disillusioned admirers descry within these hallowed tracks, though the one about the late Lowell George (think it's him, any other El Lay rocker die recently?) is unusually rank."[9] Even Kit Rachlis's takedown of the album in the paper of record, *Rolling Stone* ("*Hold Out* is probably the weakest record he's ever made—an album on which all of the big decisions are carefully considered, but many of the small ones backfire. What we have is a song cycle with scarcely a single tune that has the moral imagination, pop grace or writerly precision of Browne's best material"[10]) didn't keep it from becoming Browne's first US number 1 album. In 1981, he toured to promote it, this time punctuating the usual arena shows with appearances in humongous festival environments in Ireland, England, and Switzerland, as well as at the US Festival in San Bernardino, California, helping headline a show before a quarter million fans. In July 1982, "Somebody's Baby," a song he cowrote with Danny Kortchmar, was released as a single from the soundtrack from Cameron Crowe's teen sex comedy, *Fast Times at Ridgemont High*. Blatantly commercial but liltingly sweet and good-hearted, the song became a Top 10 hit (his last), and so Browne was again all over the radio in the last half of the year.

He was never more famous than at the exact time when he was never more uncertain about his future musical direction. As a man, a husband, and a father, he was even more uncertain. In January 1981, he married Lynne Sweeney, the woman to whom he'd dedicated *Hold Out* and the one who would give birth to his second child, Ryan, the following January. But by the time he started work on *Lawyers in Love*, in 1983, Sweeney had returned to Australia and the couple started divorce proceedings. And there was a new woman in his life, actress Daryl Hannah.

LAWYERS IN LOVE

Hold Out would be the last album for a while where Browne's private life would be its primary focus. *Lawyers in Love* has its relationship songs, but aside from "Cut It Away," which Browne has confirmed is about his life with Lynne Sweeney, and maybe "Tender Is the Night," they're pretty much impersonal: "On the Day" and "Knock on Any Door" are about people struggling with their passions, but the characters in those songs could be anyone, with broadly recognizable but nonspecific emotions. Jackson simplifies and abstracts them so that they can be relatable to fans across arenas and stadiums. The days of *For Everyman* and *Late for the Sky* were long gone.

Which was pretty much Jackson's intent. He'd made six albums now that were often wrenchingly confessional, and he was ready to step out of the role of sensitive poet-rocker that he'd been saddled with (and that he helped create). "The intimate, confessional and introspective song really had its time," Browne said in 1983. "The middle of the Seventies, the first half. But then you got a lot of really bad examples of it. . . . So it always interests me to hear from people who liked *Late for the Sky* best, because those songs—at least six out of the eight—were really the culmination of a period that I just don't feel anymore."[11] For the time being, it seemed, he'd squeezed all the juice he could out of the travails of his personal life.

He also felt uncomfortable writing about himself now that he was a pop star. Aware that his stardom made him fodder for *Entertainment Tonight*, he didn't want his songs to encourage tabloid gossip. "I began by writing about myself," Browne explained, "but after a certain point, celebrity catches up with you, and it looks like you're opening your life up like a book. That's not so great. Not great at all. So this time, there was a conscious effort not to serialize my life and times. It's not interesting to me, and if it's interesting to other people, maybe that's not so healthy. I've often thought, 'What can these people be interested in?' It's . . . *unhygienic*."[12] By the time *Lawyers in Love* came out, he was in divorce proceedings with Sweeney and being photographed all over Hollywood with actress Daryl Hannah, whose career, given the buzz about her upcoming role in *Splash!*, was blowing up at the time. The *Rolling Stone* review of the album noted just how unhygienic Browne's fans were getting: "Plenty of people," it noted, "will choose to read the songs that follow 'Lawyers in Love' as romans à clef about Browne's troubled marriage,"[13] and Browne had had enough of it. Though Hannah would appear in the "Tender Is the Night" video and feature in the hit video for "You're a Friend of Mine" that Browne made with Clarence Clemons, he wouldn't write (or release) songs about Hannah for another decade.

Browne's artistic gaze, in any case, was shifting more and more to the social and political world. His activism for safe energy, nuclear disarmament, and the peace movement was taking up more and more of his time and imaginative energy, and that shift would naturally reflect itself in his music.

His decision to write booming, up-tempo, arena-sized rock also had its effect in another way: it branded him as a mainstream rocker, which made him less appealing to a new generation of listeners that might otherwise have been attracted to a sensitive, intimate pop poet. By 1983, "alternative rock" had arrived. Bands like R.E.M. and Sonic Youth were exploring emotional textures that were oblique and slippery but, in their way, as intimate as what Browne, whose lyrical approach was more direct, was doing. These bands tapped into a rich vein of dense, often inchoate feeling that Gen Xers, raised on irony and more comfortable with vagueness, embraced as their own. If Browne was modern, exploring in his lane of rock music the same complexities of self that modern art generally did, these alt-rockers were postmodern, going after structures of feeling where identity is fractured, the meaning in language scattered, ideas of truth untrustworthy, and where all discourse, musical or otherwise, swirls in a bottomless vat of mystery and uncertainty. R.E.M. and Sonic Youth were speaking to a daydream nation in styles that grooved off the flat affect and mediated ironies of Andy Warhol, the Rimbaudian performance poetry of Patti Smith, the New York avant-garde generally. Browne had brushed shoulders with Warhol in 1967 during his brief sojourn in Manhattan with Nico, and he knew even then that he had nothing in common with that scene. That wasn't Browne's turf, and it affected his ability to grow his audience with the Gen Xers.

I know my love of Browne's music began to waver during the early 1980s, when I was just out of college. I was living in LA now, in my first apartment, and the albums my friends and I bought—usually at used record stores—were by The Clash, the Jesus and Mary Chain, the Minutemen, the Plimsouls, "college radio" stuff, and they had to jockey for turntable time with R.E.M.'s *Reckoning* and *Murmur*. I bought *Lawyers in Love*, of course, but by then Browne had lost his hipness factor, and my expectations, already downsized by *Hold Out*, weren't terribly high.

It was a good thing that I expected so little, because *Lawyers in Love* has only two standout tracks (maybe three), one that's so-so ("On the Day"), one that's a surprise, and three absolute duds. The duds include "Downtown" and "For a Rocker," two Springsteen soundalikes that, like "Boulevard," were written with big concert halls in mind and are by-the-numbers rock songs that were, by 1983, being done far better by even superficial hitmakers like Rick Springfield ("Jesse's Girl"). The third, "Say It Isn't True," was Browne's first bit of explicit political commentary, a song focused squarely on a single political issue, and it's awful. It bemoans the very real possibility of nuclear war—in 1983 the Bulletin of Atomic Scientists' doomsday clock was set at a paranoia-inducing one minute to midnight—in lyrics that are confoundingly soft-headed: they sound like a naive kid's high school graduation speech, backed by a buzzing synthesizer track. It's a most inauspicious entry into a world of political outspokenness that would consume Jackson's music for the next decade.

The surprise is "Knock on Any Door." The title, taken from an early Nicholas Ray film noir (1949) starring Humphrey Bogart, refers to a line spoken late in the movie where Bogart, a lawyer defending a murderer before a jury, tries to elicit sympathy for his client, Nick Romano, who was raised in poverty by a criminal father, sent to a reform school plagued by violence, and is subject throughout his life to an environment likely to turn anyone criminal and nihilistic. (The murderer's motto is, famously, "Live fast, die young, and have a good-looking corpse.") "Knock on any door" in the slums, Bogart tells the jury, and "you'll find Nick Romano." In Jackson's song, the speaker urges a woman to go ahead, "knock on any door," presumably to convince her that no matter where she goes, the same conditions obtain. "It's a cold world" out there, he warns, and it's better to "keep your heartache to yourself." He advises that she should "trade your memory for . . . [her] health"—that is, suppress her past in order to keep her sanity. It's by far the harshest song Jackson had ever written—as hard bitten as a noir film, in fact—and manages, interestingly, to avoid the liberal sentimentality that creeps into the film (which sentimentality so mars "Say It Isn't True."). But what makes the song work is the arrangement: the vocal melody is compelling, and the lyrics overlap in a way that gives the song urgency and momentum. Finally, the guitar work—presumably by Danny Kortchmar, who cowrote the song and is thanked in the liner notes for "arranging and playing on these songs"—has genuine power and resonance.

"Tender Is the Night" is another stolen title, this one from F. Scott Fitzgerald's last completed novel, though Fitzgerald in turn stole it from John Keats's "Ode to a Nightingale." Keats's poem is about a young man, besieged by the sickness of his dying brother, who escapes the misery of his earthly life "on the viewless wings of poesy"—that is, by entering, through the power of his poetic imagination, into a higher plane of transcendent and immortal beauty. "Tender is the night" is the phrase he uses to describe what it feels like when he suddenly reaches that transcendent realm. It's not certain that Browne has read either Keats or Fitzgerald, but it doesn't really matter, since, from way back, he took in their strain of Romanticism through an instinct and cultural osmosis, if nothing else. The "transcendent realm" in Jackson's work is the tenderness of love, as it is with Fitzgerald, and it's almost always achieved in "darkness" and at "night." (Think of Jackson's long list of songs about the night: "The Night Inside Me," "Sky Blue and Black," "Enough of the Night," "The Arms of Night," "You Know the Night," "Still Looking for Something [in the Night].") In "Tender," the protagonist urges his lover to forgo the "angry sun" of day-light (when they're always fighting) and to enter ("reenter" would be the better word) the world of night, where mystery, tenderness, and forgiveness abide. The song would have worked better had it not, after its promising quiet opening, pushed electric guitars into the arrangement, however: the tenderness the song is trying to evoke is muddled by the punch of those guitars. It would be interesting to hear the song in a solo acoustic format.

"Cut It Away" has punchy guitars, not to mention synthesizers, but also real power, thanks to an agonized lyric and impassioned singing; it's the album's sole success in mixing a contemporary rock sound with the penetrating insights of his previous relationship songs. The protagonist here scourges himself for ruining his relationship: he has "hid" and "schemed and lied," showing his lover only a "fantasy" of himself in order to keep her in love with him. But as time went on, she naturally began to see who he really was, and he's tortured that he can't live up to the fantasy, and that his "crazy longing for something more" is destroying what they have. It's that "crazy longing" and "hunger for something I can't see" that he wants to "cut away" from himself. The metaphor is violent, and Browne sings as if carving out a piece of his heart with a knife just might be what he deserves. At song's end, his lover has left him—they're in widely spaced cities, and he can only wail, as if across hemispheres, that he still loves her. Unlike "Hold On Hold Out," the pronouncement is absolutely credible.

The title track is something new in Browne's work, a fully ironized satire about American cluelessness in the face of potential apocalypse. "I can't keep up with what's been going down," the song begins, and Jackson sings it straight, as if this were going to be another "Running on Empty." But suddenly he's going on about "designer jeans" and the "screams and the strangled cries / of lawyers in love"—and we find ourselves back in the land of the Pretender, only now the Pretender's become a joke. (We're primed for this by the album cover: look at that well-groomed yuppie there, paddling in his sinking Mercedes in New York Harbor, trying to keep his tailored suit dry while the world ends.) In the second and third verses, things get goofily surreal: "God sends his spaceships to America"—that is, to his chosen people—which sends the Russians packing—"The Russians escaped / While we weren't watching them" (they know God isn't on *their* side)—which leaves the entire USSR vacant and available to become "vacation land for lawyers in love." Written at the height of Cold War tensions, when the Soviet Union and the United States were provoking each other to levels not seen since the Cuban Missile Crisis, Browne manages to parody Cold War fears (and his own apocalyptic tendencies) at the same time that he insists that it's not just Russian aggression that's the problem but that American materialistic excess is intrinsic to the dangers the planet is facing.

The song was also prophetic in its way: when the Soviet Union fell apart in 1991 and began to welcome Western investment in order to rebuild its economy, Americans (many of them lawyers, some of them presumably in love, at least with money) jumped in to colonize the place in the name of late-stage capitalism. It's a great song. For a moment Browne exploded the bounds of his sincerest sensibility: the "ooh sha la la ooh-oooh" background vocals, and Browne's imitation of a David Lindley soprano howl, are hilarious and finally reveal the sense of humor that everyone who knows Browne says is a big part of his character. It's unfortunate that he didn't develop this irony in his songwriting—it may have saved him from releasing "Say It Isn't True" or from the artistic cratering we will see on the next two albums.

The album went platinum, and "Lawyers in Love" and "Tender Is the Night" went Top 20 and Top 30, respectively, so Browne's hold on the marketplace was still strong, if weakening. "Jackson Browne" was beginning to mean something different from what he meant in the 1970s, though; he was a hitmaker making mainstream American rock music alongside Seger and Petty and Henley, but his distinctiveness was waning. He'd regain that distinctiveness, becoming one of the few American rock stars to dedicate himself, on his next two albums, to a sustained critique of American domestic and foreign policy, but artistically, he'd sink to the nadir of his career.

6

ALL IN ON THE POLITICAL

We make out of the quarrel with others rhetoric, but of the quarrel with ourselves, poetry.

—W. B. Yeats

It's like I have to *do* something, right?

—Jackson Browne (1987)

For fans who stuck with Browne through the early 1980s as he transformed himself from paragon singer-songwriter to mainstream rock star, the explicit politics of *Lives in the Balance* (1986) and *World in Motion* (1989) were almost as big a chore to listen to as Bob Dylan's Christian Evangelist albums were to his fans. Not that people weren't aware of Jackson's politics; as we've been saying all along, some of his major songs—"Rock Me on the Water," "For Everyman," "Before the Deluge," "The Pretender," and "Hold On Hold Out"—made clear that he was a countercultural holdout for a fervent romantic liberalism: for a belief in the inherent dignity of human beings; for a freedom that had to be wedded to equality (social, racial, economic) for it to mean anything; for transparent, responsive, honest government; and for what came to be called social democracy. Anyone who went to his shows were used to hearing him talk about these things. By the 1980s, his political activism was well known, not just for spearheading the No Nukes shows but for his busy charity concert schedule, lending his support to everything from saving old-growth redwoods and assisting Native American tribes to promoting community health centers.

But the near-exclusive focus on politics in *Balance* and *World*—they absorb him on eleven of the sixteen tracks—suggest that Jackson had been holding something back for years. All through the 1960s and 1970s, his political concerns were jelling into a coherent point of view, but by the 1980s, they'd grown into full-blown commitments to action. And by the mid-1980s, they shunted aside the personal concerns that had fueled most of his music. Part of the shift in focus had to do with a certain exhaustion with all the psychological excavation he'd undertaken on the early albums. "What happened to me," he said in a 1987 interview, "is that I changed in terms of what I wanted to talk about. I have less of a capacity to talk about internal things."[1] (He also wanted to protect his privacy, which his fame now threatened.) Part of it was his discovery that acting on his convictions gave him an anchored sense of meaning and purpose that eluded him when he was sitting alone with a guitar, trying to get at the mysteries of love and selfhood. Journalist Steve Turner teased that admission out of him in another 1987 interview:

> For Browne, political campaigning has become a form of salvation. In "The Fuse," the opening track on *The Pretender*, he'd said that "the fear of living for nothing strangles the will" and "Running on Empty" was a confession of a man without faith. The search for purpose, disguised in many phrases, has been a persistent Browne theme.
>
> Has his politicisation been more than simply a matter of maturing? Has it fulfilled his quest? "Ah!" he says, as if found out at last. "I guess so." Surely he'd thought about it before? "Well, I think about it in, er . . . yes, I've thought about it a lot. You do want to find the meaning of your life."[2]

And part of it, finally, had to do with what was happening in the United States under Ronald Reagan, whose administration was bulldozing just about everything that the countercultural Left had built and which Browne had held out for.

But that shift in focus came at an aesthetic cost. You can make the argument—Browne certainly did—that his albums of the late 1980s were designed to inspire people to political activism, or at least to prod them to investigate the albums' themes of American imperialism in Central America (or American materialism or whatever). Again, from a 1987 interview:

> It's like I have to *do* something, right? And if it's, say, going to Central America, I felt like I had to try to put in perspective something that was really unclear. . . . I thought it would be worth anything to get a point across, perhaps to let people know that the issue is not whether or not one of the poorest countries in the world is a threat to our security but whether or not they have to the right to the same opportunities we have.[3]

To "let people know" about political issues, especially complex ones that have been demagogued to death by politicians, is a laudable thing, but it's the rare songwriter who can walk the fine line between alienating listeners with agitprop on one hand and preaching to the choir on the other. *Lives in the Balance* and *World in Motion* trip over that line; they contain some of Jackson's least effective music, and it's because of what W. B. Yeats pointed out: quarrels with others make rhetoric while quarrels with ourselves make poetry. (And Yeats would know: his lifelong political involvement in Irish politics, some of it dangerously reactionary, was even more intense than Browne's political activity has been.) These two albums frankly lack poetry. They try to make a persuasive argument for certain ideas, but even as rhetoric they're too obvious: Joyce Millman of the *Village Voice* was unsparing but mostly on point when she likened *Lives in the Balance* to a "ponderous, overblown editorial . . . a well-intentioned but stifling lecture."[4] Jackson Browne is a stubborn artist and man—bless him for it, because he couldn't have sustained a fifty-year career if he weren't. But in the late 1980s he had the idée fixe that the music he was writing was politically *necessary*, that he had "to *do* something" as an activist and in his music to address the increasing perniciousness of American military power and the deadening of American ideals he saw all around him. You can't fault his ambitions, or the urgency and sincerity of his convictions. But you can certainly bemoan the results.

THE REAGAN YEARS

It's hard, in a Trumpian age of unprecedented political polarization, to remember that the 1980s were plenty polarized too: it's tough to recapture the extent to which Jackson and his fellow American liberals were appalled by the Reagan years. Many on the Left felt blindsided, and betrayed, by the Reagan administration's frontal assault on liberal policies that had been carefully set in place by administration after administration starting in the 1930s. Reagan's massive tax cuts in 1981 and 1986 may have put a stop to the long period of stagflation, but that came at the cost of a rapid rise in income inequality and the choking off of government benefits for children, the poor, and the working class. Unemployment and inflation were cut in half between 1983 and 1987, but the benefits of an improved economy were parceled out unequally: the megacorporations, the white-collar world of finance, and the idle rich prospered, but those in manufacturing (especially those in labor unions) and small business went into a decades-long slump that left entire swaths of the Midwest—the "Rust Belt"—reeling. Lyndon

Johnson's "Great Society"—the liberal vision of a country compassionate toward the poor and the historically underserved—was never fully funded in the first place, but the Reagan administration did its best to dismantle what was left of it. And Reagan—the "Great Communicator"—performed a neoliberalist magic act, convincing huge sectors of the American public that a deregulated "free market" somehow meant the same thing as "freedom."

Then there was the transformation of foreign policy. Richard Nixon's policy of détente toward the Soviet Union, designed to lower Cold War temperatures and cautiously embraced by liberals, was replaced by Reagan's aggressive evil-empire rhetoric and policies that brought the two superpowers closer to nuclear confrontation than they'd been since the Cuban Missile Crisis. Though Reagan's bellicosity toward the Soviets eventually palled after Mikhail Gorbachev took power, his warlike posture in the Americas didn't. Part of Reagan's foreign policy agenda was to undo the "Vietnam Syndrome"—the American people's post-Vietnam revulsion toward US military intervention in other countries, and their desire for the "peace" that the counterculture had advocated. That meant aggressive moves in Central America—first a military invasion of the tiny island of Grenada, followed by an assault on Panama, both of them rationalized by trumped-up claims that their governments were "communist" or otherwise hostile to vital American interests. These incursions were warm-ups for Reagan's extraordinarily inhumane and confused policies in El Salvador and Nicaragua, which prompted Jackson Browne's ire more than anything.

But the outrage that Browne and his fellow liberals felt toward Reagan's economic and foreign policies was hardly the end of it. His administration's environmental policies reversed many of the protections enshrined in the Environmental Protection Act of 1972 and aggressively promoted the expansion of offshore oil drilling and nuclear power, as well as the leasing of ecologically fragile federal lands and waters to developers. Reagan's Interior Secretary, responsible for implementing environmental policy, was James Watt. Watt, a fundamentalist Christian, admitted during his confirmation hearing that he wasn't much concerned with protecting the environment because the Second Coming was on the horizon: "I do not know how many future generations we can count on before the Lord returns."[5] (He resigned in 1983 for racist comments he made and, a decade later, was found guilty for multiple felonies involving his lobbying for developers.) Despite increasing international recognition that global warming was occurring—and occurring due to human activity—the Reagan administration entirely ignored it, even when dire warnings about climate change were presented before Congress, as they were in 1986 and 1988.[6]

If the Reagan administration's policies left progressives like Jackson flailing, trying to shore up whatever liberal programs remained in place, Reagan's influence on the broader culture was just as dispiriting. Reagan's undeniable charisma and naive optimism inspired a sense of jingoistic patriotism that radically shifted the American mood toward a simplistic us-versus-them-ism. "You hear it all the time, 'my country wrong or right,'" Browne noted, headshakingly, in "For America." In Oliver Stone's *Born on the Fourth of July* (1989), the main character Ron Kovic blindly repeats, "America love it or leave it"—at least until his horrific Vietnam experience convinces him that love of country is a complicated matter. The Sylvester Stallone film *Rambo: First Blood Part II* (1985) was a decade-defining phenomenon of nationalistic (and racist) fervor: the main character was a muscle-bound symbol of a new American triumphalism, spraying machine gun fire and toppling hundreds of anonymous Vietnamese soldiers in his one-man attempt to rectify the shame of the Vietnam war. Even Bruce Springsteen's echoing howl of despair, "Born in the U.S.A," was misinterpreted as a paean to American pride, no less than by Reagan himself, who said on the campaign trail, "America's future rests in a thousand dreams inside your hearts. It rests in the message of hope in the songs of a man so many young Americans admire: New Jersey's own Bruce Springsteen."[7] Needless to say, Springsteen demurred.

There was, naturally, a dialectical response to all the simplistic flag-waving, much of it fomented inside the liberal-leaning pop culture industry itself. Oliver Stone's best 1980s movies (*Salvador, Platoon, Born on the Fourth of July, Wall Street*), while ham-fisted in their polemics and melodramatic in their plots, were still powerful antidotes to the prevailing jingoism. Hollywood had a brief love affair with rural America and the working class (*Norma Rae, All the Right Moves, Places in the Heart, Country*) that highlighted the increasing disparity between urban and rural America, the "coasts" and "flyover country," college graduates versed in business and sophisticated technology and high school graduates working on farms or in low-tech retail—disparities that reflected the Reagan revolution's transformation of the American economy.

And the rock world (re)discovered a political conscience in the 1980s. Browne's work on the No Nukes concerts may not have singlehandedly kickstarted rock's devotion to social causes, but he and his colleagues certainly influenced it. Band-Aid's "Do They Know It's Christmas?" (1984), USA For Africa's "We Are the World" (1985), Live Aid (1985), Farm Aid

(1985), the Amnesty International tours (1986), and the rash of benefit concerts, films, and albums that followed, tainted as they sometimes were by pop star egos and questionable accounting, poured millions into drought-starved Ethiopia, into the pockets of American family farmers, and into coffers of groups advocating for human rights.

For Jackson, however, the biggest spur to writing politically committed music was Steve Van Zandt. Van Zandt, a guitarist in Bruce Springsteen's E Street Band, quit the band and went out on his own in 1984. His album from that year, *Voices of America*, featured the blistering "Los Desaparecidos" (about those whom government death squads had made "disappear" in El Salvador and Nicaragua) and "I Am a Patriot," a bold if simplistic statement of faith in American ideals that Browne liked so much he covered it on *World in Motion*. Van Zandt was the brains behind Artists United against Apartheid, which released one of the most potent songs (and videos) of rock 'n' roll politics in the 1980s, "Sun City." Van Zandt's example, along with Springsteen's *Born in the U.S.A.*, the blockbuster album that, more than any other, helped define the pop culture discourse about Americanness during that decade, nudged Browne into his most unequivocal political music.

LIVES IN THE BALANCE

There was a lively pop discourse about "America" in the mid-1980s, most of it inspired, pro and con, by the Reagan revolution. Punk rockers were the most vitriolic (the Dead Kennedys' "We've Got a Bigger Problem Now," the Ramones' "Bonzo Goes to Bitburg,") and hip-hop the most searing (Grandmaster Flash's "The Message," N.W.A.'s "Fuck tha Police," Public Enemy's "Black Steel in the Hour of Chaos"). But mainstreamers got into the act too: Springsteen started it off with the bleak landscapes of *Nebraska* (1982), followed by the anthemic *Born in the U.S.A.* (1984), but there was also Bob Seger ("Making Thunderbirds"), David Bowie ("This is Not America"), John Cougar Mellencamp ("Pink Houses," "Rain on the Scarecrow"), Don Henley ("All She Wants to Do Is Dance," "The End of the Innocence"), and Prince ("Ronnie Talk to Russia," "America").[8] All of these artists contributed to an energized pop discussion about the fate of the American Dream, the decimation of the working class, racism, the carceral state, and imperialist foreign policy. Eventually the "America" craze got so faddish that hair-metal acts like Night Ranger or Sammy Hagar cashed in with drivel like "(You Can Still Rock) In America" and "V.O.A." That Browne would enter that discourse was natural—also treacherous: he could be accused of jumping on a bandwagon that was already creaking with heavyweight passengers.

Which is the problem with "For America." Take it out of its mid-1980s context, and "For America" reads like the ruminations of a countercultural survivor who feels guilty that when he was young, he exercised his precious American freedoms "from the comfort of a dreamer's bed / and the safety of my own head" while his fellow citizens were forced to fight and die in Vietnam. Now grown up, he believes in the "shining dream" of American possibility more than ever, and he strongly identifies with his country—"I was made for America / It's in my blood and in my bones"—but sees those ideals constantly sacrificed to a system dedicated to money and power. He also fears that a "generation's blank stare"—a swipe at the Reagan-supporting generation that followed Jackson's 1960s compatriots—will allow the nation's dream to fade away completely. The song ends with the holdout protagonist recommitting himself to that dream until the country's "conscience" is rediscovered.

Fine; on paper, "For America" works. But stick it back into its mid-1980s context and its power drains away. The guitar riff that kicks off the song is tinny and scrawny, as if Browne hadn't kept up with what 1980s rock guitar was capable of. The saxophone solo, intended to lend a certain sonic grandeur to the proceedings, is thin, and it embarrassingly echoed the meaty Clarence Clemons solos on Springsteen's albums. "I was made for America" is a tired (and belated) literalization of Springsteen's bold metaphor, "born in the U.S.A.," and Browne's attempt to steal back an ideal strain of patriotism from the Rambos and Reaganites who had appropriated it pales in comparison to Springsteen's brutal narrative of a Vietnam vet betrayed by his country. The whole song feels profoundly derivative: Browne *explains* his ambivalence toward America while Springsteen's song *embodies* it. Springsteen cast a long shadow on Jackson's 1980s rock music, but no song of Browne's was put more in the shade than "For America."

One of the concerns of "For America" has to do the Reagan administration's lies. The song's protagonist wants to "find out what's true," especially in Central America, but he wonders how that's going to happen "with everyone from the President on down / Trying to keep it from you." That desire to find out the truth led Browne to two trips to Nicaragua in 1984, where he encountered Nicaraguans who were exposed to constant intimidation and terror but, Jackson found, lived with the underlying desire for the same freedoms and dreams that Americans take for granted. Those trips, along with Browne's extensive reading and friendship with leftist activists, inform "Soldier of Plenty," "Lives in the Balance," and "Till I Go

Down," which subject Reagan's policy in Central America to Browne's brand of liberal, humanistic critique.

That critique assumes that the American government ought to care about the individual lives of Central Americans caught in the crossfire of military conflict, that "there are lives in the balance" that must be considered. It assumes that concerns of realpolitik—for example, how American business interests and military security are threatened by Central America rebel forces committed to socialism or communism—ought to take a back seat to a rock-hard devotion to human rights and human dignity. It assumes, essentially, a radically Christian orientation of love toward other humans—a position that was best articulated by what came to be called "liberation theology" in the Central American Catholic Church and has more than a little in common with Martin Luther King's beliefs.[9]

Such assumptions, it goes without saying, easily slide into slush and sentiment. Compare these songs to, say, The Clash's "Rebel Waltz" or "Washington Bullets" (from *Sandinista!* [1980]) and you see the problem. The Clash did combat rock: "Washington Bullets" engages the Nicaraguan Revolution like compatriots with boots on the ground, and so the band can share in both its horror and its (temporary) victory like the committed partisans they were. Next to *Sandinista!*, Browne's songs feel like airy liberalism, which Steve Turner, in his 1987 interview, accuses him of: "Those who criticise Browne's new politically conscious material call it 'coffee-table protest,'" Turner writes. "They find the splice of sun-kissed Californian rock and Reagan-knocking too incongruous. Is his laid back music the most appropriate vehicle? 'Not really,' [Browne] says with an honest laugh. 'But it's the only kind I know how to make.'"[10]

Turner's question is a good one, and Browne's answer unsatisfying. For anyone paying attention, America's role in Central America during the late 1970s and 1980s was rage-inducing. The United States propped up deeply corrupt Salvadoran juntas that viciously tortured and murdered thousands of people, year after year, and it did so because the juntas claimed to be "anti-communist" and were willing to do Washington's bidding. (Almost any random page of Joan Didion's astonishing report on El Salvador's early 1980s civil war, *Salvador*, is replete with horrors that should incense any reader.) In Nicaragua, the United States—frantic that the Marxist Sandinistas had toppled the Somoza regime (which had been an American ally)—had the CIA work to overthrow the new government and reinstall pro-US leadership.

How was Jackson to musically communicate his outrage, frustration, betrayal—his rage—at America's involvement in Central America? Punks could scream, spew contemptuous satire, pummel the listener with ear-wrecking guitars. But that was not Browne's way. He was a rationalist about all this. He thought he could use rock as reasonable persuasion—as rhetoric: if he could just give people information, he hoped, he could do his part to change the popular mind. Plus he was now wedded to mainstream rock methods—LA studio studs came in, played their parts, and picked up their checks. Most mainstream rock in the 1980s, being mainstream—that is, a compliant bullhorn for status quo culture, for status quo capitalism—had forsaken its 1960s roots in rebellion and, unless practiced by someone who could summon deep wells of soulful passion, was no longer equipped to deliver rage: that's why punk and hip-hop had to be invented in the first place. Browne, whose voice and songwriting have always been controlled, was hemmed in by the limitations of the form.

But the lyrics are as big a problem as the music on *Lives in the Balance*. Many of them seem as distant from their subjects as "Boulevard" was remote from "the streets." The very title "Lives in the Balance" feels banal and detached: meant to be anthemic, it's a tepid, almost bureaucratic way to refer to real Nicaraguan victims of oppression. The song makes point after analytical point—about how "they sell us" our politicians and wars the same way advertisers sell cars, or about how politicians send citizens to fight in wars but don't put their own lives on the line—that by the 1980s were already leftist bromides. "Soldier of Plenty" casts America as a "boy"—inexperienced and naive—who callously treats Central American countries as a "toy." It follows that up with another lame rhyme that describes Nicaraguan villagers living lives that are "long on hunger . . . short on joy." The credible reggae of "Till I Go Down" is marred by its trite castigation of Reagan as "the leader with the iron will / And his allegiance to the dollar bill." Never had Browne descended so blatantly into troughs of the obvious.

Things improve marginally when Browne turns his gaze to injustices closer to home. "Lawless Avenues" is a large-canvas composition about a gang-infested neighborhood, presumably the streets of Hispanic East LA during the 1980s. It contains a rarity in Jackson Browne songs: actual characters—Silent Joe, Manuelito, Rosa—plus multiple storylines that weave an operatic narrative about the desperation of kids trapped by clueless parenting, ubiquitous violence, and horizonless futures. The song, cowritten with Jorge Calderón, is sung half in Spanish (Calderón sings background vocals) and lovingly nods toward the Mexican mariachi tradition. The music rocks harder than anything else on the record, and we can see why Browne is proud of it (he included it on *The Very Best of Jackson Browne*). Still, it's hard to imagine anyone who actually lived through the 1980s in LA barrios thinking this was expressing something authentic. Did anyone who ever cruised Atlantic Avenue or Whittier Boulevard think of them as "lawless avenues"? Who on those streets talked about the "prison system" rather than "jail" or the "joint"? (One of my best friends grew up as a gun-packing gangbanger in Baldwin Park in the 1970s, and when I played him "Lawless Avenues," he just smirked and shook his head.) The song feels written by a very concerned white guy who's made a bit of a study of the troubled Latino community. It's tone-deaf, sociological slumming.

There are three nonpolitical songs on *Lives in the Balance*. "Candy," written by Jackson's boyhood pal Greg Copeland and Wally Stocker, vies with *World in Motion*'s "Lights and Virtues" as one of the worst tracks Browne ever laid down: the nicest thing one can say about it is that Browne was generous in allowing some royalties to be channeled to a friend whose musical career had stalled. "In the Shape of a Heart," however, was the one song from *Balance* that Browne fans, fidgety with his political turn, hung onto as proof that he still "had it." And it *is* a great song, written, as it were, on home ground: it's beautifully sung, meticulously detailed, and held together by a central symbol that locks together the song's meaning at the end. Browne himself called it "probably my most personal, and sometimes I think my best, song."[11]

The song mourns the end of a relationship characterized by "sorrow and regret" and marred by misunderstanding (of both oneself and the lover) as well as a hint of violence. The song's about nothing less than love's mystery and volatility. "People speak of love / don't know what they're thinking of," this master analyst of romantic entanglements sings, and he makes it clear that when he says "people," he means himself. Such people "speak in terms of belief and belonging / Try to fit some name to their longing"; they "try to think of a word for the burning." The longing and the burning between these lovers, however, eventually bear hostile fruit: one of them puts a hole in a wall, "about the size of a fist / or something thrown that had missed." When the lover finally leaves, the song's speaker sees that his lover has left behind a piece of jewelry, a ruby in the shape of a heart. He takes this symbol of their desperate love and drops it into the hole in the wall, thus bringing the tenderness and the violence together, and realizes that love's volatile mysteries reside in "the shallows and the unseen reefs / That are there from the start." Who the woman in the song is based on—Major, Sweeney, Hannah, someone else, or a composite—isn't clear, but it doesn't matter. It's the volatile, romantic Browne who's the subject of the song, and in this quarrel Browne has with himself, he's made the poetry we expect from him.

The album's closer, "Black and White," is another quarrel with the self, and *Balance*'s most overlooked song. One of the few tracks on the album that's sonically satisfying, with a brightly lyrical piano riding over a tasty bed of bass, guitar, and synthesizer, it's another look back at the paths Browne has taken in his life, the latest chapter of "Looking into You." From his vantage point, as he closes in on the age of forty, the protagonist marvels at the energy of his own youth—"you were going to burn this city down . . . ticking like a time bomb in the night"—and is bemused by the black-and-white assuredness of his early ambitions. But things are so much more complicated now, and "time is running out." He only half-remembers the "search" he was on then, and though that search is still "burning like an ember in [his] heart," those embers are threatening to go out. The track ends with the repetition of the phrase "time running out"—we actually hear it thirty times throughout the song—with the instrumentation gradually falling away until we hear nothing but the vocals echoing—an aural equivalent of a suspending ellipsis. It's a fine reminder that, for Browne, who by now, in midlife, had taken on so many responsibilities both personal and political, time was pressing ever harder—meaning that he would have to dig deeper to find the energy to commit himself to the ideals he continued to hold out for. Needless to say, the demand to dig deeper is one the listener is meant to feel too.

The reception of *Lives in the Balance* ranged from the lukewarm to the brutal. *Rolling Stone* and *Sounds* were kind, giving the kid-gloves treatment to one of the editors' favorite sons, but *Musician* noted that the arrangements sounded "forced," the musicianship of the players made up a "bland stew," and the lyrics were "vague."[12] The *LA Times*' Robert Hilburn, who in the 1970s was one of Browne's biggest fans, pulled no punches, saying that some tracks were "riddled with clumsy catch-phrases," and that "For America" "is undercut by an instrumental design straight from 'Miami Vice' and a chorus guaranteed to make you wince."[13] Browne's one-off pop duet with Clarence Clemons, "You're a Friend of Mine," had been a Top 20 hit in 1985, but *Lives in the Balance*'s sales tumbled, becoming the first Jackson Browne since the mid-1970s not to go platinum upon its initial release. Jackson, worried that Asylum wasn't doing enough to promote it, took it upon himself to pay for a video of the title track, but that didn't pick up sales either. Another kind of man would have seen all this as good reason to alter his approach next time out. Jackson Browne was not that kind of man.

WORLD IN MOTION

None of the criticism Browne hurled at *Lives in the Balance* seemed to stick, and *World in Motion* doubles down on exactly the things that made *Lives* so problematic. We have the same revolving door of studio musicians doing their best versions of "contemporary rock," the same lyric generalities expressing the same sincere liberal platitudes, the same inability to use new strategies—like irony—to express sociopolitical conditions that begged for less sincere, on-the-nose treatment. You have to be impressed in a way: the man stuck to his guns the way Dylan did in following up *Slow Train Coming* with *Saved*, or the way Bowie kept releasing unfathomable Tin Machine albums. I remember this as the record that almost made me get off the bus though. By the time of its release in 1989, rock seemed pretty healthy as a form, with a percolating mainstream (U2, Petty, Springsteen), pop megastars worth getting excited about (Michael Jackson, Madonna, Prince), an alt-rock thing so happening that it was hardly alternative anymore (R.E.M., Talking Heads, Sonic Youth), boiling local scenes in Minneapolis (Husker Du, the Replacements) and Seattle (Soundgarden, Nirvana), and a provocative hard rock/metal scene (Guns N' Roses, Metallica). Browne, at the center of the singer-songwriter movement through the 1970s, and a potent member of the rock establishment during the eighties, started to seem like a marginal figure whose music wasn't keeping up. I drifted away from him as I drifted from Joni Mitchell after *Don Juan's Reckless Daughter* or from Van Morrison after *Inarticulate Speech of the Heart.*

World in Motion has an eye-catching cover—Francisco Letelier's striking mash-up of Mark Rothko and Richard Diebenkorn color fields, behind which we glimpse shadowy portraits of distressed Central American children. Browne stares warily at the viewer, promising that this record will be a tough ride all around. Which it indeed is. Possibly to make sure that his longtime fans aren't turned off right away, Jackson, after the title cut, front-loads the album with its two nonpolitical songs, "Enough of the Night" (about his sister)[14] and "Chasing You into the Light." Both are listenable, functional pop-rock, though some of the lyrics are cliché-ridden or atypically awkward ("Don't allow . . . / Another night to close on your empty cup"?) and are lightweight compared to what we expect from Browne relationship songs.

Then, torrents of rhetoric. "How Long" whines through a mind-deadening lecture about how the US government spends its money on missiles rather than food for impoverished children, and is as bathetic as "The Word Justice," which takes up the Iran-Contra scandal, Reagan's "war against drugs," and the betrayals of American democracy in a lyric that hardly even tries to be verse—it sounds like a letter to the editor hastily rhymed up into a song. "World in Motion," with its busy guitar-and-synth arrangement and metallic percussion, announces its theme at the outset—"Sun going down on the U.S.A."—and proceeds through a familiar laundry list of national foibles (media distraction, materialism, selfishness, ignorance of other cultures) before announcing, out of nowhere, that "things like hunger, greed, and hatred / One way or another, gonna be eradicated." Where that optimism comes from is anyone's guess.

The "sun going down" notwithstanding, Browne evidently wants to be positive, so in "Anything Can Happen" and "When the Stone Begins to Turn" he goes for inspiration. "Anything" has a pleasant synthesizer-led melodic pulse, but the lyrics' scattershot generalities smear its message of hope and possibility. "Stone" invokes Martin Luther King Jr.—"In the years since they shot him down / You see changes that once were a dream begin to come around"—and then Nelson Mandela, at the time still imprisoned by South Africa's apartheid government and the central rallying figure for the worldwide anti-apartheid movement. "Stone," lifted by the tight buoyant reggae rhythms provided by Sly Dunbar and Robbie Shakespeare, is very nearly a success, though it can't quite wave away its whiff of sanctimony.

As Browne's critical bête noire, Robert Christgau, pointed out, the album's two best songs are written by others. The first, "My Personal Revenge," was cowritten by Tomás Borge, a cofounder of the Sandinista National Liberation Front who in 1978 was imprisoned and tortured by Nicaragua's Somoza government for his part in the unfolding revolution. After his release, with the help of Nicaraguan singer/composer Luis Enrique Mejía Godoy, he wrote "Revenge." Browne's story about the song's origins is worth quoting in full:

> Tomás Borge was a political prisoner who was tortured by the National Guard. After several months he was released from prison and he told the jailer who had been torturing him, he looked at the man who had done these inhuman things to him and he said, "I'm going to be back for my revenge." And the guy, you know, laughed or kicked him or something; he obviously didn't believe it.
>
> But about three years later the Sandinistas were in power and Borge went looking for the guy, and he found him, in this dark prison where all the National Guardsmen were being held. He says, "Do you remember me?" The guy says, "No." He's looking down. So Borge makes him look at his face again. "You remember this face, don't you?" And the guy still says no . . . he won't look up. So then Borge starts to speak to

> the guy. And he says, "I told you the last time I saw you that when I saw you again I would have my revenge." And he says to him: "My revenge will be that our children will get to go to school. My revenge will be that even though you tortured these hands, I give them to you and show you that you have been unable to take away their tenderness."[15]

The song's theme of generosity and forgiveness in the face of evil rouses Jackson to a strong, empathic performance. Browne doesn't often succeed in embodying someone else's consciousness in his songs, but he manages it sensitively here.

Browne and producer Scott Thurston give Steven Van Zandt's "I Am a Patriot" a spry, syncopated rhythm and stirring gospel vocals, which allows Browne to do what "For America" couldn't, which is take back the term "patriot" from the Reaganites who had usurped it. The gospel opening—"the river opens for the righteous . . . someday"—infuses the song with an African American take on what it means to be an American, that is, an unending struggle to face realities which contradict the ideals the country says it stands for: "What I believe in my soul / Ain't what I see with my eyes," sings the speaker. And later: "I want to run with the lions released from the cages / Released from the rages burning in my soul tonight." There's a warmth in the melody and in Jackson's delivery that draws on a basic love of family and of life itself that helps him transcend his frustrations and reaffirm his love of country, despite everything.

The song falters only at the end, when the speaker tries to identify what the American ideal is. "I ain't no communist / And I ain't no capitalist," he begins, and starts listing the ideologies—imperialist, socialist, Democrat, Republican—that serve more to divide than to define the country's spirit. After disposing of these, he affirms, in the song's climax, "I only know one party / And it is *freedom*." Which is nonsense. The word is used as if it had a magical radiance, when in fact it means nothing without context—communists and capitalists, Democrats and Republicans all have very worked-out ideas of what they think it means—so Van Zandt's use of it at the end is pure cant.

"Lights and Virtues," which ends the album, signals its bathos in its title. A near-fragment of a lyric which does little more than laud a series of virtues—truth, knowledge, hope, purpose, strength, honor, love, friendship—and does so as drily as the list I've just made, is the record's low point, with an arrangement that's only lifted above the level of elevator music by Kevin Dukes's tasty guitar solo.

Jackson toured for a month during the summer of 1989 to promote the record, which did little for sales. (*World in Motion* was Browne's worst-selling album to date.) He followed it up with performances at the Nelson Mandela International Tribute for a Free South Africa at London's Wembley Stadium as well as at Amnesty International concerts in Santiago, Chile. Back home, he did benefits for Neil Young's Bridge School, for the Christic Institute, and for Native Americans commemorating the one-hundredth anniversary of the massacre at Wounded Knee. (In 1991, he contributed dobro guitar and background vocals to Bruce Cockburn's "Indian Wars," from Cockburn's 1991 *Nothing but a Burning Light* album.) For an Electra Records compilation CD—*Electra's 40th Anniversary*—he contributed a lovely, loose-limbed version of the Incredible Strings Band song "The First Girl I Loved," whose autobiographical lyric, penned by Scotsman Robin Williamson, remarkably mirrored many of Jackson's own experiences as a young musician on the make. It was a harbinger of a much-hoped-for (by critics, by fans, certainly by me) return to the personal that would be the hallmark of Jackson's albums of the 1990s.

7

TURMOIL, THEN RENAISSANCE

By the mid-1980s, Jackson Browne may have thought he'd said his piece about the turmoil of the inner life, but his own turmoil didn't stop just because he'd turned his gaze toward politics. In fact, it finally erupted in a most publicly unpleasant way.

Since his separation from Lynne Sweeney in 1982 (they divorced the following year), he'd been seeing actress Daryl Hannah, who was on the crest of major stardom, (she'd star in a string of 1980s hits, including *Splash*! [1984], *Wall Street* [1987], and *Steel Magnolias* [1989]). During their relationship, the couple were careful to confine the media's exposure of their relationship to the occasional celebrity or charity event and to her modest appearances with him in a few music videos. That control, however, evaporated all at once on the morning of September 23, 1992, when Browne called the police to report that "someone was ransacking" the Santa Monica home he shared with Hannah.[1] It turned out to be a domestic dispute between him and Hannah, but one that got so muddled in the press, particularly when the tabloids got hold of it, that no entirely satisfactory explanation has ever emerged. Even today, no version of the story quite holds together; it unfolded over the course of many months in a way that must have been nightmarish for both of them and would have personal and legal repercussions that would last for years.

A few indisputable facts about that night: Hannah had just flown into Los Angeles from New York and evidently had gone to their Santa Monica house to break off her relationship with Jackson. She'd been having an on-again, off-again affair with John F. Kennedy Jr., the son of the former president, whom she'd met in 1988 while she was living with Browne. The couple argued, some sort of physical altercation ensued, Browne called the police, the police responded. From here on, narratives diverge. A few hours after the altercation, Hannah's press representative released a maddeningly ambiguous statement: "Daryl Hannah received serious injuries incurred during a domestic dispute with Browne for which she sought medical treatment." The statement did not say that Browne beat Hannah or caused any of her injuries, only that the she "received" injuries "during" their dispute. Browne didn't immediately address the incident in the press at all.

Hannah made no other statement—she never would—and didn't file a complaint with the Santa Monica police. But photographs of her bruised face began to appear in the tabloids.

From there, the celebrity press took over. In October, *People* magazine published a confusing and frankly insidious report on the matter. Browne had indeed called the police, it said, but when they arrived—this is according to "friends of Hannah"—she was hiding in a guesthouse and didn't talk to the police (who, therefore, couldn't confirm her injuries). Browne, however, told them, "Everything is fine," and the officers left without filing a report. Then, according to Hannah's associates, she called her sister, who accompanied her to a hospital where doctors treated her injuries—a black eye, bruises on her chin and ribs, a broken finger. Pictures were taken and Hannah's ambiguous press statement was released. In the *People* piece, Hannah's mother is quoted as saying, "I saw [Daryl] shortly after in the hospital. I saw the damage that was done to her. The doctor was very concerned. Jackson was a very, very good friend of mine, but when I saw Daryl, I just felt betrayed." This implicates Browne more than the press statement does but, again, doesn't flatly state that he was responsible for her injuries. In the time-honored tabloid way, *People* wove an aura of guilt around Browne by quoting unnamed friends of Hannah accusing him in general terms of being subject to "blind rages" and of having an "explosive personality." Another said that "this has happened before, but never this bad." For "balance," friends of Browne were contacted who were quick to defend him. J. D. Souther claimed that "he is just not a violent guy. As far as I can tell, he was just trying to protect himself. *He* was getting chased around by *her*." Don Henley added, "I would bet everything I own that Jackson did not batter Daryl." Publications even less principled than *People* ran a flurry of articles over the succeeding months, none of which featured comments from either Browne or Hannah.

There things stood until Browne released *I'm Alive* in late 1993, an album that was so obviously about the relationship that he couldn't escape talking about it to the press. In a revealing interview—to Rob Tannenbaum of *GQ* magazine—he opened up, but in a way that still left lots of questions unanswered. "I was accused of violence, and I deny it," he said. "What was described in the tabloids and in *People* magazine *did not* happen. What *did* happen is not something I'm going to describe publicly."[2] He added, "I'm not gonna say what it was about because it isn't anybody's business." When asked about a photograph that appeared in the tabloids showing Hannah with a black eye, he responded, "I realize that's very damning," but he insisted that he couldn't "describe publicly how that might have happened" without explaining the full context of their argument, and he was not about to do that because it violated his and Hannah's privacy. Realizing that his reticence about the details of the episode didn't inspire confidence that he was an innocent party, he finally asked in exasperation, "Had I beaten her, would I have summoned the police?"

A few months later, Browne sat down with Fred Schruers of *US* magazine and again addressed the incident. Again he denied the allegations and again declined to offer much context, though he did maintain that the police *did* see Hannah during their visit and that they both spoke to the police "for a long time." In fact, Santa Monica police officer Sgt Gary Gallinot is quoted in the article as saying, "A male and female officer went to the house. It was an argument, what we call a family disturbance, and when we left, everything was OK. [Hannah] never made indications she was assaulted . . . if there are any signs of domestic violence, we take a report, but in this instance there were no signs. It could have happened later, but she never filed charges."[3]

That interview, in any case, prompted Haskell Wexler, Hannah's uncle (and the famed cinematographer) to write a fierce letter to the editor in April 1994: "Jackson beat Daryl in September 1992," he wrote. "I was with her in the hospital. I saw the ugly black bruises on her eye and chin and on her ribs. The examining doctor reported she had blood in her urine. The doctor was shocked by the severity and noted Daryl as 'a badly battered woman.' I photographed her at the hospital." This was the first time a named (and supposedly credible) source had directly accused Browne of abuse on that night.

Browne's response was printed in the same issue. First, Browne offered up a November 1992 letter, written by Lt. John Miehle of the Santa Monica police department, about what happened that night:

> The Santa Monica Police Department went to the house where Jackson Browne lives regarding a possible disturbance. We resolved the situation in about five minutes. There was never any assault. There are no charges pending and no prosecution sought by or intended by the District Attorney. It is this department's intention that no citizen, regardless of

> who she is, suffer any kind of abuse, whether it be domestic violence or any other kind of assault. But in this case, absolutely no assault occurred. Our investigators tell us nothing happened. Nobody has even alleged that Daryl Hannah was even touched. If they had, we'd be investigating. We're not hiding anything. The press is trying to make more out of this than there really is, and it's unfair, not just to Browne, but to us. We did our job, and repeat, no crime occurred here. This whole thing is ridiculous.

The statement contradicts much of what had previously been reported by *People*, and it certainly contradicts Wexler. But it isn't an official document of the department, since no report was made on the night of the incident, and it feels casual, if not defensive, in tone. Still, along with Gallinot's statement, it's the only account of the incident by a sworn-in officer of the law.

Then Browne addressed Wexler himself, saying that since he and Wexler were (or at least until that time had been) friends, to accuse Browne publicly was no way to resolve the issue: "I suggest," he said, "that you allow me to describe Daryl's actions to you and then judge for yourself as to how those injuries may have occurred. I repeat: I did not beat her. I have no desire to expose Daryl to public scrutiny in this matter. I have avoided describing her actions or characterizing her behavior so far. It has been hard. I would have preferred to talk to you." Though his main contention—"I did not beat her"—is clear, Browne's reluctance here, as elsewhere, to discuss the details publicly suggests that what occurred on the night of September 23, 1992, was so private and complex that to air it all in the distortive atmosphere of the media would be unfair to Hannah. Indeed, in his *US* interview, he said that discussing the affair in public constituted a "breach of faith in a covenant [with Hannah] that is many, many years old."

We're left with a few salient points. It was Browne who called the police, not Hannah—it defies credibility that a batterer would call the police on himself. Though Hannah's injuries were real and documented, again, neither she nor her spokesperson ever claimed that Browne beat her, only that she "received injuries incurred during" their argument. Only Wexler claimed otherwise. There was doubtless a physical encounter between the two, but how her injuries came about is something only the principals themselves know. And to reiterate, Hannah never filed charges and never addressed the incident in public. For what it's worth, John F. Kennedy Jr., who one might think would defend her, doubted that Browne had beat her. In an interview, he hemmed and hawed about how complex Hannah's personality was, and about how she could inspire anger in men, only to finally say, "Do you mean do you think he, um, hit her? No."[4]

My own sense is that Hannah initiated the aggression and Browne defended himself, which resulted in her injuring herself. Hannah's spokesperson released the curious statement trying to explain her injuries, but Hannah knew better than to pursue it, either legally or through the press. As for Browne, I suspect his reluctance to explain the matter in detail came from his sense that it really was no one's damn business and that, in any case, if he did try to explain it, he would be laying the blame on Hannah herself as the initiator of the violence, which he didn't want to do. It was all too private and complex a matter, and to explain it to the popular press couldn't result in anything but more distortion and hysteria.

Wherever the truth lay, the episode sullied Browne's until-then pristine reputation as a sensitive and peace-loving male, and there were those, like Browne's lover from the early 1970s, Joni Mitchell, who were publicly eager to pile on the hate. In an uncharacteristically cruel song from her *Turbulent Indigo* album (1994), "Not to Blame," Mitchell, without mentioning Browne's name, declares that his "fist marks were on her face," and that he was cowardly in his "whitewashed claim" that it was Hannah who "was out of line" (a claim Jackson never made). But her anger at Browne didn't stop there. The song drags Jackson's son Ethan into it, strangely suggesting that his father trained him up from birth to become some woman-stalking lothario unaffected by his own mother's suicide (Mitchell writes that she remembers the three-year-old boy saying, "Daddy let's get some girls / one for you and one for me"). Finally, she brings up Phyllis Major herself, saying that she had "the looks you despise / and love to drive to suicide."

A confounded Browne responded three years later in a 1997 interview:

> Joni Mitchell is, unfortunately, she's not really well. At this point in her life, you know, she has had deep fallings-out with many people in her life. I think there's quite a few people that she's no longer on speaking terms with. She's not a happy person, and what she says in that song is absolutely, 100 percent wrong. And it's really very nasty, very, very ill, you know, very bad-spirited of her to make this kind of conjecture when in fact as she and every one of her friends knows it's all about carrying a torch for 20 years.[5]

He went on to say that "it was abusive to employ that image of my son as somebody who treated his mother's death lightheartedly. I mean, he was a three-year-old baby, you know. This is inexcusable."

Jackson knew that the fallout from the incident with Hannah would linger, but except when he felt forced to defend himself, he kept quiet about it. (When a TBS movie about JFK Jr.'s life, *American Prince, the JFK*

Jr Story, was aired in 2002 and included references to Browne having battered Hannah, Browne threatened to sue, and he got the producers to cut those references. Subsequent showings of the film removed the scene and appended an apology to Browne at the beginning of the film.[6]) The relationship was, in any case, over by the time he went into the studio to record *I'm Alive*. And by the time it came out, he told Tannenbaum, "The things I have to say to her have been said—in these songs."[7]

I'M ALIVE

Whatever the immediate context of the album's release, *I'm Alive* is the album that longtime fans had been hoping for since *Running on Empty*. It's his most thematically coherent record, sequenced in a way that tells the story of a relationship's joyous beginning, troubled middle, and painfully messy end, followed by a group of songs that reach for understanding, forgiveness, and acceptance. The album's highlight, "Sky Blue and Black," concludes with Browne wailing repeatedly, "That's the way love is / That's the way love is," as if he himself can't believe what he's gone through, or that the word can cover such wild swings of pleasure and pain, intimacy and disconnection, trust and lies, sky blue and sky black. *I'm Alive* doesn't cut quite as deep as *Late for the Sky*: there's some mediocre music in its middle stretches, but it stands with that album, *The Pretender*, and *Running on Empty* as one of his best.

While an exploration of a complex love's rise and fall is what the fans were waiting for, the music might be the most gratifying thing about the record. *I'm Alive* is Jackson's first album since *Running on Empty* where he seems done with the idea of keeping up with rock fashion; he's not chasing anybody else's sound or style. And it's a good thing, because by 1993, the year of the album's release, hip hop and hip hop–inflected R & B had moved to the center of the pop universe, dominating airwaves, MTV, and the consciousness of the young, even the smart white males who had for so long been Browne's primary audience. Rock's mainstream, to which Browne belonged in the 1980s, had given way to the styles and ethos of grunge: Nirvana and Pearl Jam changed the musical landscape almost overnight. Lollapalooza and Furthur festivals replaced US and Live Aid festivals, and a generation of aging boomers were replaced by tattooed Gen Xers sporting Doc Martens and backward baseball caps.

I'm Alive blithely sidesteps all of that. Eschewing the rock bombast of the two previous albums, it embraces a warm, updated folk-rock sound that feels altogether Browne's own, acoustic, electric, and synthetic elements smoothly crystallized in Scott Thurston's calm, clean production. It's Browne's first record in a decade and a half where he seems comfortable in his own musical skin. It's also the record where he begins to assemble the group of players—bassist Kevin McCormick, drummer Mauricio Lewak, and guitarists Scott Thurston and Mark Goldenberg—who would record and tour with him for the next two decades.

Jackson dives right in on the opener, "I'm Alive." The title suggests that he can hardly believe he's emerged from a romantic maelstrom: "I'm going to have to block it out to survive," he sings at one point, "I thought that it would kill me," at another. It's set up as another SoCal road song: the protagonist is "rolling down this canyon drive" or "rolling down California 5," (the state's main north-south interstate) finally free of the torment of a failed love. He mulls over it all as he drives: the "lies" she told him, his own "insane" behavior, the "beautiful plans" he made while ignoring troubling warning signs in their relationship, the acknowledgment that now "those dreams are dead," all while marveling at "the pleasures we once tasted." Sensual pleasure, not incidentally, is a leitmotif on the record: sensuality as lure, trick, astonishment. The song features a firm, crisp attack: the drums smack and crack, acoustic and electric guitars are nicely interwoven, and the rhythm section re-creates the chugging cadence of an Eagles road trip. Jackson's vocals, alternately tender and bitter, bring out the nuances of the relationship's intricacies, and embodies the grief, relief, regret, and wonder that the protagonist feels now that it's all over. One of Browne's two dozen best songs, it serves as a kind of pull-no-punches opening statement.

"My Problem Is You," which follows, is one of Jackson's wiliest, most self-aware songs, full of an irony that pokes fun at his romantic and political obsessiveness. Working off a light and airy organ riff by Benmont Tench (sitting in from Tom Petty's band), and featuring a super low-register bass harmony vocal that bends the song toward the comical, Browne flips the seriousness of the title track so we can see the relationship's absurd side. Any sane person, the protagonist sings, knows that when a relationship begins to feel like a prison, you need to get out of it. But he admits he's not that guy: "To go on attempting to break into the prison / You've got to be me." He's fine with "this crooked world," he sings; he's got no problem "telling right from wrong." All that's fine: "My problem is *you*." The song's self-satire is a delight, but what makes it even better is that he places it side by side with convincingly earnest expressions of desire ("I need your wonder and I need your light"). And then he throws in one of the best quatrains he ever wrote. The second verse begins with the protagonist saying he wanted to "live in the realm of the senses" but knows that few people are genuinely prepared for doing so, because "for some kinds of pleasures there are no defenses / I know that now." Pleasure is something that he needs to defend himself against but can't; sensuality is something overwhelming, out of control, and incomprehensible. This is the album's strongest clue that the experience of extraordinary sensual pleasure characterized his years with Hannah, and perhaps plagued them. Despite all this, the song drifts off to a comic conclusion, the protagonist muttering about how the hole in the ozone layer doesn't bug him and neither do Madonna's exploits. Again, "my problem is you." Of course, by now the listener gets it: the singer ought to be singing, "My problem is me."

The songs that follow form a sort of trilogy, inscribing a rise-and-fall arc to that relationship. "Everywhere I Go" is one of Browne's proficient homages to reggae, McCormick and Lewak holding down a plausible riddim while Waddy Wachtel's guitar briskly chops away on the two and four. It's cheerful and self-deprecating, about a guy who can barely see what's in front of him because his lover seems to be everywhere. With Browne giving a light-hearted Caribbean lilt to the two spoken-word breaks, the song nicely conveys the loopy happiness of romantic beginnings. "I'll Do Anything," which follows, is another song of romantic fixation, but darkness and mystery now creep in, signaled by John Leventhal's eerie guitar line. "You hold a life there in your hands," the protagonist solemnly tells his lover, and his vulnerability only builds from there. "I'll do anything," he says, to get her to "see what I'm imagining," to "keep the light from vanishing." He'll even do the ridiculous—"fly this airplane upside down," "steal a tank," "rob a bank." Somehow the absurdity of his need doesn't, as in the previous two songs, seem funny or preposterous, but dire and increasingly obsessive. "Miles Away," the album's most guitar-driven and hardest-rocking song, tells us where that obsessiveness took the couple. It's Browne's latest entry in the we're-breaking-up-but-neither-of-us-can-leave-yet genre that he practically invented. The song's protagonist pleads with a lover who won't hear him; she's either "got this rage choking up [her] voice" or she's "staring at the far horizon . . . miles and miles away." Scott Thurston, the album's producer, supplies a wild caustic squall of a backing vocal (worthy of a career that included work with Iggy and the Stooges), repeating the title phrase, and Browne paints a picture of a relationship in utter disarray, complete with fights "when you're so mean and wild" and a sense of "innocence betrayed," the album's first reference to infidelity.

The rest of the album deals with the consequences, morning-after reevaluations, and "attempts to understand a thing so simple and so huge," as he put in another context in "Before the Deluge." The next three songs are decent midperiod Browne, agreeable-enough folk-rock that, however, relies too much on fussily crafted images and tasteful musical touches to fully convey the devastation of failed love evident in the album's best songs. "Too Many Angels" finds our protagonist alone at home, in the relationship's aftermath, among multiple artifacts of angels—tiny statues, bibelots, pictures—that stand in silent witness to the relationship's failure. The angels are obvious symbols of innocence lost, of love's possibilities forsaken, and can't carry the burden of desolation they're meant to. "Take This Rain" is better—the vocal melody is strong and memorable, and it addresses Jackson's reaction at discovering Hannah's infidelities—but it too gets mired in indirect and distancing metaphor. Jackson sings of two pairs of footprints in the sand, walking side by side, that gets invaded by a third pair—too obvious. The song is trying to get at the "madness" of the discovery that she was cheating and how it makes the protagonist go "crazier every day." But it settles for clever resolution—he suggests that the rain will wash away the remnants of all those footprints—and a forgiveness that doesn't feel adequately earned. "Two of Me, Two of You" is weak all around: the spare melody and arrangement wrap around a lyric dedicated to the banal insight that the lovers each had two sides to them, one true and loyal and loving, the other selfish and capable of betrayal. It too reaches for forgiveness but runs out of gas before the listener can feel it.

What those three songs try to do "Sky Blue and Black" accomplishes all at once, and gloriously. A postmortem of singular intensity, it looks back at the rubble of the love Browne and Hannah left behind with acute pain and regret but discovers in the process a persistent yearning that ultimately gives way to a reaffirmation of romantic love that's filled with awe and wonder. Singing over a simple piano riff and tender synthesizers, the protagonist—the defeated lover—finds himself on a beach, haunted by everything around him: the sounds of waves, the sight of circling seagulls, fragments of songs from nearby radios. The details come in a hurry, in a first verse so word-crammed that Jackson has to rush to get all the syllables in. All that detail reminds him of "the sound of the world where we played," of a sky blue with promise and beauty. But while the lovers were enjoying their halcyon days, "the heavens were rolling / Like a wheel on a track," ultimately turning their sky black. That image of the sky turning from blue to black, from day to night, from promise to disappointment, from birth to death and back again in an eternal circle, is a powerful and durable one that suggests an awe before time and creation itself. But that awe is intensified by the protagonist's promise to continue to love despite the dark nights, the black disappointments, the failures of love he's experienced. In the final stanza, he again catalogs the things that remind him of his lost love—for example, "you're the color of the sky / reflected in each store-front window pane"—and then sums it up with this: "You're the hidden cost and the thing that's lost / in everything I do." By song's end, he knows she's gone forever. To me, at this point the real-life lover he's lost has, as it were, dematerialized and become Love Itself, which he promises to pursue "in the sunlight and the shadows"—that is, under skies blue and black. In that sense, the song portrays Browne again as permanent holdout, eternally committed to romantic love despite its Janus face and manifest riskiness. Because, he understands, "that's the way love is." He sings that concluding line three times as if it stunned by the courage—foolhardiness?—it takes to pursue love this vulnerably. It's a song sung de profundis, seeking an all-embracing acceptance of things as they are. Albert Camus once wrote, "There is the will to live without rejecting anything of life, which is the virtue I honor most in the world."[8] "Sky Blue and Black" embodies that virtue in a ravishing six minutes of great popular art.

The album concludes, anticlimactically, with "All Good Things," which reiterates, without the passionate desperation, what "Sky Blue and Black" dramatizes: that "all good things have to come to an end." It appends to that clichéd sentiment the thought that those good things "come 'round again," but it pleads its case with a sort of distance and reserve that make it, after "Sky Blue and Black," an irrelevance. And as an album-ender, it comes off as self-conscious—the good thing coming to the end here is also, presumably, the album itself, which seems awkwardly self-referring.

I'm Alive satisfied critics and diehard fans, but those fans were dwindling: much of his 1970s audience had either abandoned him after his 1980s political records or grown up and, like most adults focused on family and career pursuit, had gotten out of the record-buying habit. The album topped out at number 40 on the Billboard charts, yielded no hit singles, and took a very long time to finally go gold. But no matter: it gave Browne back his muse and laid the groundwork for a millennial renaissance that he would ride through *Looking East* and *The Naked Ride Home.*

WATCHING THE WORLD WAKE UP FROM HISTORY

I'm Alive is so personal that you'd hardly guess it's a 1990s record: its inward gaze is as impervious to the social, political, and cultural world as Jackson's late 1980s albums are blind to the personal. *Looking East* restores the balance, letting the world back in without ignoring Browne's ongoing personal development. And there was a lot to let back in. Between 1989's *World in Motion* and the new album in 1996, the world had transformed in ways it hadn't since 1945. The forty-five-year Cold War ended with the breakup of the Soviet Union and the demise of communism in Eastern Europe. Historian Francis Fukuyama said we'd reached the "end of history" as we knew it, the end of a historical process that had now concluded in the triumph of liberal democracy. George Bush Sr. declared a "new world order" of American hegemony and sent a half million American soldiers to the Middle East to fight a war to prove it (and to keep oil supplies flowing). In Washington, top environmental scientists warned Congress that industrialization was on an unmistakable collision course with the climate. (Hardly anyone listened.) Meanwhile, a restless and fickle populace, mid-Right in disposition but unhappy with an economy that didn't pop and fizz with Reaganesque effervescence (and whose savings-and-loan industry had to be bailed out by the government to the tune of $200 billion) elected a Democrat to the presidency for only the second time in twenty-eight years. And something called the Web happened.

These years, spanning the Bush Sr. administration and Bill Clinton's first term, began hopefully. Mikhail Gorbachev, the Soviet leader, had in the mid-1980s introduced the policies of glasnost (openness/transparency) and perestroika (restructuring) that radically transformed Soviet society, shifting away from authoritarian rule toward ideas of freedom and self-determination both for Soviet citizens and those in Eastern European countries who had been under Moscow's thumb since the end of World War II. By the time Bush assumed office in 1989, there were genuinely substantive talks between the United States and the Soviets to reduce their nuclear arsenals and to loosen Cold War tensions. (An arms reduction agreement was signed in 1990, reducing nuclear stockpiles by more than 25 percent.) To many of us, the idea that the Cold War might end without a major hot war (or a nuclear conflict) seemed too good to be true. But that's what happened.

Poland, spurred by the Solidarity labor movement, threw off its Soviet shackles, held free parliamentary elections in 1989, and installed a new leader committed to democracy. A year later, on November 9, 1990, the Berlin Wall fell, starting a chain reaction in Eastern Europe that led to similarly peaceful democratic revolutions in Hungary, Czechoslovakia, and Bulgaria. (Romania's revolution was not peaceful: its dictator Nicolae Ceausescu and his wife were arrested, tried, and executed by firing squad on Christmas Day 1989. My father, Romanian-born and a fierce anti-communist, made this a big part of our holiday celebrations that year.) The

Soviet Union itself finally fell apart in late 1991. The end of communism and the wave of democracy sweeping through Europe promised enormous positive change: an end to the sword of Damocles hanging over the planet ever since the first atomic bomb was dropped on Hiroshima; the possibility of significant "peace dividends" that would allow nations to shift resources from military expenditures to education and social services for their people; the opportunity for expanded trade and cooperation between East and West that would benefit all classes.

That promise, alive in parts of Europe for many years afterward, didn't much take root in the United States. The Bush administration, looking to solidify its geopolitical primacy in the Western Hemisphere, invaded Panama in late 1989, deposing its dictator Manuel Noriega and installing a pro-American leader. After Iraq's invasion of Kuwait in August 1990, the United States and its coalition partners responded, in January 1991, with a massive invasion and a bombing campaign of "shock and awe" that defeated the Iraqis within weeks and left no doubt about American military supremacy in the world. A "no blood for oil" protest movement against the war petered out quickly once the war started, emblematic of an American Left that was in tatters in the post-Reagan years. For a time, Bush Sr.'s approval ratings skyrocketed; "the Vietnam syndrome," the country's reluctance to enter into military conflict overseas, was finally put to rest, replaced by an expansionist foreign policy eager to take advantage of the Soviet retreat from world affairs. No significant "peace dividend" materialized in the United States, and conservative sentiment for a time hardened.

But internecine battles among Republicans, Bush's reneging on his promise not to raise taxes, and a short recession in 1990 and 1991 dried up much of his support, clearing the way for "New Democrat" Bill Clinton to win the presidency in November 1992. Young and charismatic, a political centrist from Arkansas, a wily manipulator of public sentiment able to swat away countless rumors of womanizing, and a magnetic presence to young people (he donned shades and blew a jazzy saxophone on MTV, and he got R.E.M. to play at his inauguration party), Clinton dispelled the conservative portrait of Democrats as out-of-touch bleeding hearts catering to minorities and weak on defense. Though a social liberal, on matters economic he fully embraced neoliberal principles (deregulation of the finance industry, privatization of government services, free trade, unleashing the powers of the free market) and signed, with only token emendations, the North American Free Trade Agreement that his predecessors Reagan and Bush had negotiated with Mexico and Canada. His presidency made clear that the American middle had shifted, more or less permanently, to the right, and that even the Democratic party, since FDR the defenders of the downtrodden, had little use for the working class. The plight of working people was for a time hidden, however, as the broader economy boomed during the 1990s, thanks largely to the extraordinary innovations of the Information Age—seven-hundred-channel cable television, the rapid digitization of information, the relentless wiring of the economy, and the breathless expansion of the internet into business and in everyday life.

Plenty of the songs on *Looking East* attest that Jackson, however embroiled in his personal troubles, was paying careful attention to what was going on during these years. Like Mike Edwards, the singer of Jesus Jones's "Right Here, Right Now," who in the hit video watches in amazement as a TV screen shows the Berlin Wall falling and the Soviet empire crumbling, Browne, too, watched "as the world [woke] up from history," but he watched from his perch "at the edge of my country, my back to the sea, looking east." Being the holdout humanist he was, he wasn't jaundiced by the dread so pervasive among 1990s rockers (sometimes sincere, as in Nirvana or Radiohead; sometimes faked, as in Stone Temple Pilots or Bush); the brutalism, misogyny, and bling worship of so much East and West Coast hip-hop; or the slicker and slicker hedonism of pop. Having (re)discovered on *I'm Alive* that he needed to make music that was folk-based rock 'n' roll in collaboration with musicians he knew and trusted, Browne devoted himself, in *Looking East*, to a philosophically expansive but detailed examination of the America he knew best—with emphasis on Los Angeles—and taking care to anchor his observations in his own experience.

LOOKING EAST

Looking East is a band record—it's a pity that the CD package contains no pictures of his players; Browne would correct the oversight on future albums—and firmed up the group he had been gathering since before *I'm Alive*. The lineup now included Kevin McCormick on bass (who also coproduced), Maurice Lewak on drums, guitarists Mark Goldenberg and Scott Thurston (who coproduced), Jeffrey Young on keyboards, and Luis Conte on percussion. Other players dropped in for a session or two (David Lindley, Waddy Wachtel, Ry Cooder, Benmont Tench and Mike Campbell from Tom Petty's Heartbreakers, plus a bevy of background singers), but Browne maintained the same basic ensemble throughout an entire album for the first time since *Lawyers in Love*. More important was that Browne opened up the songwriting process. Eight of the ten tunes were cowritten by the band while in the studio: the rock steady reggae of "It Is One," the funk lite of "Culver Moon," and the celebratory salsa of "Niño" are all products of players whose musical reach significantly extend Jackson's own. Even the slinky blues of "Baby How Long," one of the two songs written by Browne alone, benefits from the pros he's assembled.

The album, then, is musically of a piece. Not that it's uniform in quality: "Alive in the World" is tepid (it's the other song Jackson wrote himself) with a vocal melody that's wan if achingly sincere. The protagonist "wants to live in the world, not inside my head," wants to feel all its "beauty and cruelty," but he worries he's so captive to his own self-doubts that he won't be able to break out of himself. The song invokes "the infinite power of change" but doesn't generate much power itself: it's hard to imagine the protagonist breaking through his self-imposed prison to be "alive in the world."

"It Is One," the album's closer, and "Some Bridges," the record's first single, are pleasantly professional, with hummable melodies and catchy arrangements. They're easy on the ears, especially Goldenberg's guitar on "It Is One," but their sweet cheeriness don't make up for the clichéd sentiments about the need for unity in a time of increased political fragmentation. "Culver Moon," a modified blues animated by a sharp, chugging guitar riff, is considerably better. It takes for its satirical subject the LA suburb of Culver City, which in the 1990s had to be one of the most nondescript cities in Southern California, a loose amalgam of housing tracts built in the 1940s, a movie studio, aviation factories, big box stores, mini-malls, and wide, heavily trafficked streets that made walking anywhere impractical. (I know: in the late 1980s, I was a UCLA grad student, and I lived under that Culver moon for a good stretch.) Jackson gets at its nowhere smogginess and meretricious connections to low-end Hollywood: he points out the Chippendales dance hall, and devotes a whole verse to Angelyne, an "actress" who never acted in anything but who was well known in Los Angeles because of the ubiquitous billboards featuring her impossibly enhanced body and surgically modified face. She looked down upon the city like the eyes of Dr. T. J. Eckleburg in *The Great Gatsby*, and Browne uses her similarly as a symbol of spiritual emptiness. Back then, Culver City was a characterless LA backwater, filled with the displaced ("everybody here's from someplace else") and people who couldn't afford housing in better parts of the city, but Browne, with his gently satirical treatment, defines it as shrewdly as Quentin Tarantino did LA's South Bay in *Pulp Fiction*.

The other song about Los Angeles is "Niño," an energetic salsa that takes place in a Hispanic neighborhood somewhere west of downtown, perhaps East Hollywood. Browne tells the story of a musician, based on the experiences of his percussionist Luis Conte, who came to LA to make a career in music but for a time was so down on his luck that his passion for playing the music of his Cuban homeland could only be satisfied by banging hubcaps with a stick on Sunset Boulevard or "keeping *tumbao* [rhythm] on the hood of some car." The song is infectious—Conte's dazzling percussion is all over it—and features a chorus sung in Spanish, with harmony vocals provided by Jorge Calderón, who previously had cowritten "Lawless Avenues" with Jackson. It's a song that celebrates the immigrant dream of America ("Niño, people will know you one day / Niño, they're going to call you El Rey" [the king]) in a way that he'll return to years later in "The Dreamer," but this is the best Latin-influenced song Browne had yet done.

The album's major songs are "Looking East," "The Barricades of Heaven," and "Information Wars," but before we turn to them, a word on "Baby How Long" and "I'm the Cat." Critics loved the latter for its pop melody—everybody compared it to "Somebody's Baby" and noted its clever buoyancy. As we've been saying all along, Jackson Browne is a melancholic artist, and whenever he's able to (convincingly) lift himself free of the sadness deep in his DNA, that's something to applaud. As for "Baby How Long," it's a traditional blues, dedicated to the oldest blues theme there is—my woman done me wrong. It's impossible not to pull Daryl Hannah back into the discussion here, but this song's different from "I'm Alive," "Take This Rain," or "Two of Me, Two of You," songs which reference her cheating on *I'm Alive*. Whereas the pain of being cuckolded is raw on the earlier album, on "Baby How Long" it feels distant, even studied: Jackson's precise vocal phrasing, the slow stinging guitar, the cheatin' heart clarity of the lyrics—all of it feels less like an exploration of the pain of infidelity than a solid exercise in blues form, suggesting that the suffering he endured has faded. Good for Jackson Browne, not as good for his music.

I discussed "The Barricades of Heaven" at length in chapter 2. As clear-sighted and openhearted a song that Jackson has ever written, it chronicles the birth of his own idealism, rooted in a Keatsian and Wordsworthian Romanticism, locating it first in the love of his mother and then in the excitement of his adolescent obsession with music, which gave him a voice, an orientation (a belief in love, "hope that never ends"), and a future. Given a sturdy, vibrant musical setting that perfectly suits its meditation on a past that's unrecoverable except through art, and then only as art, "Barricades" is one of the five or six songs that best defines Jackson Browne as man and artist. When it first came out in 1996, I listened to it with special interest. The year before, I myself had moved to Orange County—to take a job as an English professor at Cal State Fullerton, located no more than a mile or two from the house where Browne spent his teen years, and so Jackson's old stomping grounds were now pretty much my own. I grew to know OC's conservatism very well indeed and had no trouble understanding Browne's motivation to leave or in writing about it as he did. It took me a lot longer to break the barricades than it took Jackson—I didn't move back to LA until my sons finished school and went off to college—but the song often sounded in my head as I endured the county's sterile suburban smugness and rampant consumerism.

The title track and "Information Wars" provide Browne's take on the state of the union circa 1996. The latter is one of Browne's most ambitious compositions, taking up the theme of the saturation of American life by advertising, cable news and "infotainment," and the political and social distortions they create. Building off multiple guitars phased to create an aural atmosphere of electronic media overload, Jackson puts together a lyric whose first eight lines are entirely borrowed from commercial slogans: "Give us twenty minutes and we'll give you the world" was taken from an ad for KNX news radio (an LA station); "we bring good things to life" from a General Electric commercial; "the heartbeat of America" (a Ford commercial); "your true voice" (AT&T), and so on—all of it suggesting that mass media batters viewers into believing that it's not only an unbiased, transparent window into the world ("your true voice") but that the world it displays is a beneficent conveyor of solid American values. These lines are followed by Jackson's commentary: that the mass entertainment matrix of mid-1990s America gives us "the world every night as a TV show." It gives us the "latest war as a pay-per-view," an allusion to how the Iraq war of 1991 was the first war that Americans watched live on their TV screens, and whose images of bombing campaigns over Baghdad were ruthlessly controlled by the military so that only a sanitized American perspective was allowed on air. And in the line "the more you watch, the less you do," Browne suggested that all that information and media imagery, far from bringing the world closer to us, actually made us existentially and politically passive and thus more susceptible to political demagoguery and media manipulation.

Now, to be sure, by 1996 these ideas were common coin among intellectuals and the media savvy. Don DeLillo's great novel *White Noise* (1985) dramatized them with great satirical shrewdness and philosophical power and, as a bestseller, circulated them to a large readership. Douglas Coupland's novel *Generation X* (1991) watered them down but made the ideas available for a new generation raised on 24/7 TV, mall culture, designer drugs, and personal computers. As did Hollywood, in trailblazing features like *Blue Velvet* (1986), *sex, lives, and videotape* (1989), and *Pulp Fiction* (1994). Pop music got into the act by the 1990s, too. U2's massively successful Zoo TV tour, which ran from 1992 through 1993, was a spectacular demonstration of the ubiquity, uncanny ecstasies, and confusions of a life lived through the lens of mass media. And Radiohead's brilliant *OK Computer* (1997) (and early videos like the one for "Fake Plastic Trees") put a capstone to pop music's ability to embody the dystopian tendencies of the new media environment.

Given all that postmodern discourse about mass media, Browne's "Information Wars" felt to many both tame and belated. It seemed so to me at the time: I was teaching many of the works mentioned above to my students, and Jackson's contribution to the discussion seemed simplistic, even moralizing. It doesn't seem like that to me anymore. What typifies most postmodern works on mass media is the insistence that it is all-pervasive, that as DeLillo put in *White Noise*, it is impossible "to get outside the aura" of advertising, entertainment, consumerism, and the like.[9] It's the idea that there is no privileged vantage point outside the media matrix from which we can critique it; that is, we're trapped in it so we better get used to it. There's even the prevalent notion, often proffered in a way that's a little proud of its own hipness, that we secretly, ironically, self-consciously love our existential enmeshment in mass media, that we're seduced by its blandishments and pleasures, and that we no longer have the will—or the ability, even the need—to resist them.

This is exactly where Browne rejects the postmodern position. Jackson, the unreconstructed humanist, schooled in an Old Left analysis that the power of capitalist propaganda can and must be resisted by employing rational thought and collective will, applies the same stance to the power of mass media. We *can* and *must* resist its seductions; we can break its ubiquitous influence by refusing to participate in it, by saying no to it. In fellow humanist Bruce Springsteen's "57 Channels (And Nothin' On)" (from 1992's *Human Touch* album), the protagonist is inundated by so much TV choice—bad, boring choices—that, like Elvis, he takes a .44 magnum, points it at the TV, and "let[s] her blast." Browne isn't so dramatic, but his message is the same: "The generations [will] go . . . into the failing light" if they don't stand up to media's soul-sucking power. Given the exponential increase in media saturation in American life—our addiction to "screens"—in the last three decades, and the scientific evidence piling up that those TV, video games, and social media are causing dangerous levels of anxiety, depression, and social isolation, particularly among young people, it's no surprise to find that many experts are asking us to severely limit exposure to them if not to just say no to the domination of screens in the culture.[10] In the 2020s, with the rise of social media and Trump-era disinformation, Browne's old-school resistance has renewed significance and utility.

Finally, the title track. Large-souled, as poetic as anything he's ever written, uniting personal, political, and spiritual themes in a way that his most demanding fans have always hoped he would, and backing up its desperate romantic hopes with a rock 'n' roll of genuine kinetic power, "Looking East" is one of Browne's most indispensable works, displaying his talent in full flower. Beginning with layered electric guitars chugging chords and melodic fills over a steady drumbeat and then gathering into a phalanx of rousing power chords during the choruses, the song sonically reinforces the "hunger" and "power" that are at the song's lyrical core. The protagonist places himself on the California shore, in the Pacific itself, his back to the setting sun and his face "looking east," toward "my country." (The cover photograph of Browne rehearses this image, only the partially submerged Browne is looking not at "my country" but, intimately, at the viewer—his countryman.) His pithy diagnosis: "These times are famine for the soul while for the senses it's a feast." The "feast" part of it is easy to see: in the mid-1990s, large parts of the economy were booming (the coasts, the finance and tech sectors) leading to an ever-enveloping materialism, and the country seemed to skim from one media obsession to another—the OJ Simpson trial, the *Titanic* movie, runs on Beanie Babies or the latest hi-tech gadget, Michael Jackson's troubles—in an endless succession that seemed to wipe out the memory of one fixation as soon as the next one took over. To elucidate the "famine" requires the rest of the song. It's about "the god-sized hunger" that no movie, bank balance, media event, or trinket can possibly address. It's a hunger that's everywhere—"in the mansion . . . and the rented room." It's on television and in the newspapers, it's in the hearts of the "bride and groom." It rumbles "underneath the laughing and the rage . . . underneath the questions of the age." That unsatisfied hunger, which comes about because we're not attending to our real existential needs, has led to a frightening "absence of light / and the deepening night," and so the protagonist poses these questions to himself:

> How long have I left my mind to the powers that be?
> How long will it take to find the higher power moving in me?

The fact that he's asking *himself* these questions ensures the song won't stumble into self-righteousness. Browne uses the word "power" in two different ways. In the first line it's political and asks why the protagonist has allowed his own consciousness to be usurped by the prevailing political institutions and media. In the second line it's spiritual. The higher power Browne invokes here is ecumenical, a tinge Buddhist (thus "Eastern," which gives us another way to think of the title), though Browne's own Romantic pedigree links it back to Wordsworthian notions of a "spirit and a power" he explored previously in "For a Dancer" (see chapter 3); in the Neruda poem, "Brown and Agile Child," quoted on the back cover of *The Pretender*; and in "The Fuse" (see chapter 4). That higher power is literally everywhere, and in an incantation that slowly builds in tension till it reaches an inspired climax, the protagonist tells us where that power can be found: in the tininess of the insect; in the grand sweep of wheat fields (an image he borrows directly from Neruda); in seas, stones, snows, silences, sunrises, and songs sung alone; in the "sound of a lover's name" and "in a prayer released." So, just as the hunger is everywhere, so are the places where that hunger can be satisfied. Only we have to be attuned to the power inherent in all these things before they can help us with the hunger. The music, which aims at once for grandeur and humility, is designed to nudge the listener to that attunement and to me is wildly successful. "Looking East" is one of Browne's great midcareer achievements.

Though neither *I'm Alive* nor *Looking East* were commercial hits—neither broke into the Top 30, though *I'm Alive* eventually went gold—they contained the best music he'd made since the mid-1970s and, particularly on the latter album, showed the ability to put together a record that put side by side some of his best political and personal music. These albums added at least four songs to his permanent concert repertoire—"I'm Alive," "Sky Blue and Black," "Looking East," "The Barricades of Heaven"—and made it inevitable that he would ultimately be admitted into the Rock & Roll Hall of Fame (he would be, in 2004). And the momentum he built during those years carried over to *The Naked Ride Home*, his first album of the new millennium.

8

MILLENNIAL HIGHS, MILLENNIAL LOWS

There's a notable contingent of nostalgists out there who look back at the late 1990s with the kind of indulgent affection we reserve for candies we loved as children, as if years were Airheads or Nerds. But there's something to it, a perceived innocence about the times before the Towers fell, before the country jumped into an endless war on terror, when the economy seemed to bestow its bounty far and wide, when pop culture painted just about everything—even a presidential impeachment—with the DayGlo colors of know-it-all irony, and every new dot-com IPO heralded utopian promise.

Jackson Browne wasn't one of those people. Since his youth he'd distrusted the blandishments of capitalism and was studiously aware, as the millennium beckoned, of the panic beneath the partying. As we've chronicled here, that distrust made his politics lean left from the beginning. As he matured, his progressivism cohered and solidified. By the 1990s, in fact, his thoughts on America past and present came right out of Howard Zinn's *A People's History of the United States*; his ideas on military and foreign policy were informed by Noam Chomsky; and his take on daily events seemed guided by Amy Goodman, the longtime news director of the lone-wolf progressive radio network Pacifica. (A bumper sticker for its LA affiliate, KPFK, is plastered on Jackson's guitar case in the lyric booklet to *Time the Conqueror*.)

Now it's true that from 1995 till early 2000, the American economy as a whole seemed to skyrocket. During that five-year period, all the major economic indices were up: gross domestic product climbed by an average of 4 percent a year; the Dow Jones Industrial average doubled; the NASDAQ, reflecting the "irrational exuberance" of the dot-com bubble, *tripled*; the unemployment rate shrunk to below 4 percent; inflation held around 3 percent. For the first time in thirty years, the US government did what for a long time seemed unimaginable: it balanced the federal budget, and for three years (1998–2001) actually coughed up surpluses. A lot of people had a lot of money and were spending it. Further, during the eight years of the Clinton administration, the United States managed to avoid major military confrontations around the world, giving rise to thinking that the New World Order—a triumphant capitalist system leavened by progressive social ideals—had indeed arrived that would allow governments to devote more of their largesse to ploughshares rather than swords. The internet was here, touting itself as "free" and not yet colonized by conscienceless money-grubbers. The Clinton administration signed on to the Kyoto Protocols, the first major international agreement to limit greenhouse gases and address global warming. (The US Congress failed to ratify the agreement, however, so the United States was never a formal party to the agreement. Nevertheless, for the rest of the world, Kyoto was an important global step in addressing climate change.) Politics was getting messier—Speaker of the House Newt Gingrich had assembled a coalition that was intent not just on foiling Clinton's more progressive agenda items but also destroying the Clintons (cf. Whitewater, the Monica Lewinsky scandal)—but the public seemed to see through it: by the time Clinton was impeached for lying before a Congressional panel, his favorability ratings were the highest of his presidency.

Progressives like Browne could acknowledge the good news but still see how it masked the structural changes neoliberalism had introduced and that had been accelerating since the passage of the North American Free Trade Agreement in 1993. Statistics and headlines hid deeper troubles, troubles that are behind the pessimistic assessments in "Casino Nation," *Naked*'s wide-ranging take on the years leading up to the millennium. The industrial Midwest continued to rust: solid union jobs in steel and auto production were lost to Mexico and Southeast Asia, and the men and women who used to work the assembly lines were now found toiling, at decreased wages and benefits, as cashiers or customer service reps at Target or Home Depot. Meanwhile, the good new jobs that *were* cropping up were in the burgeoning sectors of finance or information technology, jobs that factory workers often weren't qualified for and that were being filled by college-educated urbanites hip to the New Economy. As income and wealth inequality widened, a new social dichotomy evolved, one class consisting of educated urban professionals living either on the coasts or in select urban enclaves—Pretenders and Lawyers in Love with money enough to buy houses, send their kids to college, and retire in style. The other consisted of a downwardly mobile class of citizens living in nondescript exurbs, or else small towns and rural areas that seemed futureless, with local investment shrinking, property values falling, young people leaving, and those remaining hoping for a lottery win—or prescriptions for painkillers and antidepressants—to get them through their days. For those in urban centers, it was even worse, with gang violence at record highs and three-strike laws being passed, which created the largest population of incarcerated people—mostly people of color—on planet Earth. Liberals of the time made the grave mistake of ignoring this distressed and disillusioned underclass; Clinton addressed almost all of his rhetoric to the middle class—the ones "who work hard and play by the rules." (It's notable that the 1996 election had the lowest voter turnout since 1924, a good indicator of working-class disaffection.) In response, a nationalist, evangelistic populism arose among the forgotten class, whose heroes were reactionary firebrand Pat Buchanan and folksy billionaire Ross Perot, men who scapegoated immigrants and "elites" and encouraged the seething resentments festering among those whose fortunes were plummeting. A number of tragic events—the Oklahoma City terrorist bombing in 1995, the Ruby Ridge disaster of 1996, and the Columbine school shooting in 1999—symbolized a new kind of American despair, steeped in media addiction and paranoid extremism and inexpressible except in acts of wildly reckless and random violence.

American pop culture in the 1990s, designed (except in rare cases) to distract rather than express any of this, and now emboldened by a global reach that massively lifted profits, did what it was good at doing: it palliated the yuppies with *Friends* and the working classes with *Married with Children*, it fed everyone *Titanic* and *Star Wars* sequels, and it filled our Walmarts and Targets with warehouses full of cheap Chinese imports. In music, the reign of grunge that briefly gave voice to the anxieties of 1990s life gave way to the Spice Girls, NSYNC, and the seductive fantasies of gangsta rap. Alternative and college rock flourished among niche audiences, and the New York scene—the one that gave us the Strokes, Interpol, the Yeah Yeah Yeahs, and ultimately The National—briefly gave the impression of a rock renaissance around the turn of the century, but for the most part, pop culture churned out precisely the feel-good stuff that pumped enough endorphins for us to consume all the new product.

Browne's response to all this? He lent his name, voice, and wallet to charities on the ground that were working to hold back the tides of reactionary change—human rights groups; environmental organizations promoting solar energy, opposing nuclear energy, or educating people about plastics in the oceans; charities funding community health centers, struggling schools, arts education groups, or groups opposing American intervention in Central America; groups supporting Native American tribes; musician friends in need; even a presidential politician or two (he supported Ralph Nader in 2000 and John Edwards in 2004). There were a number of years in the late 1990s and early 2000s when I wondered how Browne made a living. Every time I opened the *LA Times*, I'd see another charity concert he was giving.

He was, of course, doing well enough—he bought a chunk of land in the Holliston Ranch area of Santa Barbara, which he kept in as natural a state as he could, running it entirely on renewable energy sources.[1] He maintained a house in foresty Aptos (inland from Santa Cruz, California) and bought an apartment in Barcelona to indulge his love of all things Spanish (seeking "a world where I hear angels play" in "The Night Inside Me," Jackson mutters, "Maybe I should go back to Spain"). For taking the trouble, he was honored with the John Steinbeck Award in February 2002, an award given to artists like Arthur Miller and Bruce Springsteen before him, which is bestowed upon "writers, artists, thinkers, and activists whose work captures Steinbeck's empathy, commitment to democratic values, and belief in the dignity of people who by circumstance are pushed to the fringes."[2] The award description could hardly have fit Browne any better. They may as well have called it the Holdout Award.

During these years he toured, both with a band—for the *Looking East* tour—and on multiple solo acoustic jaunts in the early 2000s. He also recorded tributes and duets with other musicians, among them a moving version of Lowell George's "I've Been the One" for the George tribute album *Rock 'n' Roll Doctor* (1997); a reggae-fied duet, with Bonnie Raitt, of the Weavers' ditty "Kisses Sweeter than Wine" (1998), for which they received a Grammy nomination; and his duet with Joan Osborne performing Dylan's "My Back Pages" (on the soundtrack to the film *Steal This Movie* [2006]). (And since we're on the subject, Browne rewrote "Rosie" as "Marjorie" as a comic duet with *The Simpsons*' Homer [Dan Castellaneta] when he appeared on the show in 2003.) And, of course, he continued to write new songs, though his production had by now slowed to a trickle.

Electra Entertainment, Jackson's label, with David Geffen still at the helm (until 1997, when he sold it to MCA), was at the white-hot center of the culture industry and so was eager to cash in on the increased visibility and artistic credibility that had accrued to Jackson after the releases of *I'm Alive* and *Looking East*. In 1997, *The Next Voice You Hear: The Best of Jackson Browne*, was released. By any measure, the collection's a disappointment. Trying to represent an album-oriented artist like Browne by cherry-picking thirteen standout cuts from his ten albums is an exercise in futility—actually, of frank profiteering. Only two albums, *Late for the Sky* and *Lives in the Balance*, are represented by more than one song, and the CD had to make room for "Somebody's Baby," Browne's last hit single and, to hear Browne discuss or occasionally play it in concert, something of an embarrassment to him.

Then there's the matter of the two previously unreleased tracks, neither of which belongs on a best-of. "The Next Voice You Hear," a bluesy homage to self-reliance in the face of relentless social pressure—Jackson says it was inspired by the film *High Noon*—isn't bad, but it's too sketchy lyrically to drive home its point about sticking stubbornly to one's inner convictions.[3] As for "The Rebel Jesus," it's one of the more misbegotten tracks Jackson has recorded. Ostensibly a Christmas song, it begins benignly enough, with a verse evoking "streets . . . filled with laughter and light" and families "gathering around their hearths and tables" to celebrate the holidays. But in the middle verses, Browne unloads his frustration about the hypocrisy of Christians who "guard their fine possessions," turn "the nature that I worship in / From a temple to a robber's den," and stoop "once a year when Christmas comes . . . [to] . . . perhaps give a little to the poor." The condemnations don't let up: if anyone (like a progressive) "should interfere / in the business of why they're poor," deigning to point out the structural factors keeping the poor where they are, you can be sure that they'll "get the same as the rebel Jesus." Was he really comparing the struggle of progressives with Jesus's crucifixion? Browne has said that he was trying to write "about the effect of Christianity" on the Mayan people—he had a Mayan friend who had encouraged him to write the song. "Rebel," Browne said, "turns into a statement of allegiance to Christ but not to Christianity." Genuine Christianity, he suggested, resides in Jesus's rebellion against hypocrites, materialists, and those who disregard God's command that we be good stewards of the earth.[4] Which is fine—no argument here. But the moral grandstanding is distasteful, not to mention formally inappropriate in a Christmas song. Jackson seems to recognize this in the last verse, when he sings, "Pardon me if I have seemed / To take the tone of judgment," and signs off by saying, "I bid you pleasure and I bid you cheer," but by now the song's lost any hint of goodwill, and his backtracking comes off as disingenuous. One of the greater missteps in the Browne catalog.

The Next Voice You Hear got lost in the marketplace, peaking at number 47 on the charts, but over the years, it has sold steadily and was certified platinum in 2021. By then, however, the far superior two-CD package, *The Very Best of Jackson Browne* (2004), whose thirty-two tracks were handpicked by Browne himself, had long superseded it. *The Very Best* has never achieved more than gold status, but it's the place for Browne neophytes to start.

THE NAKED RIDE HOME

The cascade of songwriting about Daryl Hannah that led to *I'm Alive* had exhausted, at least for the rest of the 1990s, Jackson's need to write relationship songs, allowing him to branch out, in *East,* into fruitful meditations that took in his early autobiography, as well as a renewed attention to social and philosophical issues. But *The Naked Ride Home* (2002), Jackson's first album in six years, finds him returning to the relationship theme with renewed ardor, not to mention a humility and mature insight that honor the pains and failures of his romantic history.

The spine of *Naked* is its four songs about love—the opening title track, two songs from the middle of the album ("For Taking the Trouble" and "Never Stop"), and the concluding song, "My Stunning Mystery Companion." A clear narrative runs through them, one where the protagonist moves, gradually, away from a love that's defined by beauty, glamour, and sensual excitement (but also lying and self-deception) toward one that's about honesty, sympathy, and a couple's mutual effort to create "a world love wants to see." Biographically, this narrative tracks with Browne breaking up with Daryl Hannah in 1992 and getting together with Dianna Cohen, an artist and environmental activist with whom Browne began a relationship that same year and who has been his "compass" and "companion" ever since (as of this writing). On the rest of the album, Jackson attends to that world loves wants to see in songs like "Casino Nation" and "Don't You Want to Be There," investigates his own creative processes in "The Night inside Me" and "About My Imagination," and even throws in an homage to spaghetti Western filmmaker Sergio Leone. It's a wide-ranging album that sustains the artistic resurgence that began in the 1990s: the trilogy of *I'm Alive, Looking East,* and *The Naked Ride Home,* in fact, boasts the strongest artistic run Browne had since the midseventies.

We can begin with that spine of love songs. "The Naked Ride Home," a sturdily anchored and melodic slice of folk-rock shimmering with layers of echoing guitar, begins like this:

> Just take off your clothes and I'll drive you home, I said
> Knowing she could never pass on a dare.

Well, this is new, no? Not only is Browne telling a story (his lyrics tend not to be narratives) but the story is blunt—and serious—about sex ("Redneck Friend" and "Rosie," among others, are essentially jokes). In fact, "Naked" is one of Jackson's most incisive songs about the delusional power of beauty and the sensual life. The protagonist's demand that his lover strip in the car isn't an opening move in a playful seduction but the act of a desperate man "too far gone to care," as if sex is the last card in his hand that might save their relationship. Perhaps unaware of this, she obeys, "with a trace of a smile and a defiant look in her eye." When she has undressed, "a vision of paradise swung into view." They are driving at night on an LA freeway, and so the scenario is sexy and glamorous, but the protagonist knows it's all deception: "Her beauty [was] a sight so misleading." He tries to touch her but she demurs, choosing instead to "[hurl] through the dark in a world of her own." Her rejection makes him realize that her heart—his, too—"was beating alone / on the naked ride home." The nakedness isn't just literal: his request that she strip and the misleading sight of her beauty strip them both of their illusions about each other. When they arrive "home"—only at the end of the song do we realize the couple actually live together—it dawns on him that the beauty and sensuality that have held them together are fictions, which will eventually "force [him] to decide" to end the relationship. The song is concise, carefully detailed, morally pointed.

"For Taking the Trouble," takes up the protagonist's life after that relationship has failed, when he is "working through / the rubble of a shattered mind." The song's point of view isn't clear—it could be a friend talking to the protagonist or the protagonist talking to himself—but we get the gist. The previous relationship trapped him and made him into a person he didn't want to be. Now, going forward, he asks himself, what kind of woman do I really want: "That girl who catches every eye / or the one you can set your compass by?" Having had enough of blinding beauty and its discontents, he chooses the latter. The decision indicates a fork in the road for the Browne protagonist. For Browne the man too. Until then, his longest, most intense relationships had been with paragons of beauty—dazzling models or actresses—but they'd also been his most destructive, one ending in suicide, another in a tabloid disaster. Now change has come.

"Never Stop" is directly addressed to the woman he found whom he can "set his compass by"—and it would be fair to call her Dianna Cohen. (In the acknowledgments sections to *Looking East* and *The Naked Ride Home*, she is thanked first, even before his two sons.) As sincere and direct a love song as Browne had written in decades, and featuring Mark Goldenberg's gleaming, echoing electric guitar, it's a song of gratitude for a woman who "had my back" when "we came through some hard places," and it's a promise to try to return the favor. This relationship is defined less by romantic passion than by common goals—"I got some things that I want to do / And I want to do them with you"—which presumably have to do with his and Cohen's mutual passion for art and environmental activism. (Cohen is a visual artist and cofounder of the Plastic Pollution Coalition, and she conducted a TED talk that helped popularize the issue.[5]) Crucially, he links the personal love they share with a larger, world-encompassing love: "Never stop coming up on the world love wants to see," he sings. It's a slightly odd verbal construction: What does "the world love wants to see" actually look like? What does love want to see? For Browne, it's the world that he's been holding out for from the beginning, an amalgam of the idealization of love as cosmic principle that he picked up from the 1960s counterculture, and of Martin Luther King's political passion rooted in Christian love. To quote again from King's 1967 speech, "Where Do We Go From Here?": "Power at its best, power at its best is love, implementing the demands of justice, and justice at its best is love correcting everything that stands against love." Love wants to see justice, and justice is nothing but the loving soul's desire writ large upon society.

"My Stunning Mystery Companion," which concludes the album, shows us how far Jackson's come from the romantic disillusionment of "The Naked Ride Home." It's another song of gratitude for Cohen, sung directly to her, but this one's more melodically robust, with a lyric that's sweetly self-satirizing and carried by a casually intimate vocal. The song begins essentially where "The Naked Ride Home" left off, with "all my expectations long abandoned" and the detritus of a life lived among boxes "where my past lives have been stowed." But then *she* shows up, stunningly, mysteriously, patiently, willing to help him through his "crash landing" and willing to "put a little more work in on me." The song's charm comes from the protagonist acknowledging what a mess he is—but it wouldn't work if his gratitude wasn't credible and if he didn't acknowledge *her* needs in this relationship, which he does. No Jackson Browne album concludes with a more positive song, and it's hard not to feel good about the man who sings it.

The sense of security that the new love in his life gives the protagonist informs the rest of the album, especially its two most world-facing songs, "Casino Nation" and "Don't You Want To Be There." Actually, "Casino Nation" is a bracing description of a world love *doesn't* want to see—a harsh assessment of the United States as "a weapons-producing nation under Jesus / in the fabled crucible of the free world," nailing some of the country's contradictions and hypocrisies in the song's opening lines. The song is replete with allusions to the desperate dreams of the underclass for some kind of media fame (recall how popular *The Jerry Springer Show* was during these years) or winning the lottery, to 1990s carceral policy that created a "permanent criminal class," and to George W. Bush as a "cowboy mogul" fooling his own supporters into defying their own economic interests. But it eventually homes in on the entertainment and weapons industries—the United States's biggest economic exports in the 1990s—as the forces that dictate America's future direction; they are the "hammer that shapes the hand." It's a striking metaphor. We may think of these industries as tools—hammers—that we control in order to create economic prosperity, but they in fact control us: they have powerful, impersonal agendas of their own that shape our economy by dictating our priorities. What Browne was offering here was a deft structural critique of the economy—something that was rare in millennial-era pop music, unless it came in the form of Rage Against the Machine's frenzied indignation or Radiohead's postmodern slipperiness. Browne's doesn't ride atop a storm of revolutionary anger or angsty pessimism; his rhetoric is reasoned and analytical, more direct than—if not as aesthetically powerful as—say, "Bulls on Parade" or *OK Computer.*

(By the way, absent from the song, or from the rest of the album, is any mention of 9/11. *The Naked Ride Home*'s recording was completed in early 2002, just months after the attack, and Browne, given his slow songwriting methods, probably wasn't ready to address the attack. Others were and did so soon after it happened: Alan Jackson's "Where Were You [When The World Stopped Turning]?" debuted live on television only weeks after the towers' collapse; Don DeLillo's great essay, "In The Ruins of the Future" appeared in *Harper's* magazine in December 2001; and Bruce Springsteen jumped on the theme, releasing an entire album about 9/11, *The Rising*, in July 2002.[6] Browne waited till his next album to address some of 9/11's effects, in "The Drums of War.")

If "Casino Nation" is swamped in gloom, "Don't You Want to Be There" is its antidote. If there's any song that suggests *how* we "come up on a world love wants to see," it's this one. Musically spacious and airy, rooted in a ringing electric piano and overlaid with quietly rising guitar lines and a feathery synthesizer, the protagonist imagines an idealized place—a "there"—where strength and love triumph over fear and where, crucially, forgiveness and self-acceptance reign. This "there" is that proverbial place "where the trumpets blow," trumpets that blow for the hungry and the downtrodden, for "those choking in anger" and those "driven insane." It's a place where love can act on those who need it most. It's genuinely uplifting music, and together with Jackson's aching voice, it succeeds in actually creating that "there" aurally. There's a patient layering of sound—including a bass line lifted, perhaps subconsciously, from the Breeders hit, "Cannonball"—that integrates beautifully with the song's hopeful lyric.

Not every tune on *Naked* works. "Walking Town," Browne's latest "walking" song about a guy walking around and picking up a sense of his surroundings (cf. the Nina Tapes' "Walking," "Walking Slow," "Boulevard"), adds little to the theme. "Sergio Leone," Jackson's tribute to the Italian film director of spaghetti Westerns, is a curiosity. Part biographical sketch, part film criticism, the song tries to suggest Browne's fascination with the man, and there are clues as to why he's fascinated: Browne shares some of Leone's thematic concerns, certainly "the darkness and the anguish," and they share an obsession with the enigmas of American violence. But at eight minutes, the song drags, and the question nags: Why Leone? Why not, say, Fellini, whose *8½* Jackson has called his favorite film?[7]

Aside from its four songs about love, the album's two strongest songs—"The Night inside Me" and "About My Imagination"—are autobiographical, "looking back" songs in the tradition of "Farther On" or "The Barricades of Heaven." "The Night inside Me" also fits Browne's tradition of "night" songs ("Late for the Sky," "Tender Is the Night," "Enough of the Night," "The Arms of Night," etc.) which portray the night as a time when veils of darkness make it possible for Browne's protagonist to explore himself in a way that daytime doesn't. Propelled by the best rock arrangement on the album—Mark Goldenberg's guitar fills are a highlight—the song presents a guy who remembers a boyhood filled with doubt, sorrow, and inexpressible confusion but at the same time recalls a saving grace amid all of it. Lying under the stars, he remembers that it was the night that could "set me free." During the day, he was bound by "the obligation, the burden and the light of day," but night "lifted the dread away." Now, looking back, he realizes that this night "full of promise and uncertainty" has always been inside him—it was, and remains now, the way to "navigate the inner reaches of my disarray"—maybe Browne's most poetic description of what self-exploration entails. The night, dark and mysterious, is what gives his imagination free rein, and the thing that's allowed him to become the artist that he is.

"About My Imagination," the album's most passionately sung and played song, develops this theme. Again looking back to his formative teen years when "the world was new" and love seemed easy, he sees that it was his imagination that helped him survive his own ignorance, that helped him develop those values of personal love and political compassion that made him the holdout he is. But he realizes that now is a time for transformation: "With so much changing, and changing for the worse," his youthful imagination, passionate but ego-driven, won't do. He needs to rededicate himself, from a position of experience, to "elevation" and "affirmation." The last two minutes of this six-minute song build on a series of call-and-response "-tion" rhymes between Jackson and drummer Mauricio Lewak, alludes to lyrics from "My Generation," "Good Vibrations," "People Get Ready," and "Dancing in the Street," and crescendos into a thrilling celebration of Jackson Browne's liberated imagination as well as rock's own history. Kevin McCormick's guitar rocks harder than anything in Browne's catalog and gives us a sense of what Browne's band was capable of in concert. "About My Imagination" is one of Jackson's best unheralded songs.

Browne credits his band as cowriters on six of the album's ten songs. As on *Looking East*, he wasn't bringing completed songs into the studio but allowed the band members to bring their talents to his lyrics and skeletal musical ideas. On "About My Imagination," the collaboration pays off in passionate ensemble playing and a great arrangement. For the most part, however, *The Naked Ride Home*'s songs are bloated in their arrangements, their momentum often blunted by longish passages of logy solo playing. Browne's instincts, more and more, were to share the writing responsibilities—you can tell that he's fired by ensemble creation—but it doesn't always come off on record. This will be a bigger problem on *Time the Conqueror*, a record that will be problematic in other ways, too.

BROWNE COMES ALIVE

The Naked Ride Home was Jackson's last studio release on Electra. When his contract with the company ended, Browne, who had ceased to be a profit machine years ago, cast about for another label before deciding to form his own—Inside Recordings—which would from then on record and distribute his work. This arrangement gave Browne complete control of his output, which he took advantage of by releasing a slew of live albums: *Jackson Browne Solo Acoustic, Vol. 1* (2005), *Jackson Browne Solo Acoustic, Vol. 2* (2008), and *Love Is Strange: En Vivo con Tino*, his reunion with David Lindley (2010). The solo acoustic records are intimate affairs, with Browne leavening the somberness of the songs by introducing them with charmingly wry anecdotes (see, for example, the comedian-grade intro to "Fountain of Sorrow" on *Vol. 1*). Recording both in the United States and Europe, Jackson deftly handles crowds that he knows are his, projecting an easy humor, political commitment, and trustworthy warmth. Without a backing band, Jackson has to rely on nothing but his voice and either guitar or piano. His piano playing is rudimentary, but his guitar is nimble and precise. His audiences are as quietly attentive as a classical music audience during the songs, though they whoop it up during Jackson's funny intros. The overall atmosphere of these albums hearkens back to the intensely personal sound of his early 1970s LPs and no doubt served to restore the bond Jackson had with his audience back in those days.

Love Is Strange: En Vivo con Tino is something else again. It was recorded in 2006 in a series of dates in Spain, where Browne over the years has maintained an enthusiastic audience. Jackson brings together his sidekick/musical muse David Lindley (on multiple guitars and fiddle) as well as a number of Spanish friends/musicians, including the Latin percussion master Tino de Geraldo. The result is a delighted Jackson heading up a high-energy show featuring all sorts of surprises: a three-song interlude of Lindley songs (including his two solo hits, "Mercury Blues" and "El Rayo X," and Jackson's all-in attempt at a real blues number, "Sit Down Servant"); Lindley's rockin' fiddle on "Take It Easy"; Kiko Veneno's Spanish translation of "Take It Easy" called "Tu Tranquillo"; Luz Casal's Spanish-accented rendition of "These Days," which has it all over Nico's German-accented one; and Jackson and Lindley's sweet/weird version of Mickey and Sylvia's 1957 hit, "Love Is Strange," which segues into a crowd-participating "Stay." The CD ends with a way too long (nine-minute) version of "The Next Voice You Hear," but his renditions of other material, especially "Looking East," "For Taking the Trouble," and "Late for the Sky," are eye-opening, and the ensemble playing rejuvenates his classics. *Love Is Strange* is great fun—Bud Scoppa in *Uncut* called it "his best album in years";[8] that might not be true, but it's certainly his most joyful album ever.

Jackson continued to work with Lindley here and there for years afterward—until Lindley's death in March 2023. Shortly after the funeral, at a small gathering in Claremont, California, Browne joined with other friends and musicians to celebrate Lindley's life. Jackson played "Call It a Loan," a song he cowrote with Lindley, and said beforehand, "Everything we did together was so much him. It was his touch and his expression. And that acted on me whenever we were together to a degree that I think just about everything I did with him was pretty much fifty-fifty. I'd play something, and then David would come along and play something brilliant that I couldn't live without, and then we'd have the take."[9] In a statement he later made for *Billboard*, Jackson gave an example of what he meant, recalling their first meeting in 1969: "We started to play 'These Days' and my world changed. His playing was so emotional, and immediate—it cast a spell over me and everyone there. It didn't matter that he had never heard the song before. What he was playing made it more emotional and more real than it had ever sounded the years I had played it alone."[10]

TIME THE CONQUEROR

Love Is Strange was released in May 2010, eighteen months after *Time the Conqueror* dropped in September 2008, but nothing from *Conqueror* makes it onto the live album, and we don't have to spend a lot of time wondering why. Along with *World in Motion*, *Time the Conqueror* is Jackson Browne's weakest record. Almost all rock artists slow down once they hit sixty—Browne hit that milestone just weeks after the record was released—but the paltriness of the material he came up with in the six years between *Naked* and *Time the Conqueror* is striking. I remember buying and listening to *Time* when it came out but putting it away after a couple of listens. I was by then a very busy divorced father with two young sons, and new music, even from longtime heroes, was hardly top of mind anymore. Still, I was puzzled, disappointed, and convinced that his muse seemed to have left him again.

Of course, Jackson had a lot beside writing new music to think about during the early years of the 2000s. In addition to an almost yearlong tour in 2002 and his continuing work for charitable organizations, in November 2002, he was part of a ten-million-dollar suit against Warner Brothers, attempting to recoup unpaid royalties from *The Eagles' Greatest Hits*, which contained "Take It Easy." (He won the case, though the terms weren't disclosed.) In 2003, he also threatened legal action against Twentieth Century Fox, which owned TBS, the company behind the made-for-cable movie, *America's Prince: The John F. Kennedy Jr. Story*, which had made those unfounded suggestions that Browne had beaten Daryl Hannah. Browne was able to get them to delete those references as well as apologize for their mistake. Similarly, he was able to get Viacom, which owned VHI, to delete suggestions that he had beat Hannah in their program *When Cameras Cross the Line*. (And, for good measure, Jackson sued the John McCain presidential campaign in August 2008 for unauthorized use of "Running on Empty" at McCain's rallies. He won that suit as well.)

In addition to his legal wrangling, Browne was dealing with the illness and death of his close friend, Warren Zevon, who died of lung cancer in September 2003. When Zevon got his fatal diagnosis, he gathered his musician friends, including Browne, to record a final album, *The Wind*. Jackson assisted in the studio and sang backing vocals on "Prison Grove" and told Warren's ex-wife, Crystal Zevon, "Warren has been a really huge feature of the musical landscape of my life for thirty years. He was always the writer who said the things I wish I said, the things I wish I could say. He was an independent thinker. I never saw himself dumb himself down or simplify what he had to say so more people would recognize him."[11] Ever since, Jackson has helped keep Zevon's music alive by consistently covering his songs in concert.

In 2004, Jackson was inducted into the Rock & Roll Hall of Fame, introduced by Bruce Springsteen. The Boss's induction speech was both insightful and funny, noting that in his early years, Jackson was a "bona-fide rock 'n' roll sex star" whose audiences were full of good-looking women (compared to Bruce's which, he noted sheepishly, was "mostly men, and not good-looking men either") but eventually gets around to talking about Browne's music. "In '70s, post-Vietnam America," he said, "there was no album that captured the fall from Eden, the long slow afterburn of the '60s, its heartbreak, its disappointment, its spent possibilities, than Jackson's masterpiece, *Late for the Sky*."[12] It's one of the most cogent things anyone had said about the way Browne's music captured the spirit of the early 1970s. Browne's own speech was a model of earnest self-effacement and gratitude—it's online—and nicely bookended the first thirty years of his career, which was then duly celebrated when Electra/Rhino released the thirty-two-song, two-CD *The Very Best of Jackson Browne*, with tracks hand-picked by Browne himself and featuring critic Dave Marsh's outstanding liner notes.

The best-of release, unfortunately, puts into sharp relief the shortcomings of *Time the Conqueror*. Here, working with the same band he used on *The Naked Ride Home* (while adding background vocalists Chavonne Morris and Alethea Mills), he renews his commitment to topical political music, takes several more looks back at his beginnings, examines his obsession with beauty one more time, includes an interesting ringer or two, and makes an attempt at a big statement in the title track. But the results are, for the most part, tepid do-overs of familiar themes, strident political broadsides with little of the nuance or wit that characterize his best political music, and overly long slabs of instrumental playing that aren't particularly interesting. (The average length of these ten songs is over six minutes.)

The trouble begins on the opener, "Time the Conqueror," Browne's latest attempt to tackle the theme of the passage of time—whose tandem theme, necessarily, is how we sustain our desire for meaning and intensity. Jackson's concerns with the theme go back to the original "These Days" and its protagonist's angsty regret over how much time he's already wasted at the tender age of sixteen. "The Fuse" lent the theme real urgency—time's burning fuse made the protagonist yearn to be "alive in eternity"—and "Black and White," with its echoing repetition of "time running out," reinforced that need to keep "burning . . . the ember in your heart." The embers of "Time the Conqueror," however, don't generate much heat. The album's cover sets the mood: a black-and-white photograph gives us a gray-bearded Jackson donning mirrored shades that hide his eyes, his trademark boyish hair lost in shadow. The photo aims for a kind of elder statesman vibe, but the title track isn't any more mature than anything he'd written for *Late for the Sky*. The song contrasts a blissful dream that the protagonist had in his youth, when "every grain of sand was casting its own shadow" (the allusion is to William Blake's "Auguries of Innocence," possibly by way of Bob Dylan's "Every Grain of Sand") with the frightening present moment, when "the world [is] about to stop breathing" and the only certainty is that "nothing's certain yet." There's the usual holdout's commitment "to decide what kind of world I believe in," but the urgency simply isn't there. The arrangement relies on a thin, wiry repetitious guitar riff that soon annoys, and the chorus's piled-up ambiguities—time heals all wounds, time steals you blind, time's a wheel, time's a conqueror—dispel any momentum the song hopes to build.

Less ambitious, if more pleasurable, are the album's two songs that look back with unabashed nostalgia on a period when Jackson was a willing "stowaway in the slipstream" of the 1960s. "Giving That Heaven Away" doesn't try too hard—Jackson knows how difficult it is to bring back the gossamer-like utopianism of the period—but the very lightness of the treatment nicely evokes a time when it was possible to believe that hot sex in a Winnebago with a hippie chick "in the flower of sweet youth" was to experience a little bit of heaven. "Off of Wonderland" leans into seriousness a bit more, suggesting that back in those halcyon days to believe in love meant to "believe in giving it away," though he notes that that got harder to believe after the deaths of Robert F. Kennedy and Martin Luther King. At the end of the song, however, the protagonist craves a return to the wonders of a 1960s Wonderland: "If we could just believe in one another / As much as we believed in John." The John here is John Lennon, who, more than anyone, lent credence to the hippie idea that love was a cosmic panacea, that "love is all you need." The yearning here is genuine, if wan.

"Wan" is not the word to describe the most overt political songs on the album, "Where Were You" and "The Drums of War." They're focused, energetic, angry, committed. The lyrics are well-meaning, well-researched, specific, and pointed; the band's arrangements are carefully constructed, if swollen by longish, rather dull solos. The songs announce themselves as Big Statements about Big Themes—the horrendous government response to Hurricane Katrina and the protracted US war against Iraq following 9/11—and take their time exploring them: "Where Were You" clocks in at 9:48 (Jackson's longest studio track to date), "The Drums of War" at 6:12. But they're awful. Jackson repeats the mistakes of *World in Motion*: his by-the-numbers attack on the American right is obvious and strident, which makes it impossible for someone like me—who *agrees with everything he says* about the corrupt collusions of government and the defense industry or about the George W. Bush administration's disgusting (and classist and racist) response to Katrina—to listen with acceptance, never mind pleasure. Disgorging political rhetoric that is deeply unoriginal, these songs lecture, they hector, they come off as smugly hermetic and self-congratulatory. The fault isn't with Browne's values—which here, as elsewhere, are the holdout values he's been promoting since day one—it's his use of pop form to articulate ideas better expressed in an op-ed. Both songs, like his mid- to late 1980s political songs, are blind to what art, as opposed to a newspaper editorial, requires: nuance, surprise, the slant of irony or wit that can reawaken an audience's feelings, originality in idea or mode of expression. It's the preaching-to-the-choir problem again: if you happen to agree with the songs' sentiments, you don't need what he's telling you. If you disagree, you'll just turn away. The fury and resentment behind Browne's (understandable) frustrations with America's rightward drift since the 1970s sometimes make him deaf to exactly the things that otherwise make him a great singer-songwriter. The album's closer, "Far from the Arms of Hunger," a vapid plea to end war and hunger, is even worse: channeling the same high school graduation speaker who seemed to have written the lyrics to "Lights and Virtues," Browne puts words to music that seems written while on Xanax, sleepy and depleted of precisely the energy one needs to fight the forces that cause the protagonist such grief.

If you can get past the dross of the political agitprop, there are flecks of gold to be found on *Time the Conqueror.* "Just Say Yeah," though too long (5:50), is a lilting and melodic paean to Dianna Cohen that traces their history back to its beginnings in "For Taking the Trouble" and "My Stunning Mystery Companion" and takes the couple into what appears to be a happy and committed present. Of the song, Browne said, "'Just Say Yeah' is a companion piece to 'My Stunning Mystery Companion.' And the hovering question is always, how do we talk about the possibility of this lasting forever?"[13] "Live Nude Cabaret," smokily atmospheric and filled with major seventh and minor chords that give it a beat-jazz tinge, has our Browne protagonist sitting stage side, watching nude dancers at a Hollywood bar. It's his newest essay on the power of female beauty. Shrewd enough to know that the dancers think of the men who stare at them as "fools," the protagonist still gets carried away by "what the female form will do." Marveling at women's power to make men "shower them with promises" or "make their vessels of creation / The temples of our souls," he marvels, too, at his own imagination's curious, maybe absurd tendency to "fashion from her nakedness / The innocence that's gone." It's a knowing treatment of desire and its mysteries from a sixty-year-old man who can analyze it almost objectively—as the astonishing and often ridiculous thing it is.

I save for last "Going Down to Cuba," the most surprising and I think best track on the album. With a Caribbean-tinged arrangement that's as fleet-footed as its lyrics, and sultry background vocals from Morris and Mills, Jackson wittily slips political commentary into a song that's otherwise about the pleasures of the tropics. The protagonist feels the lure of Cuba—where he has friends, "where the rhythm never ends," "where the women wear gardenias in their hair." But he, like all Americans, can't go down there unless he slips in through Mexico (and outsmarts Senator Jesse Helms, a longtime enemy of progressives and a major supporter of the American embargo at the time) or gets permission from the government to go on a "cultural" mission. So he's got to strategize. All the while he throws in little digs: Cubans "might not know all freedoms you and I know / But they do know what to do in a hurricane" (referring to the fact that Cuba's government response to Katrina was far superior to that of the United States). The whole song has a sense of humor that makes the politics go down easy, something he's not able to accomplish elsewhere on the album. When Jackson avoids straightforward op-ed commentary, when he uses wit, irony, even absurdity—as he does in "Lawyers in Love," "Lawless Avenues," or in "Cuba," his politics don't talk down or lecture: they're *receivable* by an audience that feels respected by the artist. It's a lesson Browne only seems to absorb fitfully. That fitfulness will continue: he'll remember it, then forget, then remember again, on his last two albums, *Standing in the Breach* and *Downhill From Everywhere.*

9

SHOULDER TO THE WHEEL, HEART IN THE DEAL

You can't exactly call it peace, or acceptance—never mind a sense of optimism. Jackson Browne is much too turbulent a soul to have arrived, in the last decade and a half, at anything like contentment, not in any sustained fashion anyway. But in certain songs—"If I Could Be Anywhere," "Standing in the Breach," "A Little Soon to Say," "Still Looking for Something"—you can hear it: a determination that's insistent without being strident or desperate, a clear-eyed sense of the dark perils the planet faces that's balanced with a willful faith that humans can turn things around. He's a realist who's learned to appreciate the small things, who ceaselessly holds out for what most realists think is unrealistic; he holds onto slender threads of hope and belief in the face of the facts, the odds, the gathering storm clouds of the roiling future. Like he sings it in "Love Is Love," in a phrase he translates from the Creole "*L'espua fe viv*," "Hope makes life."

In 2018, Jackson received the Gandhi Peace Award, given to those who've committed their lives (and/or their art) to the cause of world peace. Browne made a revealing acceptance speech, suggesting that all the struggles he has been involved in really boil down to one issue: "Whether freedom and equality, a safe healthy environment, and equality under the law belong to everyone, or just a few." Note the values here: the democratic triad of *liberté, egalité, fraternité*, plus economic opportunity and custodianship of the earth. He goes on to say that there's a worldwide network of people working for these values, "countless people dedicated to peace, to improving the lives of people in their community, and in far-flung places in the world. Paul Hawken[1] calls it 'the largest mass movement in the history of the world.' I think this award is for *believing* in peace in spite of its absence in so much of the world."[2]

This is what holdouts do: they continue to believe in certain hard-to-hold values, not because they're naive or stubborn "idealists" but because, even in the worst of circumstances, they sense something in themselves and others that warrants faith; they also sense that life without faith in something better is too barren to be borne. It's a belief in something that needs to be conjured, nurtured, fought for, even invented, so that the human story can continue.

There's a tenacity on Jackson's last two albums that pits a holdout's faith in human possibility against the threats—the climate crisis, technological innovation that outruns our abilities to control it, steroidal capitalism that militates against any dreams of peace or racial equality—that the world faces. That affirmativeness seems to come from a man who's centered enough in his personal life that he can devote himself to the hard work that he needs to do, both in the realms of music and social activism. That Browne has been with the same partner, Dianna Cohen, for over thirty years seems to have something to do with it. So does his own focused intelligence and strength of character. In "Yeah Yeah," *Standing in the Breach*'s update of his relationship with Cohen, he says that though he's "staring at the wreckage of a lifetime strewn along the track," he remains committed, "with my shoulder to the wheel / and my heart in the deal." The romance may have dissipated, but work and love are what it comes down to: the holdout's mantra.

HOPE AND CHANGE THAT WASN'T

Time the Conqueror was released two months before the election of Barack Obama as president in November 2008, too soon to note the impress that Obama's presence in American life had made, even before the election. That presence was, as his campaign slogan suggested, about "hope and change," embodied in a liberal politics that called for the end of the wars in Afghanistan and Iraq, a closing of the military prison in Guantanamo (where the US military tortured suspected terrorists), a serious commitment to address the climate crisis, and a drive to expand government-sponsored health care. But it was personified in Obama's very identity: here was a man with a black Kenyan father and a white American mother. His election symbolized for a lot of people a long-delayed acknowledgment of the country's racist history and a dedication to (finally) eradicating it. There were a few brief months there—from about September 2008, when polls began predicting a decisive Obama victory, to February 2009, when a filibuster-proof Democratic Congress passed the American Recovery and Reconciliation

Act (price tag: $787 billion)—when progressives sensed a sea change in American politics, dreaming that a new coalition was arising, of blacks and Hispanics, young people, organized labor, white urban liberals, environmentalists, feminists, and LGBTQ folks, that would form a new and formidable majority that would determine America's direction for another generation.

But it wasn't to be. Obama's "*Sí se puede*" was quickly drowned out by loud choruses of "no you don'ts" by right-wing adversaries determined to oppose just about anything Obama proposed and willing to gum up the works of government to do it. (Republican Senate minority leader Mitch McConnell announced that his whole job was to make Obama "a one-term president.") They took Obama to court over his executive order to close the Guantanamo Bay prison (and won); they ginned up opposition to his efforts to end the wars in Afghanistan and Iraq; they portrayed the Recovery Act and the Affordable Care Act (a.k.a. Obamacare) as socialist schemes that would kill off American freedoms; eventually, they refused to even consider his nominee to the Supreme Court. They even found ways to blame the Great Recession on the Democrats. Quickly, a Tea Party emerged—made up partly of libertarian fiscal conservatives and partly of populists susceptible to infection by white nationalism—that focused the angers and resentments that had accumulated in the wake of the recession and Obama's rise to power. Some of that volatile response was racist, though usually cloaked in euphemism that insiders heard as dog whistles calling to their bigotry. Though the Obama administration managed to get the Affordable Care Act passed—the most wide-ranging expansion of government health care since the mid-1960s—the Right had its revenge in the 2010 midterm elections, when Republicans "shellacked" (Obama's term) the Democrats, took control of the House, and doomed the rest of Obama's agenda for his first term.

It didn't help that Obama responded to the Great Recession with policies that propped up the banks and aided ailing corporations while doing little to help the middle and working classes that had taken the brunt of the pain of the Great Recession's economic realignments. For longtime leftists like Browne, this was par for the course. The principles of late capitalist economics weren't going to be toppled by an establishmentarian like Obama, as socially liberal as he was. "They've got subsidies for billionaires, there's a bailout for the banks," Browne complained in "Which Side?" but he wasn't grumbling about Republicans; he was singing this in 2014, six years into an Obama administration that largely did Big Business's bidding.

Then in November 2014, in the case of Obergefell v. Hodges, the Supreme Court legalized gay marriage nationwide, precipitating an uproar among social conservatives and evangelical Christians and consolidating a populist outrage at the country's longtime leftward drift regarding social and sexual issues. All of which opened a space for a master demagogue with a genius for finding scapegoats for the resentments that (mostly) non–college-educated, working- and middle-class white Americans had built up for decades, decades during which they felt their economic interests neglected, their religion mocked, their social values ridiculed by the "woke" and the "elites." Donald Trump, who had been teasing presidential runs for years while burnishing his persona as real estate tycoon, reality TV star, and tell-it-like-it-is gadfly, targeted—demonized—Hispanic immigrants, Muslims, "libtards" (white urban liberals), intellectuals, outspoken women, and "deep state" government workers and discovered that he spoke a language half the country was dying to hear. It was a language and persona he rode all the way to the White House. His rise was so swift and so total that progressives didn't know what hit them: How do you fight a man whose supporters tolerate, even praise, a man who admitted that he sexually assaulted women, saying that if you're famous enough, you can "grab them by the pussy"? Liberals, who had lost touch with white middle America back in the 1990s, found no effective political rhetoric for this kind of thing—Browne himself seemed nonplussed. On his 2021 album, released after the maniacal circus of Trump's four years in office, one of the most politically outspoken popular artists of his time doesn't mention him once. In a 2020 interview, in the midst of the COVID Crisis and the presidential campaign, Browne said, "We know that the Trump presidency is a cancer, but we don't have to sing about it."[3] It's as if he were saying that rock music wasn't adequate as a form to deal with Trump's level of absurdity and dysfunction.

STANDING IN THE BREACH

The resolute affirmation Browne's music on *Standing in the Breach* was able to keep alive during the pre-Trump years is best explored, ironically enough, in one of the songs whose lyrics Jackson didn't write, "You Know the Night." The words are, in fact, Woody Guthrie's. In the 1990s, it emerged that Guthrie had written lyrics—but not the music—to 2,400 songs(!), and Billy Bragg and band members of Wilco hustled to put music to 30 of them. The results, released on two albums (*Mermaid Avenue, Vol. I* and *Vol. II*), were highly acclaimed, and other musicians converged on the Woody Guthrie archive to do more of the same. Among them was jazz bassist Rob Wasserman, who assembled a dozen artists to write music for more of Guthrie's lyrics. The fruits of that project came on 2011's *Note Of*

Hope: A Celebration of Woody Guthrie, which included the first appearance of Jackson's "You Know the Night." (A strong live version by Browne and Wasserman is included on *Woody At 100! Live at the Kennedy Center.*) Wasserman actually assigned the song to Jackson—Jackson didn't pick it—which feels a bit uncanny. "You Know the Night" is a love letter Guthrie wrote to his wife, yet as Jackson sings it, the lyrics could just as well be about his relationship to Dianna Cohen. There's the romantic attraction, yes (the protagonist says that when he's around her he feels like "you feel when the angels are curling your hair / and you feel like the devil is scratching your heels"), but more to the point, there's the sense that the couple shares a purpose and attitude toward the world: "Did you look at me and think / here's this guy who hopes the way I hope?" Echoing the sentiment from Jackson's "Never Stop," Guthrie wonders if together "your hopes could find shape . . . your hopes and your plans for the good of the people." Wasserman and Jackson wrote the music together—a chugging rockabilly tune whose three guitars skitter loosely and lightly around Jackson's inventive vocal melody. Like the Cohen songs on *The Naked Ride Home,* this one suggests how the strength of their love provides the fuel for the work they do in the world, effectively linking the personal with the political in a way that's not usually Browne's strong suit.

The other Cohen song on the album is more direct—and more fraught. "Yeah Yeah," as the title implies, is another affirmation of their relationship, but he's no longer writing about a stunning mystery companion but about a life partner with whom he has a long history—at this point Cohen and Jackson had been together more than twenty years—and who struggles with her man: "You paid for the love that we've got, you paid" he admits, but "you made for the heart when we fought and you stayed." The protagonist wonders how she keeps to her commitment to him: "Is it faith or your will / that keeps you hanging on still," but what's clear is they're hanging on. The song is, as many of Browne's songs are in the new century, too long at six-plus minutes, with an unremarkable melody, a dullish refrain, and some noodle-y guitar work, but Jackson's vocal passion is there: his shoulder's to the wheel, his heart's in the deal.

There are two other relationship songs on the album, but neither are about Cohen. One is the closing track, "Here," a darkly atmospheric elegy about a relationship's breakup that Jackson wrote for the film *Shrek* and which is way too beautiful to play over the end credits of a Disney cartoon. The other opens the album, "The Birds of St. Mark." "Birds" is an old song, written about Nico when Browne met her in New York in 1967 and contributed songs and his guitar to her *Chelsea Girl* album. Though it's one of the best songs he wrote in his early years, he never recorded it and, in fact, forgot about it for many years. Nico died in 1988, and Jackson resuscitated the song for the 1994 DVD *Going Home*, where he plays solo piano while singing part of it. Thereafter, he got requests to hear it when he played live. In a 2014 interview, he says he finally decided to record it when he found a guitarist, Greg Leisz, who could reproduce the Roger McGuinn/Byrds twelve-string guitar sound he always wanted.[4] But it's more than a Byrds retread. Given the bright jangly backdrop, the tune emerges as a 1960s dreamsong, musically luxurious, with long melody lines on both verse and chorus and a Val McCallum solo on the outro that echoes the tune's romantic urgency. Jackson's vocal, with the throaty graininess that he's acquired as he's aged, is superb, and gives the lyric, clearly Dylan-influenced, a gravity Jackson couldn't have pulled off in 1967. Lyrically, "Birds" is a carefully constructed allegory about a sad queen (Nico), who is so isolated in her castle (the St. Marks hotel) by her own fame that she can no longer even recognize herself, and a man (evidently Jackson), who's become so weary of trying to free her of her condition that he's given up in despair, leaving her to her lonely fate. In retrospect, it's a mystery why he held on the song so long and reminds us of the extraordinary talent Jackson had from the beginning.

"Leaving Winslow" sounds like something Browne cooked up after exposing himself to Woody Guthrie's genius in "You Know the Night." Chugging along to a Johnny Cash–like country-western beat and ornamented with fine pedal-steel work by Greg Leisz, "Winslow" is filled with loose humor, long chatty lines, and witty vocal phrasing. And it's one of Jackson's rare persona songs. The song's about an old drifter who moves from one town to the next with "not that much of anything in mind"—a character so distant from Jackson's own that it seems to free his imagination to explore possibilities both comic and melancholy. This guy's got a mother who "married an oxygenarian lady's man," who takes her dancing tethered to a "tank of oxygen." Our drifter has heard about the "disappearing ozone layer" and the "disappearing middle class," but the disappearing he's more concerned about is his own—clearly he's on his last legs and wants to see Winslow "one more time." The song is modest but suggestive, and not only because it teases us that maybe this drifter is the same guy who, decades before, was standing on the corner in "Take It Easy." The song can't help but make me wonder what would have happened if Jackson had dedicated more of his writing to persona-based songs, especially ones whose subjects were political. (The comparison—inevitably—is with Springsteen, whose political commentary in, say, "Born in the U.S.A.," "Seeds," or "Gypsy Biker" is all the more trenchant for being filtered through personae.)

The rest of *Standing*—five tracks, half the album—is focused on the political situation circa 2014. The least effective, and unfortunately the most ambitious and most op-ed–y, is "Which Side?" which takes its title from the Depression-era pro–labor union song but is about more than solidarity in the face of worker exploitation. It's about "the battle for the future," and Browne casts the two sides—way too broadly—as (1) neoliberal corporate capitalists with all their money, power, and greed, and (2) humanists and environmentalists who are fighting for justice, equality, democracy, and the preservation of the earth. Choose one. The lyrics are dutifully researched—Browne makes all the connections between political power, the military-industrial complex, "the banks and their special friends," and the corporate buying of elections that any regular reader of *The Nation* makes. But Browne listeners already know which side they're on, and don't need six and a half minutes of what is fairly pedestrian music to make up their minds: the refrain fails to muster the kind of activist inspiration it hopes to, and the instrumental outro is again too long.

"Walls and Doors" is much better. Written by the Cuban singer-songwriter Carlos Varela and translated from the Spanish by Browne, "Walls" is as simplistic in its black-and-white framing of societal struggle—rich versus poor, money mongers versus spiritual dreamers, those who raise walls versus those who open doors—as "Which Side?" but its traditional Latin folk trappings allow for that simplicity. And in any case, the song has the wisest line on the whole album: "There can be freedom only when nobody owns it," which Jackson sings with the urgency of someone who knows the line unlocks an idea that's vital, even magical. Can freedom exist when one group "owns" it and thinks it can bestow that freedom upon—or withhold it from—other groups? In other words, can real freedom exist in a society without equality? It's an idea Jackson grapples with in his Gandhi Prize speech. It's an idea that I've struggled to get across to my own students for more than thirty years. The United States has been forced to contend with relative claims of freedom and equality from its beginnings, but especially after the Civil War. Thinkers like Booker T. Washington felt that freed black Americans had to wait for equality till whites were ready to grant it, while others like W. E. B. DuBois argued that it was in never in the power of whites to grant it in the first place. He made the point that the Fourteenth Amendment to the Constitution already granted it. In fact, the Declaration of Independence stated it clearly in 1776, when it held that it was a self-evident truth that "all men are created equal, and that they are endowed by their Creator"—not by any person or any group—"with certain inalienable rights, that among these are life, liberty, and the pursuit of happiness." Intrinsic to the American idea is that nobody *grants* us freedom or equality. It's what we're owed by the state simply for being born human. Browne's vocal of Varela's concise and elegant iteration of a fundamental democratic truth is quite moving, and Varela's own plaintive vocal at song's end gives it an extra poignancy. The song, sung in concert, has all the power of a spiritual, which is what makes it politically effective.

"If I Could Be Anywhere," propelled by Benmont Tench's unusually blunt piano pounding on the verses, rocks harder in the service of a lyric about how the current environmental crisis is the result of a long history of Western empires "extracting the wealth and ruling by force." Doubtless emerging from his own involvement in Dianna Cohen's Plastic Pollution Coalition, the song uses disposable plastics as a symbol of the crisis: "You have to admit it's clever / maybe the pinnacle of human endeavor," he sings, that the plastics we produce to throw away after a single use are manufactured so they'll "never . . . disappear." Jackson swerves from his usual full-frontal sincerity to make his point—irony has begun to filigree its way through his lyrics—but the most refreshing part of the song remains its resolute positivity. "If I could be anywhere, it would have to be now," says the chorus. It's *because* we're living in such a crisis that the protagonist is glad he's alive now; it gives him the chance to be a significant player in the world's outcome. It's the kind of retort that true holdouts give to those who retreat into pessimism because of our current plight.

"The Long Way Around" is, for me, the album's best song, one that embeds Jackson's political commentary in an illuminating account of his own personal struggle. Reminiscent of the richly intimate folk-rock sound he achieved on the *I'm Alive* album, and arranged around the simplest of acoustic guitar figures, the track takes its time (at more than six minutes) but for once, the song's languid pace works. The song is *about* how the protagonist's life has taken "the long way around." It's about not going straight ahead to some prescribed place to which one's been "bound" from the beginning, but moving—acting and reacting to what life's accidents and contingencies have thrown at him. As for his past, "I made my breaks and some mistakes / Just not the ones people think I made," which is a finger wag at those (like his biographers) who make it a practice to psychologize his life from afar (though he may also be pointing to the Daryl Hannah incident and saying, "That's not the mistake I'm talking about"). As for the present, the protagonist finds himself weary of the "envy" that's taken over even those "in the richer neighborhoods"—greed seems head-shakingly entrenched even among the wealthy. And as a committed social activist, he finds himself confused; the world throws so many crises at us, one after another, that it confounds our attempts at analysis, and now: "It's hard to say which did more ill / Citizens United of the Gulf oil spill." "If I Could Be Anywhere" manages a steadfast stance toward crisis; "Long Way" admits, in a way that's been rare for Browne until now, the personal toll that his activism has taken on him. "With all we disagree about / the passions burn, the heart goes out," he laments. We're taking the long way around on "this wild road we're on," and we're not done yet, so the song offers no conclusions. "The Long Way Around," in its dense ambiguity and ambivalence, can remind us of some of the best things on *Late for the Sky*.

The title track, which concludes the album proper ("Here" is a postscript), sums up Browne's holdout stance in the new century. The phrase "standing in the breach" comes down to us from Ezekiel 22, when God, angry at the sins of the Israelites, threatens to destroy Jerusalem and disperse his chosen people among the nations. "I looked for someone among them," God says, "who would build up the wall and stand before me in the breach on behalf of the land so I would not have to destroy it, but I found no one" (Ezekiel 22:30). In Ezekiel, the protecting walls of Jerusalem have been broken—breached—and God's wrath threatens to pour through it, ruining the city. Who is there strong enough to prevent it? God asks. Browne appropriates the metaphor, replacing a sinful, threatened Jerusalem with a sinful, threatened planet, and God with a civilization hell-bent on destroying itself through greed. Who are the holdouts prepared to stand in the breach to prevent that from happening?

The metaphor is sternly Old Testament, for sure, but Browne doesn't sing it that way. The song doesn't admonish, nor does it plead. It witnesses, balancing an awareness of crisis with an awareness of human possibilities in the face of crisis. Jackson, in fact, filters his message through another metaphor. The song begins by invoking, with appropriate solemnity, the devastation of the Haiti earthquake of 2010, which has been called one of the worst natural disasters in recorded history, killing upward of eighty-five thousand people (a US estimate; Haiti's government claimed that the death toll was closer to three hundred thousand) and leaving a million people homeless in one of the poorest places on the planet. "And though the earth may tremble and our foundations crack / We will all assemble and we will build them back," the song begins. The "we" here are those who are willing to stand in the breach for humanity's poor and helpless, and for a planet in peril from the climate crisis. As in "If I Could Be Anywhere" and "The Long Way Around," the protagonist is under no illusions that the "unpaid debts of history" or the "open wounds of time" will be corrected by progressive social action. "You know the world you're waiting for may not come," he admits. Yet still, he can't help but hold onto the *belief* that we must choose love and human solidarity over greed and materialism. "We rise and fall with the trust and belief / That love redeems us each," and we must believe that love "is inside everyone." That love the protagonist is talking about is transpersonal—and transcendent: it's the love that Browne has been a holdout for since the 1960s, the love that Martin Luther King Jr. taught him as a teenager, and which will "cast our souls into the heavens" and allow us to "stand in the breach" for the good of humanity and the earth. "Standing in the Breach" is the most direct holdout song of Browne's career, pulling together strands of his worldview into one of his most coherent and moving statements and suggesting that just about every album Jackson Browne ever made could have been called *Standing in the Breach.*

THE GANDHI PEACE AWARD SPEECH

On September 14, 2018, Jackson showed up in New Haven, Connecticut, to accept the 2018 Gandhi Peace Award, a prize given by the group Promoting Enduring Peace that recognizes people for their "contributions made in the promotion of international peace and good will." (This award should be distinguished from the Gandhi Peace Prize, which is granted by the Indian government.) The first winner was Eleanor Roosevelt, back in 1960, and through the years the award has been bestowed upon such luminaries as Benjamin Spock, George McGovern, Cesar Chavez, Ralph Nader, and Bill McKibben. Browne, cited for his "extraordinary contributions of time and talent to the inseparable causes of peace, environmental harmony, and social justice on local and planetary scales,"[5] was the first artist to receive the award. The speech he made in accepting the award is, at around two thousand words, the most rounded and complete public account Browne has ever made of his political commitments: it gathers into an eloquent and coherent statement the political sentiments of his music, and it's worth diving into here.[6]

After some preliminary comments, Jackson talks about how his political education started—learning as a boy from books in the public library about "Indian life and the impact that United States western expansion had on them." The Indian Wars of the nineteenth century, with their broken treaties, provocations, and aggressions, taught Jackson that behind all the rhetoric in high-minded phrases like "Manifest Destiny" and "American exceptionalism" was "a very deep and not at all hidden belief in white supremacy." But these pernicious ideas were, at the same time, all "bound up with the lofty American ideal of spreading democratic self-rule across the North American continent and eventually throughout the world." The contradictions at the heart of the American idea—a belief in individual freedom and human dignity for white males and a corresponding refusal to confer that same freedom and dignity to anyone else—were there from the start, and a young Jackson was intuiting that. He doesn't say this in his talk, but his early thinking about Native American history prepared him for the progressive politics he picked up from his mother and, later, from Martin Luther King Jr. and Bob Dylan.

As he learned more, Browne says, he came to believe that there were some Americans—he names Lincoln, Ulysses Grant, and the American Whig Party—who believed that "the true mission of America was one of democratic example." Jackson, of course, sides with them, and through a lifetime of activism, has promoted it. But the America Jackson saw develop over the course of his lifetime and which he sees around him now [2018] seems woefully unable to adequately promote that example. "Have we become morally incapacitated by our advantage, our privilege and our comfort?" he asks. "Are we dazed by our entertainments? Are we distracted by our social media and our smartphones? Are we isolated from the rest of humanity by technological advances?" The country's rightward lurch toward American exceptionalism in the Trump era—he doesn't mention Trump but he doesn't have to—makes it possible for the country to "rule out self-criticism and precludes any discussion of the consequences of our actions." The promotion of democracy, freedom and equality, at home and abroad, have taken a back seat to pure material self-interest, to the ruination of our ideals, not to mention nature itself.

As for "enduring peace" which is what he was given this award for promoting: "[W]e have been at war for 224 of our 246 years as a nation. Enduring war is more like what we have." The United States' continuing warlike posture, and its refusal to acknowledge the seriousness of the climate emergency, makes Browne pessimistic. He is particularly worried about the fate of our system of government. Given the Citizens United Supreme Court decision, which opened the door to unlimited cash contributions by the anonymous rich and superrich to the super PACs of political candidates, "whether we have a democracy at this point is an open question." He paints a dismal picture—however, not at all an unfamiliar one to anyone who's listened to "Standing in the Breach," "Casino Nation," or "Looking East."

So, what to do? In short, the answer is, put your shoulder to the wheel and your heart in the deal. Browne recounts his own activism. "My part in this work is to help bring people together. Music is good for that. It can be good for raising spirits; also for raising money." Then he gives a long list of the ways he's tried to intercede for good causes: "I have appeared and sung my songs," he says, "to

—save old-growth redwoods
—promote solar energy
—oppose nuclear energy
—promote human rights
—support civility in our public discourse
—save rivers
—save bridges
—save our oceans
—oppose the use of single-use plastic
—help fund community health centers
—help support the arts in our public schools
—defend biodiversity
—abolish the death penalty
—support commonsense gun legislation
—support women's rights
—march for peace
—demonstrate against war"

After recounting how he's been "involved in various struggles," he comes to his main point, that all these issues "are just one issue—whether freedom and prosperity, a safe healthy environment and equality under the law belong to everyone or just a few. That's it." And the only way to fight for these values is to see them as interrelated, which requires us to fight under the same banner, united in a conscious, progressive solidarity. This is where he mentions environmentalist Paul Hawken and his idea of a worldwide progressive movement. In an interview Browne gave to *The Nation* after *Standing* was released, he previewed the idea:

> Think about this writer Paul Hawken. He wrote the book *Blessed Unrest*, in which he says how the largest movement in the history of humanity went undetected because it's called by so many names. Something fundamental has to happen to people, and whether it's brought about by mass starvation or, you know, climate change or some sort of epiphany,

> you know, is yet to be seen. You have a huge amount of people who give their passion and their hope for the future to a particular, you know—a particular goal. And if you put them all together, really, it is a movement to improve the lives of people everywhere and to save the environment. I mean, it's inescapable. If you work with people who are trying to save the ocean and people who are trying to address global warming, it's really the same problem. And same with human rights—the biggest enemy of human rights is business. It's corruption and people treating other people as if they're expendable. And the word that gets thrown around all the time in our—"American interests." You can say anything as long as I'm "defending American interests." What the hell are they? What the hell are our interests if not to have a safe environment and prosperity for everybody?[7]

In his Gandhi Peace Award speech, Browne consolidates a lifetime's worth of thinking about various political issues into a unitary message: "It's really the same problem." Treat people, and the global environment we all live in, with the love and dignity they and it deserve—recognize people's freedom and dignity, and be good stewards of the planet. "That's it." It's a credo that he will draw on repeatedly on the last album he's released, *Downhill from Everywhere.*

DOWNHILL FROM EVERYWHERE

Jackson Browne's latest album was released in July 2021, six months after Donald Trump left office amid a frenzy of unsupported allegations of election fraud and having inspired an assault on the Capitol by supporters trying to prevent the electoral college certification of Joe Biden as the new president. Nearly a million Americans had by then died of COVID-19, and though vaccines were now available to stop the spread, government vaccine and mask mandates had divided the country even more than the fractious Trump administration had managed to do. The seventy-one-year-old Browne himself was one of the first public figures to acknowledge getting the virus, back in March 2020, before vaccines were available. Characteristically, he announced it as a public service rather than as self-serving publicity, suggesting in an interview that we all pitch in together: wear the mask, quarantine till symptoms subside, and make the necessary personal sacrifice for the good of all: "Everybody has a role to play in the health of the country and of the entire world," he said.[8]

At the time he made the announcement, he had begun working on his fifteenth studio album, assembling a core of musicians—Greg Leisz and Val McCallum on guitars, Bob Glaub on bass, Jeff Young on keyboards, Mauricio Lewak on drums—that he'd gotten comfortable playing with on *Standing* and on subsequent tours. *Downhill from Everywhere*, despite its title, is the spriteliest album he'd released in decades, filled with good humor and a varied, colorful musical palette: the political songs on the second half of the album have an energy and musicality that take them well beyond agitprop, the love songs dig deep, and "A Song for Barcelona," which ends things, has a vitality that suggests that Browne, seventy-two when the record was released, was hardly done as composer and performer. If *Downhill* does end up being his last studio record, he's certainly going out on a high note.

The four-chord folk-rock opener, "Still Looking for Something," sounds like, and is, a statement of purpose. Jackson's looking back at himself as a holdout and promising that he still is one. The line that tickled reviewers and interviewers at the time of release was the one that said, "I'm way out over my due date, baby," giving them a chance to speculate about whether the aging rocker still had it. The consensus was that he did—reviews were strong—and Jackson contributed to the fun by talking about his "shelf life" as an artist (and/or commodity.) The song is pretty much Browne distilled, about a seeker who is "still looking for something in the night": love, excitement, open possibilities, the fulfillment of dreams are all hinted at. He knows that seeking will cost him plenty in terms of pain and disappointment, but he believes "somewhere there's a heart in the city / and I'm out here to find it." It's another of Jackson's songs about the mystery of the night. What interests me most about it, however, is the refrain's final line, repeated for emphasis, where he insists that despite all his seeking, "If all I find is freedom, it's alright." It's a sneaky way of saying that the seeker seems to have lost his sense of romance, his expectations for love. I think back to the end of his Gandhi Award speech, where Browne offers his thanks to his managers for their support and then to his sons for theirs. He ends with thanks to Dianna Cohen, but not for her love, emotional support, or encouragement of his music or activism. He thanks her only "for giving me a lot of freedom." His phrasing is careful, and a bit odd. If it's accurate, it signals a relationship that's a far cry from the one that had him once calling her his "stunning mystery companion."

That suspicion gets reinforced by the single Cohen song on the album, "Minutes from Downtown." Given a clean arrangement full of moody sevenths and minor chords, the song evokes a restlessness that we haven't seen in previous songs about their relationship. The song begins by rehearsing the couple's history, how at its beginning Browne "didn't think you would ever be more than a friend" and that their age difference—seventeen years separates them—somehow seemed not to matter as their love changed the course of his life. But now he feels alienated in his own home, and he longs for some kind of release: "I try to fathom why home feels strange to me / More and more the other shore is what I need to see." Perhaps inspired by the fact that he and Cohen had recently moved into a house in "mid-city"[9] LA (actually, the Beverly Grove neighborhood, adjacent to Beverly Hills), Browne sings about how he now lives "minutes from downtown, minutes from the coast highway"—that is, midway between the excitement and seductions of the city, on one hand, and the contemplativeness and sense of grandeur he feels from the Pacific Ocean, on the other. He sees himself driving the city's freeways, "plotting my getaway" to either city or shore—escaping from his newly strange home and its reminders that he's not quite up to the rigors of love because his "heart was already torn in half" when they first met. It's a deceptive song: melodically pretty and soothing, Browne's phrasing of the meticulously crafted lyrics is a real pleasure, but behind it speaks a man whose restless casting about for fulfillment is as relentless and permanent—even in his early seventies—as his holding out for the moral and political values to which he's committed.

There are two love songs (of the agape variety) on the album, "A Human Touch" and "Love Is Love"—both of which were written for other projects. "A Human Touch" came out of an invitation from film director Paul Haggis to contribute to his AIDS documentary *5B* and was written in collaboration with singer Leslie Mendelson and her writing partner Steve McEwan. ("They came up with this great song, most of it, really, although I added a few lines," Browne remembers.[10]) The film tells the story of doctors, nurses, and patients as they created the first-ever care ward for AIDS sufferers at the beginning of the AIDS crisis in the early 1980s. The song, which played over the end credits, was released as a single in June 2019 and later added to *Downhill from Everywhere*. Steeped in compassion and an awareness of death, "A Human Touch" is a simple and quite beautiful paean to the need for human connection as a salve for suffering, and hearkens back, stylistically and tonally, to *Late for the Sky*.

"Love Is Love," cowritten with David Belle, grew out of Jackson's fascination with Haitian culture and music that began when he visited Haiti in the wake of its devastating 2010 earthquake. In 2016, invited by the NGO Artists for Peace and Justice, Browne flew to Haiti to donate recording equipment to a music studio but stayed on to collaborate with local musicians (and to attend, at first reluctantly, a voodoo ceremony). Over the next couple of years, Browne made subsequent visits, other musicians joined up (from Haiti, Spain, Mali, the United States, and other countries), and they began recording an album that came to be called *Let the Rhythm Lead: Haiti Song Summit, Vol. 1*, a benefit record for the NGO, which was released in 2019 and contained Jackson's contribution. "Love Is Love" is no great shakes lyrically—it's a soft-hearted, earnest first-world take on an impoverished third-world country's ability to keep love alive amid rampant suffering—but musically it's a delight. Retaining the band that played on the rest of *Downhill*, and featuring deliciously creamy background vocals by Alethea Mills and Chavonne Stewart, it's spirited and credible world music.

The album's first single, "My Cleveland Heart," a funny (even, um, danceable) rocker with Browne's most hummable melody in many a moon, lightens the mood considerably. Playing off a pop-silly metaphor of a guy getting an artificial heart that can "take a bashin' without losing the passion" and that will never break, ache, make mistakes, or even beat—"they just plug in and shine"—Jackson writes an entirely successful comedy of innocence: his protagonist seems convinced that his new artificial heart will relieve him of "this broken heart of mine." Val McCallum, who cowrote the song, contributes stellar guitar work. The song is a pleasure—not just in itself but because of the proof it provides that the ever-brooding Browne can let it loose once in a while.

Tracks six to nine swing back to the political. The simplest and most nakedly sincere is "The Dreamer," cowritten with Los Lobos' David Hidalgo and Eugene Rodriguez, a musician who is executive director of the Los Cenzontles Mexican Arts Center in California. Originally recorded by Browne and Rodriguez's roots band Los Cenzontles and released as a single in 2017 (the version on *Downhill* has been rerecorded by Browne's band), the song is meant to address the plight of Mexican and Central American child immigrants who came to the United States through no choice of their own but because of decisions their families had made for them. During the George W. Bush years, many of these children were targeted for deportation, even though many of them had lived in the United States for most of their lives and called America home. In 2012, President Obama announced an executive action called Deferred Action for Childhood Arrivals (known as DACA), which granted children of immigrants deportation deferrals and work permits that allowed them to stay in the country to complete their educations and potentially obtain permanent residence status. But there was—and remains—immense resistance to this policy from conservatives, who have taken it to court, and from the Trump administration, who tried to reverse the action. This prompted Rodriguez, Hidalgo, and Browne to record a song about it. Jackson's concerns for Latino immigrants has been long-standing—along with the material on *World in Motion* and *Lives in the Balance*, there's a deeply affecting recording on YouTube of his performance (along with Bonnie Raitt and Bruce Springsteen) of the John Hiatt/Ry Cooder song "Across the Borderline" at the legendary Christic Institute concerts in 1990—and though "The Dreamer" lacks the grit of that song, it's a restatement of his commitment to the cause of fairness for *centroamericanos* seeking opportunity in *el norte*.

"Until Justice Is Real" has a cringeworthy title and contains lyrics that are basically a rehash of Browne's longstanding frustration with the nation's continuing struggle to make its reality one with its ideals, but its rehash is part of its point. In a 2020 interview, Browne said:

> Many of us believed that we were on a track going forward, that civil rights have improved. But nothing could be more obvious than that is really not actually the case. We're still, we're still settling the Civil War. We're still talking to people who believe in white supremacy. They want to go backwards and—see, I don't know quite how to say this. All the while I was thinking that we were getting somewhere, people were being ground up in the wheels of our society and police were killing black motorists. There were injustices that went on and on and on and on. And that's what I'm saying. We don't have the time for these to go on and be swept aside. That's what the song is talking about.[11]

The same things, in other words, need to be said again and again, and time is running short, given the country's Trumpian slipslide into worsening economic inequality, entrenched racism, climate emergency, and erosions to democratic discourse due to the proliferation of dis/misinformation on social media, all of which the song evokes. It helps, though, that "Until Justice Is Real" contains the most stirring rock music Browne has made in years. I've heard it in concert twice since its release, and Browne's band expertly builds up its country rock foundation into a thick-slabbed guitar rocker that, together with the best and most soulful background vocals Chavonne Stewart (formerly Morris) and Alethea Mills have ever contributed, whips up an excitement rare to hear at a Browne show. Hearing it live gives its message—"Putting your shoulder to the wheel / Keeping it turning until justice is real"—a driving conviction that the studio version hints at but doesn't quite deliver. Live, it's a genuine showstopper.

The classics of the album, though, are "A Little Soon to Say" and the title track. "Downhill from Everywhere" has some of the rock guitar bite of "Justice" (thanks to Greg Leisz, credited as cowriter) and big-lunged, complementary vocals from drummer Jeff Young (also a cowriter). The song's trenchancy, however, comes from its idea, which is that (except for places below sea level like California's Death Valley or Jordan's Dead Sea) "the oceans are the last stop for gravity." The oceans are literally downhill from everywhere, the end-of-the-line trash dump for all the pollution and refuse that human societies, in this age of the "Anthropocene"—a crucial first mention of that term in the Browne canon—neglect to control, limit, or recycle. The song documents all the places from which that refuse comes—literal trash generators like malls, stadiums, theme parks, factory farms, grocery stores—to more symbolic garbage creators like "K Street" or "the Senate floor" (or, when Browne really decides to let his partisan anger fly, "the GOP," "the NRA," or "ICE"). After the point has been made, Browne goes further. He slows down the song to ask, "Do you think of the ocean as yours?" It's a question at the root of environmental thought: Whatever our stated values, what is our real relationship to the natural world? Is it exploitational, or do we recognize that we're literally part of nature? Can we afford to think of that relationship as anything less than custodial? If we have any doubt, Browne reminds us that one of the oceans' jobs is to replenish oxygen in the atmosphere, and that "Every second breath you take is coming from the sea."[12] Jackson's question about our relationship to the seas is sung, with help from Stewart and Mills, with gospel solemnity and fervor, appropriate for an environmental passion that is nearly religious in intensity. But it doesn't feel like preaching or agitprop, just the ardor of the committed holdout.

"A Little Soon to Say," a bit like "The Long Way Around," combines that commitment with an acknowledgment that there's a profound emotional cost to fighting so long and so hard for what could very well be a losing battle. It's a song written in the middle of a crisis. Several lines suggest that it's about the country's battle with COVID-19 in 2020 (or even the George Floyd protests)—"Beyond the sirens in the broken night / Beyond the sickness of our day"—but it's easy enough to see the crisis as the same one "Downhill" is about. Here, though, the emphasis is less on diagnosing the problem than mobilizing those involved in the struggle against it. The singer says he came to some public event (presumably a concert) "looking for inspiration," but the song ends up being about inspiring others: "I want to see you holding out your light," the chorus begins, "I want to see you light the way." Here he's asking others to be holdouts, though in the end he's a realist: "I wanna think it's gonna be alright / It's just a little soon to say." Those last lines evoke an exhausted warrior smiling wearily while urging on fellow warriors to keep up the good fight.

The politics of tracks six to nine give way, in the album closer, "A Song for Barcelona," to cathartic celebration, eight and a half minutes of some of the liveliest music Jackson has ever put down. Partly sung in Catalan and cowritten with his core band, who give each other plenty of space to stretch out, it's a festival of pleasure and a salute to the city's culture—its streets, its architecture, its music, and, crucially, its youthfulness: "I see the searching eyes and youthful bodies pass / And my own vanished youth becomes my central truth." Barcelona reminds Jackson of the passions that made him a holdout in the first place, and being there "ignited my desire, and temporarily, my soul." That "temporarily" is pure Jackson Browne, of course; no one thing, certainly no city, holds the key to one's forever struggle to keep hope and meaning alive. Browne has kept an apartment in Barcelona for twenty years, and it seems to give him the jolt of energy that a city like LA no longer can. (See "Minutes to Downtown.") "Barcelona," in fact, gives back that jolt of energy that the city gives him and, in concert, is a neat example of the exchange of passion that the best rock music has always circulated between creator and audience.

GOOD THINGS

The last half of the twentieth century and the first quarter of the twenty-first—the years that constitute Jackson Browne's lifespan—have been studded with disasters and crises that test the credulity, never mind the goodwill, of any socially sentient American. Beginning in the shadow of the most destructive war in human history (with its concentration camps, atom bombs, and millions dead), the United States almost immediately embarked on an extraordinary economic boom that encouraged people to forget the horrors of the previous years. The new prosperity allowed for suburbs to crop up all over the country that promised a piece of the American dream to a burgeoning middle class. But boomer kids like Jackson growing up with a sense of security and future opportunity were quick to notice the vast gulf between what America promised and what the real conditions were for millions of (mostly poor, nonwhite) people. The recognition of that gulf was one of the big spurs for the social revolutions of the 1960s, where, as Marx suggested about a different era, everything solid melted into air. In a few short years, attitudes toward authority, state violence, race, sexuality, religion, success, what it meant to live a meaningful life—all were up for grabs, and young people of Browne's generation were highly susceptible to both the era's existential risks and its opportunities. The instabilities of Jackson's own family life as he grew up drew him to countercultural rebellion, and exposure to influences like Bob Dylan and Martin Luther King Jr. planted him firmly as a holdout for progressive values that would become lifelong.

Browne's music has for more than five decades traced his engagement with the running history of his country and, as time has passed, more and more with the fate of the earth itself. A boy who began his education by studying Native American culture—its loving attachment to the land, its brutal exploitation by white expansionists—enthusiastically embraced the countercultural critique and began to apply it in his life and his music. At first, his instincts told him to write about what he knew, to ground his values in the complexities of emotional experience, which led him to write the songs that made him a fixture of early 1970s popular culture, elucidating the experience of boomers eager for purpose, love, and a meaningful context to understand their lives. He named crucial experiences for that generation—what it felt like to sense that countercultural ideals were slipping away ("Before the Deluge"); what it felt like to compromise values that used to matter so much ("The Pretender"); the emotional panic when you discovered that so much of your life had fallen apart ("Running on Empty"); the recognition that in order to continue you'd have to regather your lost sense of value ("Hold On Hold Out").

As the counterculture fell apart in the 1970s and the country lurched rightward in the 1980s, Browne's life and art took on a more activist tenor. Addressing the country's myriad problems was like playing whack-a-mole—the dangers of nuclear power, the prospects for nuclear war, US imperialism in Central America, racism at home, a new nationalism, the imperiled state of immigrants, pervasive capitalist greed—and Browne crisscrossed the country (and more and more, internationally) playing benefits and drawing attention to his holdout values in his 1980s records. Though there was a brief lull in the sheer volume of planetary crises as the Cold War ended in the 1990s, which allowed Jackson to readdress exclusively personal concerns, after *I'm Alive*, his music was almost equally divided between the personal and the political, with his best music fusing the two. Into the new century, the climate crisis loomed larger and larger for Browne, and, combined with his sense that it was technology and capitalism in its late (neoliberal) stages that threatened not just the environment but freedom, equality, and democracy for everyone, it came to occupy a central role in his activism. It also lent a special poignancy to his music, which often seemed poised between a sense of futility and a determination not to succumb to it.

Browne's career didn't have to go this way. His natural songwriting talent is for intimate portraits of couples in crisis—he's never been able to live down *Late for the Sky*, though he's come close—and he could have stuck to his strengths. But his sense of citizenship got in the way. Yes, his political music has too often been hobbled by preachiness or mere editorializing—it's been his Achilles heel—but it's also something that couldn't be helped. Plenty of people in and outside the music industry told him that his politics would devastate his sales, would make him not just less of a star but less of an influence on the culture. That Browne didn't listen is as much a testament to his stubborn clinging to a not-always-effective style of protest music as it is a measure of his sense of responsibility of what it meant to be an American. You can criticize Browne's brand of liberal politics from the other direction, of course; you can say he's too cautious, as many leftists have. With Trumpian authoritarianism and climate catastrophe on the horizon, Browne's charity work, or his musical efforts to reasonably persuade people of the need to change our ways, can come across as tepid drops in the bucket, ineffective responses to the direness of the need for wholesale structural change. But, again, it couldn't be helped: he is who he is. Jackson Browne is a sincere holdout for love, freedom, equality, justice, democracy, compassion, and custodianship of the earth. These are good things. But he's not a revolutionary. He's a humanist: he fights fair—with reason and human sympathy—and assumes (hopes?) that fighting fair will win out in the end. Is his style of engagement appropriate to our times? It's a little soon to say.

NOTES

INTRODUCTION

1. *Going Home*, Pioneer Artists, 1994, DVD.

2. Lionel Trilling, *Sincerity and Authenticity* (Cambridge, MA: Harvard University Press, 1972), 2.

3. Trilling, *Sincerity and Authenticity*, 9.

4. J. D. Salinger, *The Catcher in the Rye* (1951; New York: Bantam, 1964), 211.

5. See Sheffield's sharp and often hilarious entries on these artists in *The New* Rolling Stone *Album Guide*, 4th ed., ed. Nathan Brackett, with Christian Hoard (New York: Simon & Schuster, 2004).

6. Jeff Giles, "Why Jackson Browne Became Political with *Lives in the Balance*," Ultimate Classic Rock, February 8, 2016, https://ultimateclassicrock.com/jackson-browne-lives-in-the-balance.

CHAPTER 1

1. For some of the biographical detail here, I'm indebted to Rich Wiseman's *Jackson Browne: The Story of a Holdout* (New York: Doubleday, 1982), the first full-length biography written about the singer. Long out of print, it still holds up as a thoughtful, professional, and well-researched guide to Browne's life through 1980.

2. Mike Boehm, "Most Likely to Secede: If Nothing Else, Jackson Browne's Orange County Days Gave Him Something to Move Away From," *LA Times*, August 25, 1994, https://www.latimes.com/archives/la-xpm-1994-08-25-ol-30855-story.html.

3. Lisa McGirr's *Suburban Warriors: The Origins of the New American Right* (Princeton, NJ: Princeton University Press, 2001) makes the case that an army of "suburban warriors"—a group of almost entirely white, middle-class Protestant

Orange Countians—emerged in the 1950s as a part of a widespread grassroots movement that heard the clarion call of Joe McCarthy's anti-communism in the late 1940s and the 1950s, dug themselves a deep ditch of paranoia where they could hunker down with suspicions that communists (and later blacks, or hippies on drugs) were plotting a takeover of *their* (i.e., "God's") America, and then went about the serious business of building the political base that would throw into national prominence Barry Goldwater and Ronald Reagan as well as help elect Richard Nixon and the George Bushes. Orange County was, in many ways, the very center of American reactionary activism in the years Browne lived there.

4. Wiseman, *Holdout*, 20.

5. Colin Irwin, "Jackson Browne These Days . . . ," *Melody Maker*, December 11, 1976, http://www.rocksbackpages.com/Library/Article/jackson-browne-these-days.

6. Both speeches can be found in Martin Luther King Jr., *I Have A Dream: Writing and Speeches That Changed the World* (New York: Harper, 1992).

7. Martin Luther King Jr., "Facing the Challenge of a New Age," in *I Have a Dream: Writing and Speeches that Changed the World* (New York: Harper, 1992), 22.

8. Martin Luther King Jr., "Where Do We Go from Here?" Martin Luther King, Jr. Research and Education Institute, Stanford University, https://kinginstitute.stanford.edu/where-do-we-go-here, retrieved January 22, 2023.

9. *Going Home*, Pioneer Artists, 1994, DVD.

10. Noonan and Copeland both went on to release albums in the 1960s and 1970s, sometimes covering Browne's songs and, in Copeland's case, using Browne as a producer. It's not often that three high school friends end up with recording careers. The folky coffeehouse subculture Noonan and Copeland helped start in Orange County was crucial in creating the supportive environment that led to Browne's eventual emergence.

11. Cf. "A Prefatory Paper—Heroes and Leaders," in Norman Mailer, *The Presidential Papers of Norman Mailer* (New York: Bantam, 1964), 1–8.

12. Cf. "1964: The Year That Changed America," *American Experience*, PBS Films, 2014.

13. Patrick Doyle, "Jackson Browne, Patti Smith, Others Celebrate Lennon," *Rolling Stone*, November 13, 2010.

14. Steve Boltin, "Sunday Conversation: Jackson Browne on His New Album and How John Lennon Informed His Whole Musical Life," *Forbes*, July 18, 2021, https://www.forbes.com/sites/stevebaltin/2021/07/18/sunday-conversation-jackson-browne-on-his-new-album-and-how-john-lennon-informed-his-whole-musical-life/?sh=23965ff62a02.

15. Wiseman, *Holdout*, 20–21.

16. This quote, and the preceding one, is from Rob Tannenbaum, "The Return of the Pretender," *GQ*, November 1993, https://www.rocksbackpages.com/Library/Article/jackson-browne-the-return-of-the-pretender.

17. The version I've managed to locate is called *Jackson Browne: The Nina Music Demos: Studio Demo Recording in New York, 1967* (Vintage Masters, 2009).

18. Todd Gitlin, in his essential chronicle, *The Sixties: Years of Hope, Days of Rage* (New York: Bantam, 1987), was, besides a crucial participant in the 1960s movement as a leader in Students for a Democratic Society, also a professional historian with rigorous academic standards. But even he wonders whether the counterculture really "happened" or was all in some sense a magical dream. "In the Sixties," he writes, "it seemed especially true that History with a capital H had come down to Earth, either interfering with life or making it possible; and that within History, or threaded through it, people were more than themselves, they were supercharged; lives were bound up with one another, making claims on one another; drawing one another into the common project" (7). Yet, a bit earlier, he concedes that he's always had the suspicion that it might all have been a "collective hallucination" (3).

19. Tom Hayden cites Mills's *The Power Elite* as one of the biggest influences on the thinking that led to his writing of the Port Huron Statement. See Louis Menand, *The Free World* (New York: Picador, 2021), 695.

20. In the section of the Statement that proclaims the values of the SDS, it reads, "We would replace power rooted in possession, privilege, or circumstance by power and uniqueness rooted in love, reflectiveness, reason, and creation." See "The Port Huron Statement," in *Takin' It to the Streets*, ed. Alexander Bloom and Wini Breines (New York: Oxford University Press), 67. Part of what made the New Left "new" was its insistence on taking individual feelings seriously—something that Old Left Marxists more or less dismissed; for the New Left, the personal was political, and any project that hoped to liberate a society politically or economically needed to address personal, existential liberation as well. Thus, political power needed to be fundamentally "rooted" in feeling, imagination, and love. We don't know if Browne ever read "The Port Huron Statement," but almost his entire body of work suggests that he would have wholeheartedly endorsed it. Sometimes, when I reread it, I think he could have almost written it.

21. "1989 Jackson Browne Interview," VH1 Special, YouTube, https://www.youtube.com/watch?v=uyDoh3nLFXg, retrieved January 8, 2023.

22. Mark Bego, *Jackson Browne: His Life and Music* (New York: Citadel, 2005), 28.

23. David Rensin, "Jackson Browne: Such a Clever Innocence," *Crawdaddy!*, January 1974.

24. I found this quote in Bud Scoppa's "Jackson Browne: A Once and Future Fan's Notes," *Paste*, June 1, 2004.

CHAPTER 2

1. Joan Didion made "The Second Coming" the epigraph to her seminal book of 1960s essays, *Slouching toward Bethlehem* (New York: Washington Square Press, 1968). And the next couple of years made her look more astute than she knew.

2. Alan Jackson, "Portrait of the Artist," *New Musical Express*, November 30, 1985, https://jonimitchell.com/library/view.cfm?id=661.

3. Cf. Aldous Huxley, *The Doors of Perception* (New York: Harper & Row, 1954); also William Blake, "The Marriage of Heaven and Hell" (1793), in *Blake's Poetry and Designs*, ed. Mary Lynn Johnson and John E. Grant (New York: Norton, 1979), 81–102. In Blake's exuberant poem, he writes, "If the doors of perception were cleansed every thing would appear to man as it is, Infinite. For man has closed himself up, till he sees all things thro' narrow chinks of his cavern." Blake believed that in his time (the rational, scientific Enlightenment), human beings had begun to limit their awareness to the five physical senses, which deprived them of spiritual vision and sustenance. They needed to open up the doors of perception to admit spiritual, visionary experiences that would again allow them to see the infinite. Blake seemed to have no need to take drugs to have those experiences, but Huxley saw mescaline as the road toward Blakean vision, and his book, along with Timothy Leary's proselytizing for LSD, were profound influences on the counterculture.

4. Tom Wolfe, "The Me Decade and the Third Great Awakening," in *Mauve Gloves and Madmen, Clutter and Vine* (New York: Bantam Doubleday), 1976. Christopher Lasch expands the thought in his more intellectually rigorous book, *The Culture of Narcissism* (New York: Norton, 1979).

5. Cf. Browne's introduction to "Something Fine" on *Jackson Browne, Solo Acoustic, Vol. 2*, Inside Recordings, 2006.

6. Michael Watts, "Jackson Browne: Survivor," *Melody Maker*, January 12, 1974, http://www.rocksbackpages.com/Library/Article/jackson-browne-survivor.

7. The song leaves unanswered the question of whether Saylor's death was suicide or the result of an accident, but years later Saylor's father confirmed it was indeed suicide. Cf. Tim Grobaty, "'Song for Adam' a Bittersweet Memory," *Long Beach Press-Telegram*, March 17, 2011, https://www.presstelegram.com/2011/03/17/tim-grobaty-song-for-adam-a-bittersweet-memory.

8. Adam Sweeting, "Ten Questions for Songwriter Jackson Browne," *Arts Desk*, November 17, 2014, https://theartsdesk.com/new-music/10-questions-songwriter-jackson-browne.

9. Editors of *Rolling Stone*, *The* Rolling Stone *Record Review, Vol. II* (New York: Pocket Books, 1973), 416.

10. Robert Christgau, *Christgau's Record Guide: Rock Albums of the 70s* (New York: Ticknor and Fields, 1981), 63.

11. Wiseman, *Holdout*, 81

12. Louis Menand, "Making the News," *New Yorker*, February 6, 2023, 63–64. Here Menand is rehearsing the argument that Godfrey Hodgson makes in his book, *America in Our Time* (Princeton, NJ: Princeton University Press, 2005).

13. Wiseman, *Holdout*, 88.

14. Bill Flanagan, "The Last Elvis Costello Interview You'll Ever Need to Read," *Musician*, March 1986. In his 1993 interview with Browne, seven years later, Rob Tanenbaum brings up the Costello quote and makes it clear that the jibe hit its mark: "When I begin to repeat this quote to Browne, he finishes my sentence. He knew about Costello's insult, and he remembers it, word for word." Cf. Rob

Tannenbaum, "Jackson Browne: The Return of the Pretender," *GQ*, November 1993, http://www.rocksbackpages.com/Library/Article/jackson-browne-the-return-of-the-pretender.

15. Dave Zimmer, *Crosby, Stills & Nash: The Biography* (Cambridge, MA: Da Capo Books, 2008), 153.

16. Christgau, *Rock Albums of the 70s*, 64; Janet Maslin, review of *For Everyman*, *Rolling Stone*, November 22, 1973.

17. Ronald Brownstein, *Rock Me on the Water: 1974: The Year That Transformed Movies, Music, Television, and Politics* (New York: HarperCollins, 2021), 344.

CHAPTER 3

1. Jaan Uhelszki, "Jackson Browne: *Late for the Sky*," *MOJO*, October 2002, http://www.rocksbackpages.com/Library/Article/jackson-browne-ilate-for-the-skyi.

2. Bud Scoppa, "Jackson Browne: Album by Album," *Uncut*, August 2010, http://www.rocksbackpages.com/Library/Article/jackson-browne-album-by-album.

3. Wiseman, *Holdout*, 82–84.

4. Mark Bego, *Jackson Browne: His Life and Music* (New York: Citadel, 2005), 88.

5. Scoppa, "Album by Album."

6. Aaron Timms, "The Unquiet Ghost of the 1970s," *New Republic*, November 2022, 25.

7. Cf. https://www.americanrhetoric.com/speeches/jimmycartercrisisofconfidence.htm.

8. Cf. https://www.robertchristgau.com/xg/rock/audience-77.php. Christgau may not have cared much for Jackson Browne, and I lay into him in this book whenever I think he's blind, but the fact is the man is a great critic.

9. Wiseman, *Holdout*, 100.

10. Brownstein, *Rock Me on the Water*, 346.

11. Browne discusses these books briefly in an English radio interview. See "Jackson Browne Talks about *Late for the Sky* LP," November 30, 2014, https://www.youtube.com/watch?v=XHW58A-6Gdw (site discontinued), retrieved April 2, 2023.

12. Otto Friedrich, *Before the Deluge: A Portrait of Berlin in the 1920s* (New York: Harper Perennial, 1995), xxi.

13. Editors of *Ramparts*, *Eco-Catastrophe* (San Francisco: Canfield Press, 1970). The quotes in this paragraph come from pp. v, 20, 45, and 51.

14. Katherine Barkley and Steve Weissman, "The Eco-Establishment," in *Eco-Catastrophe*, 20.

15. Murray Bookchin, "Toward an Ecological Solution," in *Eco-Catastrophe*, 45.

16. Bookchin, "Toward an Ecological Solution," 51.

17. In a 2020 interview, Browne suggested another writer who had an influence on "Before the Deluge": "That song was inspired by a writer named Paul Ehrlich. . . . He laid forth a scenario in which the world's dysfunctions compound and create an apocalyptic outcome." (Jackson was likely talking about "Eco-Catastrophe," the opening essay in the book *Eco-Catastrophe*, which Erlich expanded upon in his book, *The Population Bomb*.) Kevin E. G. Perry, "Jackson Browne: My Generation Were Idealistic and Naive but We Were Right about So Many Things," *Independent* (UK), January 30, 2020, https://www.independent.co.uk/arts-entertainment/music/features/jackson-browne-interview-new-album-haiti-donald-trump-us-election-2020-a9305846.html.

18. Christgau, *Rock Albums of the 70s*, 64.

CHAPTER 4

1. These three quotes come from Wiseman, *Holdout*, 118 and 140.
2. Tannenbaum, "Return of the Pretender."
3. Anthony DeCurtis, "As Jackson Browne's 'World' Turns," *Rolling Stone*, October 5, 1989.
4. Paul Nelson, "The Pretender," in *Stranded*, ed. Greil Marcus (New York: Knopf, 1979), 121.
5. DeCurtis, "As Jackson."
6. Paul Nelson, review of *The Pretender*, *Rolling Stone*, March 9, 1978.
7. Brownstein, *Rock Me on the Water*, 346.
8. Wiseman, *Holdout*, 116–17.
9. Nelson, "The Pretender," 125.
10. Tannenbaum. "Return of the Pretender."
11. Andy Gill interviewed Browne about the songs that made it onto *The Next Voice You Hear*, including "The Pretender." Cf. "Jackson Browne: The Next Voice You Hear—The Best of . . ." *MOJO*, November 1997. https://www.rocksbackpages.com/Library/Article/jackson-browne-ithe-next-voice-you-hear--the-best-ofi-elektra.
12. Dave Marsh, review of *The Pretender*, *Rolling Stone*, January 27, 1977.
13. Christgau, *Rock Albums of the 70s*, 64.
14. Wiseman, *Holdout*, 125.
15. Sam Sutherland, "Jackson Browne: *The Pretender*." *Phonograph Record*, November 1976. http://www.rocksbackpages.com/Library/Article/jackson-browne-ithe-pretenderi-asylum-7e-1079-2.
16. Nelson, rev. *The Pretender*.
17. The comment comes from an interview Browne did with England's *Zigzag*, no. 64 (September 1976). The quote is found in Wiseman, *Holdout*, 132.
18. Steve Pond, "Jackson Browne Adapts: No Booze, No Drugs, No Marriage: Just Rock & Roll," *Rolling Stone*, September 15, 1983.

19. "Jackson Browne Accepts the Gandhi Peace Award," 2018, https://www.youtube.com/watch?v=sEkn4qGhFgo.
20. Wiseman, *Holdout*, 145.
21. Ibid., 146.
22. Ibid., 147.
23. Abe Peck, "Entertainers Protest in Anti-nuclear Crusade," *Winnipeg Free Press*, June 13, 1979, https://jonimitchell.com/library/print.cfm?id=2152.
24. Quoted in Bego, *Browne: Life and Music*, 118.

CHAPTER 5

1. Bego, *Browne: Life and Music*, 131.
2. E. P. Thompson and Dan Smith, eds., *Protest and Survive* (New York: Penguin, 1980), 223–26.
3. Jonathan Schell, the author of the bible of the antinuclear movement, *The Fate of the Earth*, wrote a thoughtful retrospective on the event in *The Nation*, June 14, 2007.
4. Mark Rowland, "Life Lessons: Bonnie Raitt and Jackson Browne," *Musician*, August 1989, http://www.rocksbackpages.com/Library/Article/life-lessons-bonnie-raitt-and-jackson-browne.
5. From an interview with WIOQ's Ed Sciaky, quoted in Wiseman, *Holdout*, 157.
6. Ibid., 151.
7. Paul Nelson, "Jackson Browne: The *Rolling Stone* Interview." *Rolling Stone*, July 8, 1980.
8. Ibid.
9. Robert Christgau, *Christgau's Record Guide: The 80s* (New York: Pantheon, 1991), 73–74.
10. Kit Rachlis, Review of *Hold Out*, *Rolling Stone*, September 15, 1980.
11. Steve Pond, "Jackson Browne Adapts."
12. Ibid.
13. Christopher Connelly, Review of *Lawyers in Love*, *Rolling Stone*, September 29, 1983.

CHAPTER 6

1. "Jackson Browne on Music and Politics," in Anthony DeCurtis, *In Other Words: Artists Talk about Life and Work* (Milwaukee, WI: Hal Leonard Corporation, 2005), 337.
2. Steve Turner, "A Dixie Cup of Nuclear Waste Could Kill the Planet," *Q Magazine*, January 1987, http://www.rocksbackpages.com/Library/Article/jackson-browne-a-dixie-cup-of-nuclear-waste-could-kill-the-planet.

3. DeCurtis, *In Other Words*, 335.

4. Joyce Millman, "Jackson Browne: Blandanista," *Village Voice*, April 29, 1986.

5. Michael Hiltzik, "A Farewell to James G. Watt, Environmental Vandal and Proto-Trumpian," *Los Angeles Times*, June 13, 2023, https://www.latimes.com/business/story/2023-06-13/farewell-to-an-original-gop-environmental-vandal-james-watt.

6. Chris Mooney, "30 Years Ago Scientists Warned Congress on Global Warming. What They Said Sounds Eerily Familiar," *Washington Post*, June 11, 2016, https://www.washingtonpost.com/news/energy-environment/wp/2016/06/11/30-years-ago-scientists-warned-congress-on-global-warming-what-they-said-sounds-eerily-familiar.

7. "Ronald Reagan—Bruce Springsteen (19.09.1984)," YouTube, https://www.youtube.com/watch?v=z8BRWNaOdlc.

8. Maybe the most interesting of all the America songs from that period is Leonard Cohen's extraordinary "Democracy." Cohen began writing it in 1989, after the Tiananmen Square massacre, and finally released it in 1992 on his *The Future* album. Its fierce compilation of detail about American strengths and weaknesses rides that razor-thin line between critique and celebration as much as "Born in the U.S.A." does, but, at seven minutes in length, it paints with a broader, more intellectually rigorous and ambivalent palate. The song's almost unknown except among Cohen's small fan base. As of this writing, the song has garnered all of 2,300 views on YouTube in the last thirteen years.

9. For a fine primer on liberation theology, see Olivia Singer, "Liberation Theology in Latin America," Brown University Center for Digital Scholarship, https://library.brown.edu/create/modernlatinamerica/chapters/chapter-15-culture-and-society/essays-on-culture-and-society/liberation-theology-in-latin-america, retrieved June 24, 2023.

10. Turner, "Dixie Cup of Nuclear Waste."

11. Gill, "Next Voice You Hear."

12. Jon Young, "Jackson Browne: *Lives in the Balance*," *Musician*, May 1986, http://www.rocksbackpages.com/Library/Article/jackson-browne-ilives-in-the-balancei-asylum.

13. Robert Hilburn, "Browne's Balancing Act," *Los Angeles Times*, February 23, 1986, https://www.latimes.com/archives/la-xpm-1986-02-23-ca-10897-story.html.

14. Cf. the intro to "Enough of the Night," on *Jackson Browne Solo Acoustic, Vol. II.*

15. Rowland, "Life Lessons," *Musician*, August 1989, http://www.rocksbackpages.com/Library/Article/life-lessons-bonnie-raitt-and-jackson-browne.

CHAPTER 7

1. The information in the next few paragraphs about the September 23, 1992, incident with Hannah comes from the following publications: Karen S. Schneider et al., "White Knight," *People*, October 19, 1992; Elizabeth Gleick et al., "Two of a

Kind," *People*, August 16, 1993; Fred Schruers, "Interview with Jackson Browne," *US*, February 1994; Letters to the Editor from Haskell Wexler and Jackson Browne, *US*, April 1994.

2. Browne's quoted comments regarding the incident with Hannah come from his interview with Tannenbaum, "Return of the Pretender."

3. Schruers, "Interview with Jackson Browne."

4. The quote comes from a 1996 television interview with JFK Jr., cited in Larry Philpot, "Jackson Browne Backstory: 'Sky Blue and Black,'" *Onstage Magazine*, October 9, 2016, https://onstagemagazine.com/jackson-browne-back-story-sky-blue-black.

5. "Jackson Browne Responds to Joni Mitchell's Lyrics," *Tampa Bay Times*, September 27, 1997, https://www.tampabay.com/archive/1997/09/27/jackson-browne-responds-to-joni-mitchell-s-lyrics. The *Tampa Bay Times* story reported on a *Dallas Morning News* interview with Browne that is no longer available.

6. Gary Susman, "Jackson Browne Wins Apology from JFK Jr. Filmmakers," *Entertainment Weekly*, July 18, 2003.

7. Tannenbaum, "Return of the Pretender."

8. Albert Camus, "Return to Tipasa," in *The Myth of Sisyphus* (1957), trans. Justin O'Brian (New York: Vintage, 2018).

9. Don DeLillo, *White Noise* (New York: Vintage, 1985), 12.

10. See, among countless examples, the work of Jonathan Haidt, especially *The Anxious Generation* (2024) and *The Coddling of the American Mind* (cowritten by Greg Lukianoff) (2018), both published by Penguin Random House.

CHAPTER 8

1. Wayne Hoffman, "Jackson Browne Q & A," *Nature Conservancy*, 2003.

2. John Steinbeck Award, https://www.steinbeckaward.com.

3. Gill, "Next Voice You Hear."

4. Ibid.

5. Cf. Dianna Cohen, "Are We Being Consumed by Plastic?" TED Talk, https://www.youtube.com/watch?v=SO4axNuoPis, retrieved April 14, 2024.

6. For a comprehensive treatment of the voluminous—and often prematurely created—pop works about 9/11 through the 2000s, see Jeffrey Melnick, *9/11 Culture* (Chichester, UK: Wiley-Blackwell, 2009).

7. "The Questions, Vol. 6: Jackson Browne," https://www.youtube.com/watch?v=JhrRs02UAGs, retrieved February 15, 2024.

8. Bud Scoppa, "Jackson Browne & David Lindley: Love Is Strange," *Uncut*, July 2010.

9. Randy Miller, "'Farewell, Mr. Dave': A Hometown Bids Goodbye to David Lindley," *Fretboard Journal*, June 2023, https://www.fretboardjournal.com/columns/farewell-mr-dave-a-hometown-bids-goodbye-to-david-lindley.

10. Rania Aniftos, "Jackson Browne Mourns 'Genius' Instrumentalist David Lindley: 'No One Ever Played Like Him,'" *Billboard*, March 17, 2023, https://www.billboard.com/music/music-news/jackson-browne-mourns-david-lindley-statement-1235289094.

11. Crystal Zevon. *I'll Sleep When I'm Dead: The Dirty Life and Times of Warren Zevon* (New York: Harper, 2007), 430.

12. "Bruce Springsteen Inducts Jackson Browne Rock and Roll Hall of Fame Inductions 2004," https://www.youtube.com/watch?v=8YFyC6pnz-k, retrieved January 11, 2024.

13. Cf. https://www.rollingstone.com/music/music-news/jackson-browne-just-say-yeah-243364 (site discontinued).

CHAPTER 9

1. Paul Hawken is an environmentalist whose work has involved thinking about how the values of ecologists and social justice activists can transform capitalism through the application of their concerns to business decision-making. His best-selling book *Blessed Unrest, or How the Largest Movement in the World Came to Be and How No One Saw It Coming* (2007), recounts the formation of a largely sub rosa worldwide movement for social change that is serving to counteract the predations of capitalism and the climate crisis, and has influenced Browne's thinking in his last two albums, as well as influenced his Gandhi Prize speech, which we will discuss in more depth in the next section of this chapter.

2. "Jackson Browne Accepts the Gandhi Peace Award," https://www.youtube.com/watch?v=sEkn4qGhFgo, retrieved February 13, 2024.

3. "Jackson Browne: Live Interview & A Human Touch with Leslie Mendelson." https://www.youtube.com/watch?v=A8CZg5nr7GA.

4. "Jackson Browne Interview on *Standing in the Breach* and World Tour," https://www.youtube.com/watch?v=xyJA4liNPX0, retrieved February 15, 2024.

5. "Jackson Browne," Promoting Enduring Peace, https://pepeace.org/laureates, retrieved March 7, 2024.

6. The speech has never been published, but see note 2 for a viewing option.

7. Eric Alterman and Katrina vanden Heuvel, "An Interview with Jackson Browne," *The Nation*, October 7, 2014, https://www.thenation.com/article/archive/eric-alterman-and-katrina-vanden-heuvel-interview-jackson-browne.

8. Randy Lewis, "Jackson Browne on Testing Positive for COVID-19, His Condition and Passing It to His Son," *Los Angeles Times*, March 25, 2020.

9. Amy Kaufman, "Jackson Browne on Cancel Culture, His 'Shelf Life' and How to Survive Rush Hour in L.A.," *Los Angeles Times*, July 26, 2021, https://www.latimes.com/entertainment-arts/music/story/2021-07-26/jackson-browne-phoebe-bridgers-downhill-from-everywhere.

10. "Jackson Browne & Leslie Mendelson Team Up for Sobering 'A Human Touch': Video Premiere," *Billboard*, July 9, 2019, https://www.billboard.com/music/rock/jackson-browne-a-human-touch-video-8519074.

11. Tom Casciato, "Jackson Browne: We Could Have a Society in Which Justice Is Real," *PBS Weekend*, July 25, 2021, https://www.pbs.org/newshour/show/jackson-browne-we-could-have-a-society-in-which-justice-is-real.

12. Browne's lyric is backed up by the science. "More than 50 percent of the oxygen we breathe comes from the ocean," says Alan Deidun, an environmental expert with a European Union commission on the environment called Mission Starfish. He adds, "And another thing is that the ocean is soaking up a lot of that extra carbon dioxide and other greenhouse gases that we're spewing up into the air through the burning of fossil fuels; if it wasn't for the ocean, climate change would be much worse because of higher CO_2 concentrations in the atmosphere." See "Every Second Breath You Take Comes from the Ocean, Expert Says," *Euronews.green*, February 22, 2022, https://www.euronews.com/green/2022/02/22/every-second-breath-you-take-comes-from-the-ocean.

BIBLIOGRAPHY

Included below is most of the source material I used in order to write this book. I have left out a few references that are strictly incidental to the story, as well as references to reviews of Jackson Browne's albums, except in a few cases where those reviews helped shape my thinking, influenced the long-term reception of his work, or were interesting in their own right.

BOOKS

Bego, Mark. *Jackson Browne: His Life and Music.* New York: Citadel, 2005.

Bloom, Alexander, and Wini Breines, ed. *Takin' It to the Streets.* New York: Oxford University Press, 1995.

Brownstein, Ronald. *Rock Me on the Water: 1974: The Year That Transformed Movies, Music, Television, and Politics.* New York: HarperCollins, 2021.

Christgau, Robert. *Christgau's Record Guide: Rock Albums of the 70s.* New York: Ticknor and Fields, 1981.

———. *Christgau's Record Guide: The 80s.* New York: Pantheon, 1991.

———. *Is It Still Good to Ya?: Fifty Years of Rock Criticism, 1967–2017.* Durham, NC: Duke University Press, 2018.

DeCurtis, Anthony. *In Other Words: Artists Talk about Life and Work.* Milwaukee, WI: Hal Leonard, 2005.

Editors of *Ramparts. Eco-Catastrophe.* San Francisco: Canfield Press, 1970.

Eliot, Mark. *To The Limit: The Untold Story of the Eagles.* Rev. ed. Cambridge, MA: Da Capo Press, 2005.

Gitlin, Todd. *The Sixties: Years of Hope, Days of Rage.* New York: Bantam, 1987.

Hoskins, Barney. *Hotel California.* Hoboken, NJ: John Wiley and Sons, 2006.

Menand, Louis. *The Free World.* New York: Picador, 2021.

Thompson, Dave. *Hearts of Darkness: James Taylor, Jackson Browne, Cat Stevens and the Unlikely Rise of the Singer-Songwriter.* Milwaukee, WI: Backbeat Books, 2012.

Trilling, Lionel. *Sincerity and Authenticity*. Cambridge, MA: Harvard University Press, 1972.

Wiseman, Rich. *Jackson Browne: The Story of a Holdout*. New York: Doubleday, 1982.

Zevon, Crystal. *I'll Sleep When I'm Dead: The Dirty Life and Times of Warren Zevon*. New York: Harper, 2007.

Zimmer, Dave. *Crosby, Stills & Nash: The Biography*. Cambridge, MA: Da Capo Books, 2008.

ARTICLES

Aniftos, Rania. "Jackson Browne Mourns 'Genius' Instrumentalist David Lindley: 'No One Ever Played Like Him.'" *Billboard*, March 17, 2023. https://www.billboard.com/music/music-news/jackson-browne-mourns-david-lindley-statement-1235289094.

Boehm, Mike. "Most Likely to Secede: If Nothing Else, Jackson Browne's Orange County Days Gave Him Something to Move Away From." *LA Times*, August 25, 1994. https://www.latimes.com/archives/la-xpm-1994-08-25-ol-30855-story.html.

DeCurtis, Anthony. "As Jackson Browne's 'World' Turns." *Rolling Stone*, October 5, 1989.

Doyle, Patrick. "Jackson Browne, Patti Smith, Others Celebrate Lennon." *Rolling Stone*, November 13, 2010.

Flanagan, Bill. "The Last Elvis Costello Interview You'll Ever Need to Read." *Musician*, March 1986.

Giles, Jeff. "Why Jackson Browne Became Political with *Lives in the Balance*." Ultimate Classic Rock, February 8, 2016. https://ultimateclassicrock.com/jackson-browne-lives-in-the-balance.

Gill, Andy. "Jackson Browne: The Next Voice You Hear—The Best of. . . ." *MOJO*, November 1997. https://www.rocksbackpages.com/Library/Article/jackson-browne-ithe-next-voice-you-hear--the-best-ofi-elektra.

Gleick, Elizabeth, et al. "Two of a Kind." *People*, August 16, 1993.

Grobaty, Tim. "'Song for Adam' a Bittersweet Memory." *Long Beach Press-Telegram*, March 17, 2011. https://www.presstelegram.com/2011/03/17/tim-grobaty-song-for-adam-a-bittersweet-memory.

Irwin, Colin. "Jackson Browne These Days. . . ." *Melody Maker*, December 11, 1976. http://www.rocksbackpages.com/Library/Article/jackson-browne-these-days.

Jackson, Alan. "Portrait of the Artist." *New Musical Express*, November 30, 1985. https://jonimitchell.com/library/view.cfm?id=661.

"Jackson Browne Responds to Joni Mitchell's Lyrics." *Tampa Bay Times*, September 27, 1997. https://www.tampabay.com/archive/1997/09/27/jackson-browne-responds-to-joni-mitchell-s-lyrics.

Kaufman, Amy. "Jackson Browne on Cancel Culture, His 'Shelf Life' and How to Survive Rush Hour in L.A." *Los Angeles Times*, July 26, 2021. https://www

.latimes.com/entertainment-arts/music/story/2021-07-26/jackson-browne-phoebe-bridgers-downhill-from-everywhere.

Lewis, Randy. "Jackson Browne on Testing Positive for COVID-19, His Condition and Passing It to His Son." *Los Angeles Times*, March 25, 2023.

Maslin, Janet. Review of *For Everyman. Rolling Stone*, November 22, 1973.

Miller, Randy. "'Farewell, Mr. Dave': A Hometown Bids Goodbye to David Lindley." *Fretboard Journal*, June 2023. https://www.fretboardjournal.com/columns/farewell-mr-dave-a-hometown-bids-goodbye-to-david-lindley.

Millman, Joyce. "Jackson Browne: Blandanista." *Village Voice*, April 29, 1986.

Nelson, Paul. "The Pretender." In *Stranded*, edited by Greil Marcus. New York: Knopf, 1979.

Peck, Abe. "Entertainers Protest in Anti-Nuclear Crusade." *Winnipeg Free Press*, June 13, 1979. https://jonimitchell.com/library/print.cfm?id=2152.

Pond, Steve. "Jackson Browne Adapts: No Booze, No Drugs, No Marriage, Just Rock & Roll." *Rolling Stone*, September 15, 1983.

Rensin, David. "Jackson Browne: Such a Clever Innocence." *Crawdaddy!*, January 1974.

Schneider, Karen S., et al. "White Knight." *People*, October 19, 1992.

Scoppa, Bud. "Jackson Browne: A Once and Future Fan's Notes." *Paste*, June 1, 2004.

———. "Jackson Browne: Album by Album." *Uncut*, August 2010. http://www.rocksbackpages.com/Library/Article/jackson-browne-album-by-album.

———. "Jackson Browne & David Lindley: Love Is Strange." *Uncut*, July 2010.

Susman, Gary. "Jackson Browne Wins Apology from JFK Jr. Filmmakers." *Entertainment Weekly*, July 18, 2003.

Tannenbaum, Rob. "The Return of the Pretender." *GQ*, November 1993. https://www.rocksbackpages.com/Library/Article/jackson-browne-the-return-of-the-pretender.

Turner, Steve. "A Dixie Cup of Nuclear Waste Could Kill the Planet." *Q Magazine*, January 1987. http://www.rocksbackpages.com/Library/Article/jackson-browne-a-dixie-cup-of-nuclear-waste-could-kill-the-planet.

Uhelszki, Jaan. "Jackson Browne: *Late for the Sky*." *MOJO*, October 2002. http://www.rocksbackpages.com/Library/Article/jackson-browne-ilate-for-the-skyi.

Watts, Michael. "Jackson Browne: Survivor." *Melody Maker*, January 12, 1974. http://www.rocksbackpages.com/Library/Article/jackson-browne-survivor.

INTERVIEWS

Alterman, Eric, and Katrina vanden Heuvel. "An Interview with Jackson Browne." *The Nation*, October 7, 2014. https://www.thenation.com/article/archive/eric-alterman-and-katrina-vanden-heuvel-interview-jackson-browne.

Boltin, Steve. "Sunday Conversation: Jackson Browne on His New Album and How John Lennon Informed His Whole Musical Life." *Forbes*, July 18, 2021. https://

www.forbes.com/sites/stevebaltin/2021/07/18/sunday-conversation-jackson-browne-on-his-new-album-and-how-john-lennon-informed-his-whole-musical-life/?sh=23965ff62a02.

Hoffman, Wayne. "Jackson Browne Q & A." *Nature Conservancy*, 2003.

"Jackson Browne Interview on *Standing in the Breach* and World Tour." https://www.youtube.com/watch?v=xyJA4liNPX0. Retrieved February 15, 2024.

"Jackson Browne: Live Interview & A Human Touch with Leslie Mendelson." https://www.youtube.com/watch?v=A8CZg5nr7GA.

"Jackson Browne Talks about *Late for the Sky* LP." November 30, 2014. https://www.youtube.com/watch?v=XHW58A-6Gdw (site discontinued).

Nelson, Paul. "Jackson Browne: The *Rolling Stone* Interview." *Rolling Stone*, July 8, 1980.

"1989 Jackson Browne Interview." VH1 Special. YouTube. https://www.youtube.com/watch?v=uyDoh3nLFXg.

Perry, Kevin E. G. "Jackson Browne: My Generation Were Idealistic and Naive but We Were Right about So Many Things." *Independent* (UK), January 30, 2020. https://www.independent.co.uk/arts-entertainment/music/features/jackson-browne-interview-new-album-haiti-donald-trump-us-election-2020-a9305846.html.

Rowland, Mark. "Life Lessons: Bonnie Raitt and Jackson Browne." *Musician*, August 1989. http://www.rocksbackpages.com/Library/Article/life-lessons-bonnie-raitt-and-jackson-browne.

Schruers, Fred. "Interview with Jackson Browne." *US*, February 1994.

Sweeting, Adam. "Ten Questions for Songwriter Jackson Browne." *Arts Desk*, November 17, 2014. https://theartsdesk.com/new-music/10-questions-song-writer-jackson-browne.

DVDS

Going Home. Pioneer Artists. 1994.

I'll Do Anything: Jackson Browne In Concert. Inside Recordings, 2013.

"1964: The Year That Changed America." *The American Experience.* PBS Films. 2014.

VIDEOS

"Bruce Springsteen Inducts Jackson Browne Rock and Roll Hall of Fame Inductions 2004." https://www.youtube.com/watch?v=8YFyC6pnz-k.

Casciato, Tom. "Jackson Browne: We Could Have a Society in Which Justice Is Real." *PBS Weekend*, July 25, 2021. https://www.pbs.org/newshour/show/jackson-browne-we-could-have-a-society-in-which-justice-is-real.

Cohen, Dianna. "Are We Being Consumed by Plastic?" TED Talk. https://www.youtube.com/watch?v=SO4axNuoPis. Retrieved April 14, 2024.

"Jackson Browne Accepts the Gandhi Peace Award." 2018. https://www.youtube.com/watch?v=sEkn4qGhFgo. Retrieved February 13, 2024.
"The Questions, Vol. 6: Jackson Browne." https://www.youtube.com/watch?v=JhrRs02UAGs. Retrieved February 15, 2024.
"Ronald Reagan—Bruce Springsteen (19.09.1984)." YouTube, https://www.youtube.com/watch?v=z8BRWNaOdlc.

INDEX